# THE SELF-COACHED
# CLIMBER

# THE SELF-COACHED
# CLIMBER

## the guide to
## movement
## training
## performance

**DAN HAGUE**
**AND**
**DOUGLAS HUNTER**

STACKPOLE
BOOKS

Published by
STACKPOLE BOOKS
5067 Ritter Road
Mechanicsburg, PA 17055
www.stackpolebooks.com

Printed in China

First edition

10 9 8 7 6

*Cover photograph by Philippe Maurel.*
*Cover design by Caroline Stover.*
*Photographs by Dan Hague and Douglas Hunter, except where otherwise noted.*
*Illustrations by Kerry Handel and Douglas Hunter.*

**Library of Congress Cataloging-in-Publication Data**

Hague, Dan.
    The self-coached climber : the guide to movement, training, performance / Dan Hague and Douglas Hunter.
        p.      cm.
    Includes bibliographical references and index.
    ISBN-13: 978-0-8117-3339-7
    ISBN-10: 0-8117-3339-4
    1. Rock climbing—Training.   I. Hunter, Douglas.   II. Title.
GV200.2.H34 2005
796.52′23—dc22
                                                    2005012794

# Contents

# Acknowledgments

Over my years as a climber, I have been privileged to work alongside many talented climbing instructors who helped me develop the Fast Forward instructional program in movement and training, much of which is the basis for this book. Jay Young and Jennifer Bruursema were early contributors. Tom Lee, Gary Land, and Colin McCaffrey helped along the way.

Leslie, my wife, favorite climbing partner, and the best Fast Forward instructor Washington, DC, has ever known, deserves much of the credit for this book. Without her encouragement, insight, and willingness to play devil's advocate, the effort may never have begun, nor would the book be as readable or useful.

To my children, Victoria and Dylan, who patiently gave up afternoons, evenings, and weekends with their father so he might put in more time on his book.

To my friend, climbing partner, and colleague Doug Hunter, whose complementary knowledge and skills in climbing movement ensured the depth and breadth this book required. His devotion to producing the finest work possible pushed us both to rethink and rewrite whole sections, ensuring a comprehensive and thoughtful treatment of each subject.

Lastly, to all the climbing partners I annoyed by studying and critiquing and to the thousands of Fast Forward students who taught me that the greatest joy in climbing is not sending projects, but passing on what you've learned to others.

*Dan Hague*

The famed philosopher Jacques Derrida once expressed the idea that the acknowledgments section is where the author offers his book back to the people who have already given it to him in the first place. This indeed is the case here. Over the years, I have worked with thousands of climbers who have shaped my experiences, challenged my thinking, and taught me a great deal. There are far too many to name, but I hope you all know who you are and in some way see yourselves reflected in these pages.

This book would not have been possible without the opportunities provided to me over the past twenty-five years by numerous individuals, including Chris and Tim Shipley, Douglas Wistendahl, Marc Gravatt, Dale Goddard, Bob Richards, and Jeff Clapp. I also want to acknowledge the many wonderful instructors who worked at Rockreation in Salt Lake in the 1990s and who made valuable contributions to climbing pedagogy, among them Jonathan Knight, Amy Irvine, Danny Schambach, Nancy Fagan, Dan Casaboon, and Lynn Peas, as well as Steve Hynes for encouraging us to innovate. It is also necessary to acknowledge all the participants and instructors involved with Pro Camp over the years, as well as Bobbi Bensman, Hilary Silberman, Mindy Suhlack, Jim Highsmith, Aaron Shamy, Drew "the Icon" Bedford, Wendy Jones, Bob MacMillan, Peter Lenz, Ryan McDermott, "Perky," Jason and Tiffany, Nancy McCullough, Paula Child, Paul Harvey, Joe Klewiciky, Tom Adams, and all the rest of my clients, friends, and climbing partners in the huge and wonderful Salt Lake City climbing community.

To Craig Berman for introducing me to kinesiology. To Mia Axon, Mike Anderson, and Jay Tanzman for their precise readings and feedback. A very big thanks goes to Kenny Suh for being a patient model and for continuing the tradition of movement pedagogy. We also need to acknowledge Tom Wright and Kate Howe for their friendship and generosity in letting us use Jungle Gym. Thanks to Michele and Addison for putting up with the lengthy process of creating this work.

Most of all, I need to acknowledge Dan Hague, who was the catalyst that made this project happen, with whom it was a true pleasure to work, and whose insights and intelligence I respect more now than ever before.

Thanks to you all,
*Douglas Hunter*

# Introduction

The defining conceptual model of climbing performance today is that the two most fundamental abilities a climber can possess are strength and technique. It's nearly impossible to be a climber without having been exposed to these ideas and developing an opinion about which is more important. The distinction in thought between strength and technique in the climbing community has become an ideological division, and the two concepts are not often used in their correct senses. The ideas of strength and technique undoubtedly form two poles in a philosophical debate about the nature of climbing, but these positions are both very general and built upon abstractions, resulting in a misrepresentation of climbing movement.

Those who believe that, at its essence, climbing is most dependent on strength are referring to a general notion of the ability to apply force from the upper body and forearms. Their most fundamental argument is that at some point, no matter how good a climber's technique, he will find holds so small that he will lack the physical strength to hold on. On the other side, proponents of technique provide examples of moves, such as those found on friction slabs, where no amount of upper body strength will make the climber more successful. Proponents of technique will further insist that regardless of strength, the amount of energy wasted in moving inefficiently will ultimately cause the climber to fall short of his potential.

*The Self-Coached Climber* uses a different model for understanding climbing based on the four fundamental physical components of human movement: balance, force, time, and space. Our model is incompatible with the strength vs. technique dichotomy for a number of reasons. The strength argument, that forearm or upper body strength is ultimately the limiting factor on difficult moves, requires the belief that, within a certain move, on some tiny handholds, there is a pure expression of physical strength. But a single climbing move, including tasks as simple as hanging from tiny holds, is an expression of many variables, any of which will be found lacking when we attempt moves far enough beyond our current ability. For example, a consistent V2 boulderer may not be able to complete the crux of a steep V5. Naturally, there is an excellent chance the V2 climber will lack the forearm strength for moves three V grades beyond his current level, but, just as important, he will also lack the balance, motor control, timing, emotional focus, and ability to optimally select and use hand- and footholds.

Climbing movement is multifaceted, and success depends on many variables, some of which are more difficult to observe than others. We can surpass our abilities in any of them when we attempt moves sufficiently beyond our experience level. While it is possible to theorize a move that is solely dependent upon upper body strength, it is a basic fact of movement that such moves do not exist. This is not to dismiss muscular fitness. We want climbers to be extremely fit, but we also want you to understand how strength works in climbing and to use training methods that closely resemble the performance demands required by the routes you select.

The second polar argument proffers improved technique as the primary determinant of climbing performance. This contention also relies on abstractions, but does contain one sound principle: the technique argument places emphasis on efficiency. We agree. Efficiency is important in virtually all aspects of climbing, including hand and foot placement, the scheduling of performance and training days, the speed at which we can learn new moves, and the planning which goes into our most difficult climbs.

Kinesiologists such as Knudson and Morrison put significant effort into pointing out the many limitations and inaccuracies found in the visual assessment of movement in the broader world of sports. Some of these misperceptions are common in the climbing community. For example, it is often assumed that climbers who move slowly and demonstrate great control are efficient. This is not always the case; it is just as likely that climbers who exhibit great control sacrifice efficiency. They may move too slowly, resist dynamic movement, initiate most of their movement from the arms, or have other habits that require more force than necessary in every move. There is no definite link between smooth, controlled movement and the principles of mechanical efficiency.

Individual climbing moves can be quite complex, undergoing dramatic changes as they progress through space and time. There may be several changes in balance, and they may require great intermuscular coordination and precise timing. Despite this complexity, climbing moves are often represented as static body positions with little or no variation. One of the goals of this book and DVD is to use a variety of techniques to represent movement so that the reader can develop a fuller appreciation for the central role of balance, the importance of movement initiation and timing, and the way a move develops in space. The better you understand movement, the more options you will have on every climb you do. Understanding balance, force, time, and space—and their relationship with the basic physical laws that govern all movement—develops a more rigorous and useful understanding of climbing movement. These components are intertwined, interdependent, and present in all movement.

## Balance

Balance is the foundation upon which climbing moves are built. The better our balance, the less effort is required to move; therefore, understanding balance is primary to understanding movement and improving efficiency. Balance can be described as the relationship between your base of support and center of gravity. The base of support in climbing is defined by your

hand- and footholds. The center of gravity is the focal point of gravity's pull on the body. Balance has a wide range of types and qualities. Every climbing move has its most advantageous type and quality of balance, and finding and using the optimal balance for each move are central to effectiveness and efficiency.

## Force

Climbers typically think of force in terms of strength or the ability to apply pressure to holds. Our definition, however, includes any force acting on the body during movement. These include internal forces, such as body tensions, and external forces, such as gravity. The movement of your center of gravity is a result of all the forces working on it during a move. Further, you can control how force is applied and from where it originates in your body. Learning to recognize the origin and application of force is critical because, as in balance, you must be able to identify and apply the optimal forces in order to climb as efficiently as possible.

## Time

Redpoints, on-sights, boulder problems, and competitions tend to be very different in terms of their temporal characteristics and therefore call for different responses from us in our movement, tactics, and fitness. Beyond that, timing is the degree to which complex movements are coordinated and is measured by examining the relationship between different body parts at the beginning, middle, and end of a move.

## Space

Space is often overlooked in climbing, but all of our movements take three-dimensional paths through it. Where and how our center of gravity moves tells us a great deal about the balance, forces, and timing involved in a move. In addition, creating and visualizing specific paths through space is a powerful tool for creating consistent and precise movement.

These four components are the defining characteristics of movement, and they inform the concepts and activities in this book. They are fundamental to creating movement that is efficient, precise, effective, and, most of all, enjoyable. The significance of enjoying movement cannot be overstated. This is one of the greatest aspects of climbing, especially in sport climbing and bouldering, where so much time is spent learning and mastering sequences. Learning the principles of efficient movement is a process of exploration and can often take the form of play. As you incorporate the movement activities from this book into your daily climbing, use them in a dynamic manner, sometimes serious, sometimes playful, as a way of exploring the inner workings of climbing and your own movement potential.

## Efficiency

Efficiency is the one element that we retain from the strength and technique paradigm. In fact, efficiency is the most important principle in this book. Efficiency is achieved in training when the greatest gains in performance are made with the least amount of time and effort. Efficiency in tactics means learning moves and sequences in the least amount of time and gaining high-quality experience that is relevant to your performance goals. Efficiency in movement means successfully completing a move or climb with the least amount of physical exertion possible. By being efficient in these ways, all climbers can reach their true performance potential. Of course, balance, force, time, space, and efficiency are not the only important aspects of movement. Motor processing, motor learning, emotional states, and kinesthetic sensations of movement are also important elements that are explored in chapters 1 through 6. Each chapter begins with a conceptual explanation of principles and then provides activities that allow you to see and feel the concepts at work in your own movement. These activities were developed during our years as coaches and will focus your attention inward on the specifics of your climbing. This approach gives climbers the most effective method for controlling and enjoying movement and, as a result, improving overall performance.

Chapters 7 through 10 cover physical training. Our approach to strength and endurance training is based upon proven principles and practices adapted from the wider sports world. Our recommended methods focus on the demands of performing at different climbing levels. We define performance as sending a targeted route or boulder problem, or performing well in competition. Training is the means by which performance is improved. Training is not an end unto itself, and "getting strong" is not a helpful training goal. Being able to do one-armed pull-ups and radical campus moves is impressive but insignificant in terms of climbing performance because there is little or no relation between these feats and climbing at a given level. Our guiding principle is that training must be based on your climbing goals and directly promote performance. We'll show you how to do this so you can get the most out of your training efforts.

In chapter 11, we examine the emotional side of climbing. Your mental state and approach to climbing have much to do with your success or failure.

Chapter 12 contains our guide to performing a self-assessment of your climbing abilities. You simply cannot embark on an efficient journey to better climbing if you don't understand your current abilities with regard to movement, physical conditioning, and emotional constitution. We also help you determine realistic short- and long-term climbing goals. The hands-on path to self-improvement begins here.

Chapter 13 brings everything together by helping you develop a personalized training improvement plan. No two climbers are alike, so training plans necessarily differ from person to person. We teach you to create the plan that's best for your needs and goals, and we supplement our recommendations with general training plans for different climbing ability levels.

This book is the result of over thirty combined years spent studying, teaching, practicing, and coaching, and it is our sincere hope that what we have learned will help you improve your climbing.

**CHAPTER 1**
# Balance

It's nothing new to call climbing a balance sport, but the "why" behind the concept has never been fully explained. Some climbers may even question the idea, because climbing can feel like a physical battle that has nothing to do with the grace and precision associated with "real" balance activities such as walking a tightrope or figure skating. Nonetheless, balance is an essential part of climbing; it is at the heart of the kinesthetic experience of movement. The process of working out a sequence is the process of defining what type and quality of balance to use on each move. A thorough understanding of balance empowers climbers by providing a precise way to comprehend and describe the structure of movement, as well as a pragmatic set of strategies that solve difficulties and create efficient movement in any climbing situation. If you understand balance, you will always be able to find something else to try when having trouble on a difficult move.

## The Three Types of Balance

In daily life, we often act as if there were only two states of balance—we are either in or out of balance. This may be a fine shorthand description of what happens when you come crashing to the ground after slipping on a patch of ice or when you fall off a slack line, but in terms of climbing, balance is far more complex. In her important book *Dance Kinesiology*, Sally Sevey Fitt describes three types of balance: stable, offset, and dynamic, each of which has its own characteristics, and each of which can range in quality.

Before we go too far, though, we need to address a fundamental question: What is balance? In simple terms, balance is defined as the spatial relationship of your center of gravity to its base of support. The center of gravity is the point at which a body balances in all directions. It can also be described as the intersection of three imaginary planes that divide the body into halves: The frontal plane divides the body into equally weighted front and back halves, the sagittal plane splits the body into equally weighted right and left halves, and the transverse plane separates the body into equally

weighted top and bottom halves. For an adult standing with feet together and arms at the side, the center of gravity is located in the soft tissue in the middle of the pelvis. This is at about 55 to 57 percent of body height, or a little below your navel, according to Peter M. McGinnis in *Biomechanics of Sport and Exercise*.

**Balance is defined by the relationship of the center of gravity to the base of support.**

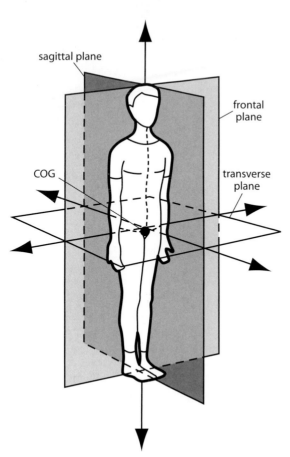

The body is divided into three planes that intersect at the center of gravity: the frontal plane, the sagittal plane, and the transverse plane.

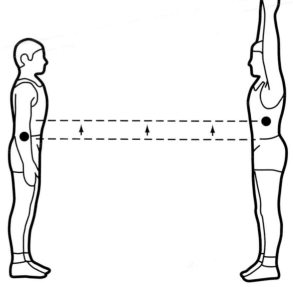

As the body moves, so does the center of gravity. Raising your arms above your head shifts your COG upward.

The center of gravity, however, is not a fixed point in the body. As you move your arms and legs and bend your trunk, the center of gravity moves as a result of the shifting weight of your body parts as they change position in space. If you're in a standing position, raising your arms out in front of you will shift your center of gravity slightly forward. Raise your arms over your head, and the center of gravity shifts upward.

For climbers, the most important thing to remember about the center of gravity is that it is the focal point of gravity's pull on the body. Gravity pulls on all parts of your body equally, but you experience that pull as concentrated on your center of gravity. Imagine gravity as a rope tied around your waist that is constantly pulling you toward the earth, and you'll quickly get the idea.

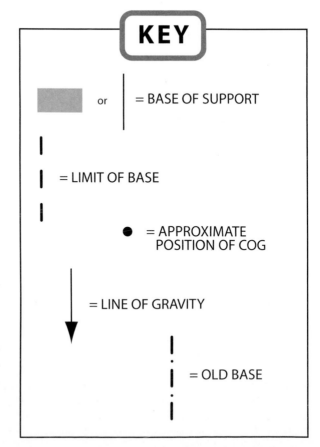

## KEY

= BASE OF SUPPORT

= LIMIT OF BASE

● = APPROXIMATE POSITION OF COG

↓ = LINE OF GRAVITY

= OLD BASE

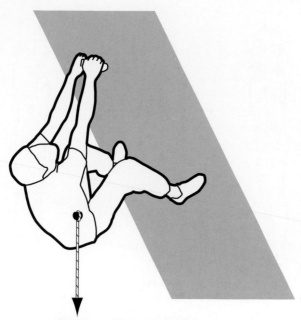

Imagine gravity as a rope tied around your waist that is constantly pulling you toward the earth. We experience gravity's pull as concentrated on our COG.

This is the line of gravity, and the orientation of the body to this line must be considered in order to understand the balance of a move. The center of gravity, then, is of immense importance to climbers and is central to every move. In order to resist gravity and make progress in movement, you need to control the location of the center of gravity in space and in relation to your base of support.

Losing control of the center or making poor decisions about where to place it can lead to a serious loss of efficiency. A fall becomes more likely because your center is actually pulling you off the rock. In competition, it can mean the difference between winning and losing. At the crag, it can result in a failed on-sight or redpoint attempt, necessitating another try. What's more, we are not talking only about gross or obvious errors. Often balance adjustments that are so small they can't be seen with the unaided eye have a powerful effect on performance.

The other component in our balance definition is the base of support. Base of support is defined as your points of contact with a supporting surface that allow you to resist the constant force of gravity. For sprinters, the base of support is their feet on the track. For swimmers, the base is the water around their bodies. For gymnasts, the base is their apparatus, such as the rings or uneven parallel bars. For climbers, the base of support is a hold or any other contact with the rock, such as a smear, that helps you resist gravity. The word *base* does not imply that your supporting surfaces must be beneath the body. In climbing, the base of support can be in front of the body, above it, to the side, or even behind it (as in a chimney). What's important is that the size, shape, and quality of your base of support are continually changing as you move from one hold to the next. This makes climbing different from many other sports, which tend to use consistent, predictable bases.

Imagine what the uneven parallel bars would be like for a gymnast if the position of the bars, the gymnast's base of support, kept changing during a routine. Many of the gymnastic moves performed today would be impossible because gymnasts depend on the stable position of the bars. Contrast this to a climber attempting an on-sight flash. The climber won't know the quality, size, or shape of his base of support or the types of balance available until he finds the holds and makes a quick decision about how to position his body relative to them. This is what we mean when we say that climbing is a balance sport.

When you are on a climb trying different holds and body positions to create an effective and efficient sequence, you are actually using your kinesthetic perception (the information your body sends you about your balance, orientation in space, muscular tension, and limb movement) as feedback to help you determine the size and quality of your base of support, as well as how to position your center of gravity in relation to this base. In climbing, the challenge of finding and using balance rises to a level of cognitive and physical difficulty that is uncommon in other sports. Finding, creating, and using effective balance are the central tasks of climbing movement.

To understand these concepts and the differences among the three types of balance, try the following activity, which will give you the chance to feel these principles at work in your body and your climbing.

*Activity 1: Experiencing the Three Types of Balance*
Stand up straight with your feet planted a little wider than shoulder width apart. Standing in this manner, you are in a position of stable balance. Stable balance

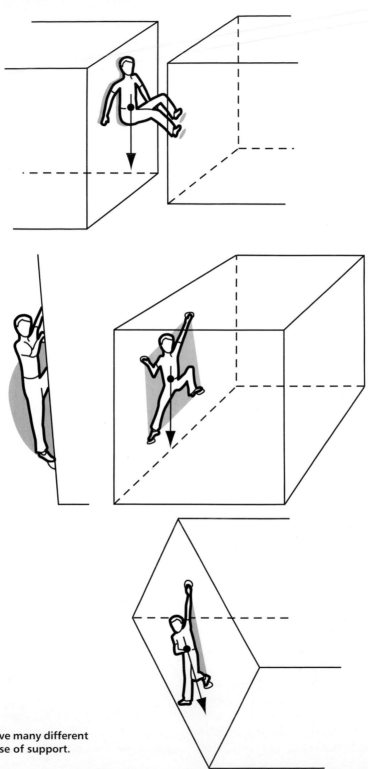

In climbing, we can have many different
orientations to our base of support.

An example of stable balance. The COG is positioned inside the base of support and moves easily within it.

ance. First, the lower the center within its base, the more stable the body will be, and second, the broader the base of support, the more stable the body will be. When we're describing balance, then, we must specify not only the type, but also the quality.

Now try something different. Stand as high as you can on the tiptoes of one foot. This is a position of offset balance, which describes any situation in which the center of gravity approaches the edge of the base of support. You may find that this position is difficult to maintain, that your leg gets jittery or that you need to make adjustments in body position to stay balanced on your foot. This position feels insecure or a little uncomfortable. You may find that it is accompanied by a mental change as well, that you are surprised by the relative difficulty of standing this way or that you must concentrate and focus in order to stay balanced. As you can feel, offset balance is less secure than stable balance. In the tiptoe position, your base of support is so small that the center of gravity is already near the edge of the base. Try to

describes any situation in which the center of gravity is positioned well within its base of support. Move from side to side, and it's no surprise that moving your center along the line from one foot to the other is no problem; you can hold your center at any point along this line with little effort. In this example, movement is easy, your weight is distributed on both feet, and you are stable and comfortable. Stable balance provides the greatest control over the center of gravity with the least amount of muscular effort, because the center is positioned within its base of support.

The most stable balance is when the center of gravity is centered and low in its base. While stable balance is more secure than offset or dynamic balance, not all stable balance movements and positions are of the same quality. For example, compare a normal standing position to lying on the floor. These are both examples of stable balance, but lying on the floor is far more stable than standing. Standing requires muscular effort to remain upright, whereas lying on the floor is so stable that no muscular effort is needed to maintain the position. This demonstrates two important concepts in bal-

**Offset balance with a very small base of support. The small base limits the movement of the COG.**

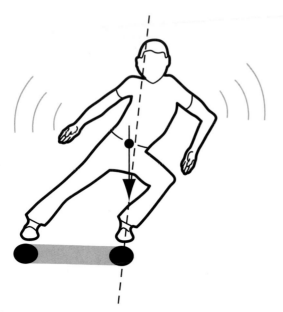

**Offset balance with the center of gravity at the limit of its base.**

ing. If you fell over you experienced the third type of balance: dynamic. Dynamic balance describes any situation in which the center of gravity passes outside the base of support. The result is that the body will continue in motion until a new base is found. In this example, the new base is the floor or whatever else you might have landed on. Dynamic balance is unique because the center of gravity must move. The center may be stationary or moving in stable and offset balance, but in dynamic balance the center must move.

Some may protest that dynamic balance is just a fancy way of describing someone who has lost his balance, but this is not the case. There are numerous examples in climbing of dynamic balance that differ from losing one's balance. The most obvious example is that of a dyno. Dynos often begin in a position of stable balance from which the climber throws his center of gravity out of the current base, creating upward momentum that allows him to latch a new hold and establish a new base of support higher on the climb. Since his center of gravity passed outside his base of support, the climber

move your pelvis around, and you will find that this base greatly restricts your range of motion. You can move up and down a little, but lateral movement of the body is impossible without counterbalancing or tipping over.

Offset balance is not limited to examples with a very small base of support. Stand again with your feet planted a little wider than shoulder width apart. Move your hips as far as you can to the right. As you slide your pelvis over the right foot and try to move past it, you will feel far more weight on that foot and notice that you are somewhat less stable. You may even feel a tiny bit of the unsteady sensation you had when standing on tiptoe. You will also notice that as you try to continue moving to the side, you find a natural stopping point, a point beyond which it seems you can't move. This point is the limit of your base of support, and as you approach that limit, your balance undergoes a transition from stable to offset. This position illustrates that offset balance is less stable; your base of support encourages movement in some directions while discouraging it in others.

From this offset balance position, try to force your hips even farther to the right. In doing so, you will either feel as if you have come up against an invisible barrier preventing you from moving any farther or fall over try-

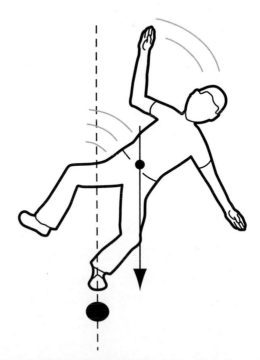

**Dynamic balance occurs when the center of gravity passes outside of its base of support.**

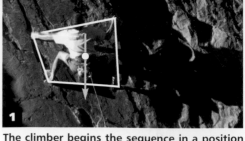

Since balance will become dynamic as soon as he lets go with his right hand, the climber must get low within his base to create enough momentum to complete the move.

The climber begins the sequence in a position of fair-quality stable balance. The base of support is large, but the holds are not very positive.

At the highest point of the move, the climber does not achieve ideal hip and trunk extension. The body does not come in as close to the rock as it could, which makes the hold difficult to latch.

Balance becomes dynamic as the climber lets go with his right hand and his base becomes much smaller. His COG is outside of his base. He only has a moment to get to the next hold.

The climber's hand reaches the hold a little late. As a result, his trunk and pelvis fall out from the wall as he makes contact.

When the climber's hand reaches the next hold, his balance becomes stable again. He can now move his left foot a little higher and clip the draw.

The climber brings up his left foot and holds his body close to the rock for the clip.

Here, the climber experiences stable balance as he makes the clip.

The quality and type of balance
can change over the course
of a single move.

Front
View

**5**

The climber matches his hands while maintaining stable balance.

**6**

The climber lifts his left foot, and his base of support changes from a large triangle to a thin line. Thus, his balance shifts from stable to slightly dynamic.

Side
View

**5**

As the climber swings to the right, he also swings out. Here his body and his center reach their greatest distance from the rock.

**7**

The climber swings slightly as the COG is pulled toward the base of support.

**6**

After the climber recovers from dynamic balance, he closes the gap between his body and the rock. This stabilizes his balance and extends his reach.

**8**

The climber steps through. Then he initiates upward movement, driving his COG up and into the base. Since the base is above the COG, this is a position of good-quality offset balance.

encountered a situation of dynamic balance, but he was never out of balance.

Not all dynamic moves use dynamic balance, however. In climbing, dynamic movement refers to the speed of the movement, not the position of the center of gravity. Dynamic movement can also be implemented in stable and offset balance moves. For example, many steep, juggy 5.10s and 5.11s in American Fork, Utah, have stable balance moves, but climbing and moving dynamically can save both time and energy.

In climbing, one type of balance is not necessarily more desirable than another. Climbs often provide you with a limited number of places to put your hands and feet. The task of the climber is to find the type and quality of balance that are most appropriate for each individual move, given the size, orientation, and location of the holds. In a typical climbing situation, you might not have a choice between stable and offset balance but you may be able to choose between different qualities of offset balance and different tactics for dealing with the available balance. Even small differences in balance can create dramatic changes in the effectiveness and efficiency of your movement. Many times the difference between being shut down on a move and being able to do it consistently is a tiny change in balance. The hard part is to find the most appropriate type and quality of balance for each movement and to know when you've actually found it. This is particularly difficult when you are working at or near your limit. Harder grades have more challenging balance problems, so you need to be sensitive to ever more subtle balance cues as you progress through the grades.

## Specific Challenges of Balance in Climbing

How the three types of balance function in climbing moves is more complex than the examples provided thus far. In the exercises above, the floor was always the same quality, which makes standing and moving around easy, and the base was always directly below the center of gravity, so gravity was pulling you toward your supporting surface. In climbing, however, the situation is more challenging.

The experience or feeling of balance in climbing can be very different from that in what we typically think of as balance activities. When you're riding a bike, slack lining, or roller blading, gravity pulls you toward the base of support. This means that although it may take energy to move forward or backward, you do not have to produce great force simply to stay on your base. In climbing, however, unless you are on a slab, gravity pulls you away from your base, which means that it can require a great deal of force just to remain on your base of support, let alone produce any movement. In addition, hand- and footholds come in different sizes, shapes, and textures, making some holds far better bases of support than others.

When you are climbing, the amount of physical effort needed to make a move will show you the quality of your balance in that move. When the quality of your balance diminishes, you need to increase your muscular effort to stay on the rock or complete the move. As your balance improves, say, by changing a foothold, the amount of physical effort necessary decreases.

In climbing, the base of support is made up of two equally important components. The first is the size, shape, and orientation of the holds. An in-cut jug provides a better base than a polished sloper, in that jugs are able to resist force in many directions, and they can resist multiple forces at once. It is possible to apply lateral, downward, and outward force simultaneously on an in-cut jug, while a poor-quality sloper may be able to resist only downward force. The second component is the position of the holds. If you were to connect the holds with lines, the resulting shape would show the size and shape of your base of support. In some moves, your base is a thin line between one handhold and one foothold. At other times, your base may look like a square or a triangle. Though drawing these lines is a good tool for understanding the size and shape of the base, they create only a two-dimensional representation of something that is three-dimensional. For the complete picture, you also need to consider the size and shape of the holds and the angle of the climb. Nonetheless, drawing the lines is an excellent starting point for understanding balance. Exploring all the possibilities of hold characteristics and their distribution in space is very complicated. Basically, the larger and more in-cut the holds and the larger the shape they describe in space, the more stable balance will be. The smaller the holds and the smaller the shape, the less stable balance will be.

A single climbing move may require any combination of stable, offset, or dynamic balance. When you let go to move a hand or foot, the size and shape of your base of support change. In addition, your center of gravity is almost constantly moving. With both of these factors in play at the same time, a move can begin with stable balance, transform to dynamic balance during a reach, and then change to offset balance when you attain the next hold. To experience these concepts at work in movement, try the following activity on a slightly overhanging wall or rock with many hand- and footholds.

*Activity 2: Climbing Balance*

First, get on the wall with your feet apart. Back-step your right foot, and keep your hands on good holds. Sink down low with your arms straight and your legs bent. Your base is a good-sized trapezoid around your body, a position of stable balance. Slowly stand all the way up, and reach for a higher hold with your right hand. What do you feel happening as you move? Letting go to reach with your right hand does not make a significant change to the size or shape of your base, and even though your center of gravity has moved, it stays within your base of support. The result is little change in the type or quality of your balance as you move. Your balance remains stable for the entire move, and you can feel this kinesthetically. Stable balance feels good and

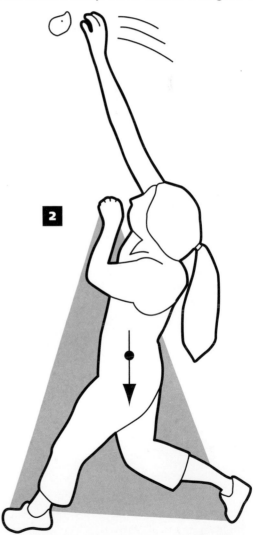

**Activity 2: In this position of stable balance, your base is a good-sized trapezoid around your body.**

In a stable balance move, your COG stays within your base of support, making the move feel smooth and comfortable.

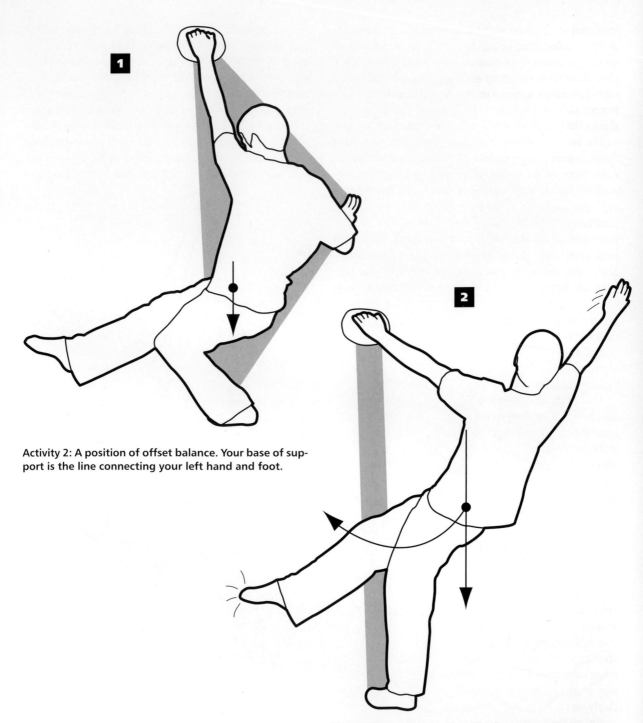

Activity 2: A position of offset balance. Your base of support is the line connecting your left hand and foot.

Your balance changes from high-quality offset balance to lower-quality offset balance as your center moves farther from its base.

solid and makes it easy to smoothly link moves together in fluid sequences, because your center of gravity is almost always well positioned within its base. Of course, skilled climbers can make any move look smooth, but it takes less effort to do so in situations of stable balance. Routes that are thought of as classics for the way their moves flow together have many stable balance moves.

For an example of offset balance using large holds, find a place on the wall where you can inside-flag your right foot while keeping your left foot directly below your left hand, with your right hand on nothing. Imagine a line connecting your left hand and foot, describing your base of support. Going by feel, position yourself so your center is as close to this line as possible. Now move your center very slowly to the right, reaching with your right hand, but not grabbing, a hold that is as far to the right as you can stretch. As you move to the right, observe what is happening to your body. How hard do you now need to press your right leg into the wall? Compare what you felt in your left arm at the beginning and end of the move. Where is the most effort required? How much body tension do you need at the end of the move compared with the beginning of the move?

In this exercise, your balance changed from high-quality offset balance to lower-quality offset balance as your center moved farther from its base. If you just looked at the line, you might think that this was an example of dynamic balance, but consider that the handhold was positive and could resist force from a number of directions, including the side. Thus your arm was functioning as a guy wire connecting your trunk to its base. As the quality of balance changed, you should have found yourself pressing into the wall harder with your right foot as well as using more body tension. You should also have noticed yourself pulling harder with your left arm. This exercise dramatically demonstrates how as balance changes, the amount of muscular effort needed to stay on the rock also changes. Try to do the same exercise again using a small handhold that is difficult for you, and you will find that you have a much smaller range of motion. If the hold you use is poor enough, you may be able to hold on only if you keep your center precisely on the line connecting your hand and foot.

Offset balance moves in climbing are often described as sketchy or technical. They feel less secure than stable balance and require more body tension to control the body and the center, regardless of the angle. Offset balance is the defining characteristic of many challenging moves. You can detect offset balance by how the move feels. If in the initial position a move feels stable but as you move your body to attain the next hold you feel your control and stability diminishing and your core tightening, this is a sign that your center of gravity is approaching the limit of its base. In such a case, trouble latching holds is not a sign of physical weakness, but it signals that you chose a sequence that ended in low-quality offset balance. In addition, as holds get smaller and the rock angle steeper, you will encounter offset balance more often.

To experience dynamic balance, find a roof and position yourself so that your hands are on jugs above the lip and your feet are extended under the roof, also on jugs. Cut loose with your feet. It's no surprise that your body swings away from the wall, but why does this happen? Why doesn't your body just stay where it is in space? At the start of the move, you are in a position of stable balance, but when you release your feet, the base of support changes from a large box connecting your hands and feet to a line connecting your hands. Your center of gravity, now far from its base of support, seeks a new base. The center wants to be directly under your hands. It will take a moment for you to be able to control the swing, and once you do, since you are on jugs, you will have achieved fairly stable balance with your center of gravity centered under your hands.

Dynamic balance also occurs frequently during moves in which letting go with one hand shrinks the base of support so that the center is left outside the box. As soon as you let go, it is not possible to hold yourself on the rock with only one hand and your feet. You will fall off. Moves like this occur all the time on difficult face routes. For an example, find a steep face where your hands are on small sidepulls on either side of your body so you are in almost an iron cross position. Your feet should be close together on small holds that feel a little high. You must make a long vertical reach with the right hand to attain the next hold. Now release your right hand and try to make the reach statically. If you have chosen your holds well, doing this move statically should be impossible—as soon as you release your right hand, you should fall away from the wall. This is a very common structure of dynamic balance moves:

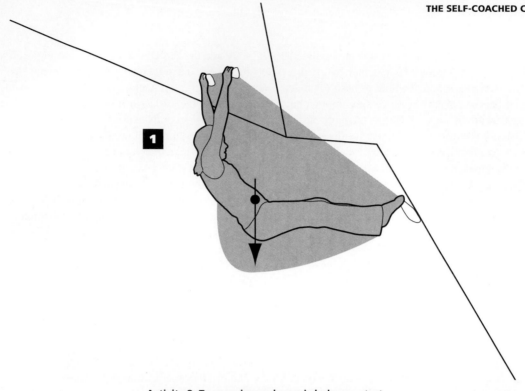

**1**

**Activity 2: To experience dynamic balance, start in a position of stable balance on a roof.**

Letting go with one hand causes the base of support to shrink enough so that the center of gravity is now outside the base and you begin to fall. And with the long vertical reach necessary to attain the next hold, the center of gravity must go even higher in order to complete the move. The only way to complete such a move is with momentum. If you identify a move as consisting of dynamic balance, commit to it and work on generating the necessary dynamic force.

Dynamic balance moves are never exclusively dynamic; they always start out as either offset or stable balance and become dynamic at the point when you release a hold and the base shrinks or when you move your center outside of its base.

These exercises serve only as an introduction to balance in climbing and a way to demonstrate that balance is essential to climbing. No move is free of balance, and the quality of your balance determines how much muscular effort a move will require. Balance is an integral part of the kinesthetic and emotional experience of climbing. These facts raise two important questions: Can balance be learned and mastered, and how can you

use your understanding of balance to learn moves, become more efficient, and send your projects faster?

These questions are difficult to answer. Research has shown that performance in activities requiring balance improves with practice, but there is little correlation between the ability to perform one type of balance activity and another, even if they are closely related. Cognitive science describes balance as consisting of both traits and skills. Traits are inherited characteristics that don't respond well to training and, like the color of your eyes, are more or less fixed attributes. So your raw ability to perceive balance may have a genetic limit, but the ability to perform a task such as climbing, riding a bike, or slack lining depends equally on learned skills. In slack lining, you need a significant amount of muscular control to keep the line steady under you. The ability to control the slack line is a skill that will improve with training. This means that with practice, you can become highly skilled at balancing on a slack line, but this skill will be specific to slack lining and does not represent a global improvement in your ability to balance. Since the skills needed for slack lining are very different from

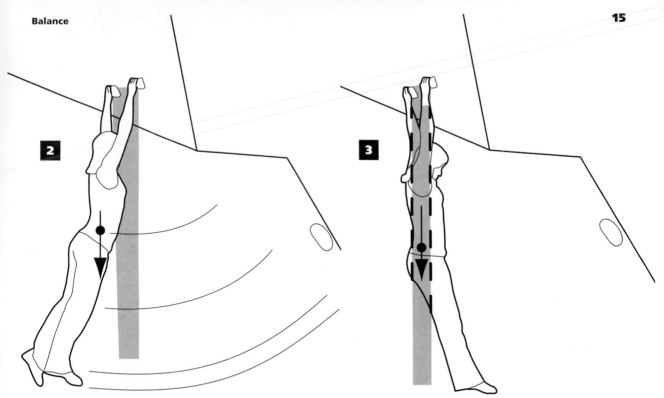

**Cut your feet loose. Dynamic balance occurs as your body swings and the COG seeks a new base.**

**When momentum dissipates, a new stable balance position is established with the COG directly below your hands.**

those used in climbing, slack lining has little or no impact on the balance skills needed for climbing.

Additionally, climbing balance skills are most likely specific to particular rock angles and other variables. For example, the balance skills developed on friction slabs may be applicable only to this type of climbing. Likewise, the balance skills necessary for steep face climbs or cracks may be just as specific. This means that in order to fully develop your climbing balance skills, you need to climb on a wide variety of routes and types of rock.

## Balance Application in Climbing

Knowledge of the principles of balance can help you find efficient sequences. The first and perhaps simplest way to gain a better understanding of balance is to learn to feel your center. For well over a century, dancers have been encouraged to "find center" by paying conscious attention to feeling the location of their centers of gravity. Some moves in both dance and climbing can't be done without this awareness, and

many more are enhanced by it even when it's not essential. In climbing, the most difficult offset balance moves require excellent kinesthetic awareness of how close your center is to the limit of your base. At times, you need to bring your center to the exact limit of your base—reaching the next hold or going too far and falling because your balance has become dynamic can depend upon a difference of millimeters. Climbers may not articulate it in these terms, but highly skilled climbers demonstrate that they possess this awareness in all their movements. New climbers, however, often show little or no awareness of this relationship. Many climbers develop the ability to find center on their own without knowing what it is, but in order to speed up this learning, we recommend the blindfolded and no-handed climbing exercises in chapter 3.

Ultimately, the point of learning about balance is to apply the understanding to sequencing difficult moves, routes, and boulder problems. Clearly the way climbers learn moves and develop sequences is largely an intuitive and kinesthetic process, but if a sequence is significantly different from what you are used to, or is close

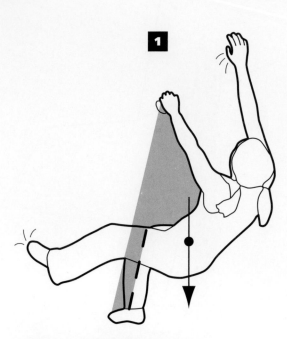

**1**

To improve balance, broaden your base of support. In this position, the base of support is narrow.

**2**

Changing the back step to a slight drop knee provides more stable balance.

**4**

This results in a barn door where momentum carries the COG beyond the base. To stay on the wall, the climber will need to exert great force on the holds.

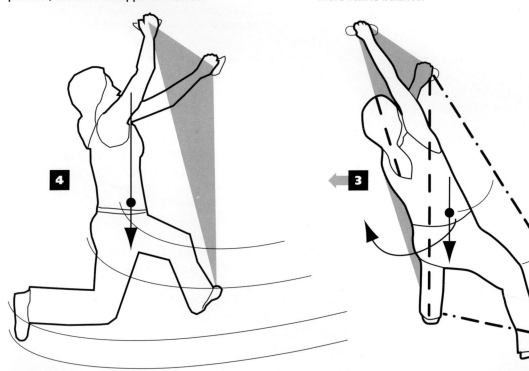

**3**

The COG will then want to swing sharply into the new base of support.

to your current limit, it pushes you beyond what you can interpret intuitively. In such cases, you can use your understanding of the physics behind balance to interpret moves and come up with different options. These balance principles interact with each other in complex ways, so they must be applied dynamically, with an understanding that there is interplay between them and that many variables govern how they are expressed. In analyzing movement this way, you will be amazed at how precise an understanding you can have of even the most difficult moves you face.

The most basic principles that govern balance in climbing are:

1. The quality of your balance is determined by the center of gravity in relation to the base of support.

2. Having a broad base of support will be more stable than having a smaller or narrower base. The size of the base is always determined by the size, shape, and orientation of the holds as well as their distribution in space.

3. The lower the center of gravity within its base, the more stable the body will be.

4. The type and quality of balance in a move determine how much muscular effort will be required.

The first strategy for improving balance is to broaden the base of support. Sometimes changing the base of support can change the type of balance altogether. Other times changing the base of support won't change the

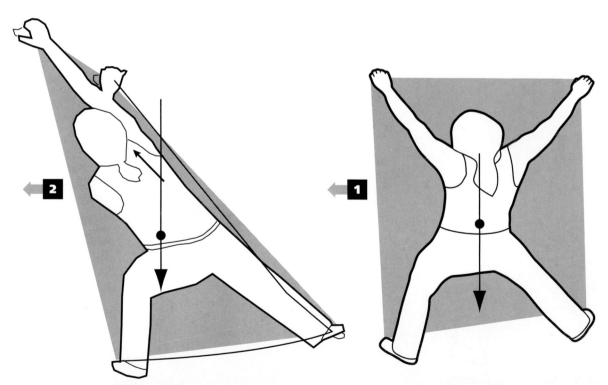

After crossing her right arm through, the climber lifts her right foot, changing the base of support and moving the COG outside the base. Stable balance becomes dynamic.

This move starts out as stable balance and then becomes dynamic as the climber attempts to move her right foot.

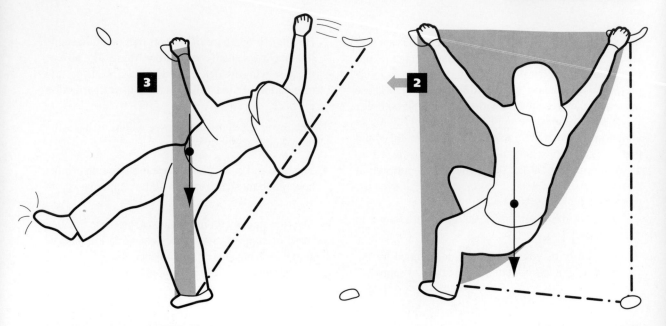

This allows a stable balance position for the next reach.

The inside flag keeps the COG within the base of support.

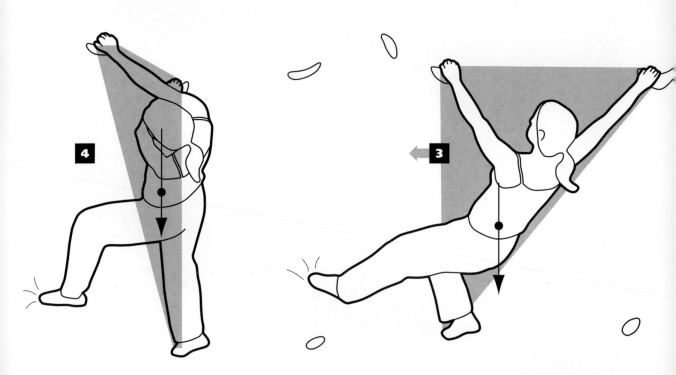

This allows a stable balance position for the cross-through reach.

The COG has now shifted under the left hand.

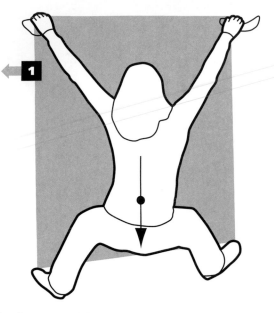

The first method for improving balance: Keep the COG within its base of support throughout the move.

type of balance, but it will slightly improve the quality of balance. Let's say you are in a back step on a steep wall. You have a bad foothold for the right foot and a small hold for the left hand. This is a move of offset balance that will feel hard because of the angle of the wall and the size of the foothold. In this situation, the base is small, and the rising center naturally destabilizes the body. If you have an adequate foothold available in the right position, a drop knee with the right leg will significantly broaden the base so that the center remains within the base for the entire move.

A slightly more complex example is found on a right-handed cross through a slightly overhanging wall. The cross-through feels fine, but you swing out and fall when you try to move your right foot. The reason for the swing is that when you take your right foot off its hold, your base of support changes size and shape so that your center is positioned slightly to the right of your new base. Your goal is to change the move so that your center is within its base at the end of the move. The

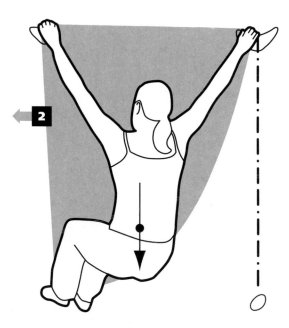

Match feet to begin shifting the COG left so it remains within the base of support.

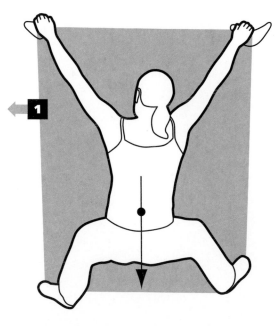

Another common way of keeping the COG within its base during a move is to match feet and back step.

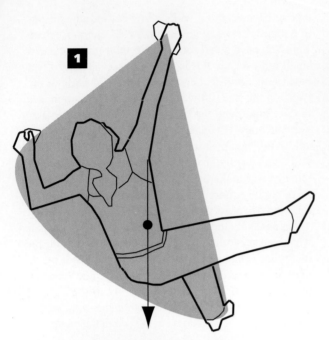

The second method for improving balance: Change the path or position of the center in space.

As the left hand releases its hold, the center is well outside the base, making the position less stable and the move more difficult.

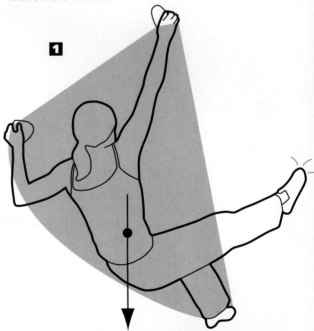

You can often change the quality of your balance simply by changing your body position in relation to your holds.

easiest way to do this is to change the move to either an inside flag by moving the right foot between the rock and your body before you reach or a back-step flag by putting the right foot where the left foot was. By using either of these options, your center remains within the base during the move and you don't swing at the end of the move. In this instance, you were able to alter the move from one that started out in stable balance and changed to dynamic balance to a move that remained one of offset balance throughout.

The second method for improving balance is to change the path or position of the center in space. Simple cases where this kind of change is helpful occur all the time in back steps. Climbers often have a fairly good base of support for a move, but they don't position their center correctly in relation to it. In the sequence

illustrated below, the climber changes a move of low-quality offset balance into one of high-quality offset balance by arching her back and driving her center closer to the line of her base.

It is advantageous to initiate a move from the position that affords the best possible balance. In the case of the drop knee on the route Dead Souls (see photos on next page), finding the position of best balance is a bit counterintuitive, since it requires bringing the body downward to a position the climber has already passed in order to place the drop knee. Notice that the climber brings his body back down and then makes the move. If he didn't bring his body so low, he would be starting the move from a position of lower-quality balance with his center very high in its base, which would make the move far more difficult.

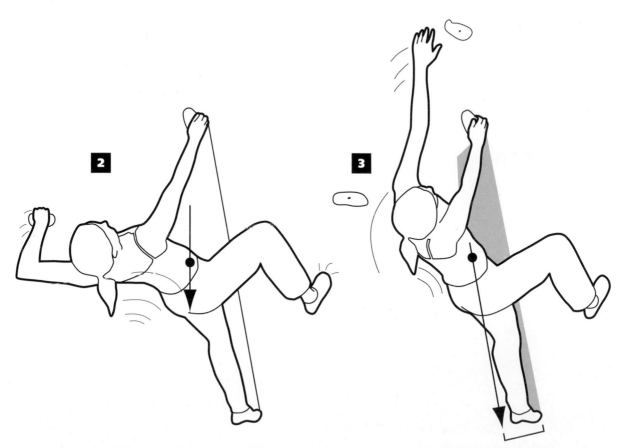

Here the climber arches her back to drive her COG closer to the base.

Notice that the move will feel easier as the line of gravity moves closer to the foothold.

Arron Shamy on Dead Souls 5.14a, American Fork, Utah. On difficult moves, it's important to start from the position of best balance. Arron's body is high as he places his foot for the drop knee.

Arron sinks down, into a position of stable balance that provides more room to create momentum.

He successfully executes the long move.

The third method for improving balance is using momentum. There are a number of uses for momentum in climbing, such as when it is necessary to move the center of gravity outside the base of support on difficult moves. In this case, your hands are matched on a right-facing sloper, your left foot is on nothing, and the right foot is on a high sloper that is poor enough that you can't pull in with it. The hold you are going for is directly up and to the right of the hold you are matched on. The hold is far enough away that in order to reach it, your center of gravity must pass outside your base. This is a difficult move because as the center crosses this plane, it creates greater outward and downward force on the handhold. If you were on a large in-cut hold, resisting these forces would be easy, but in this example the sloper provides little help in resisting these forces, which are likely to pull you right off the climb. A move like this is instructive because you can feel the exact moment when you come up against the limit of the base of support; it will feel as if you can't move any farther, but you must in order to reach the next hold. Using momentum will make it possible to get past this point and get to the next hold before falling off. Attempting to do the move without momentum will leave you stuck in a position of the worst offset balance with nowhere to go.

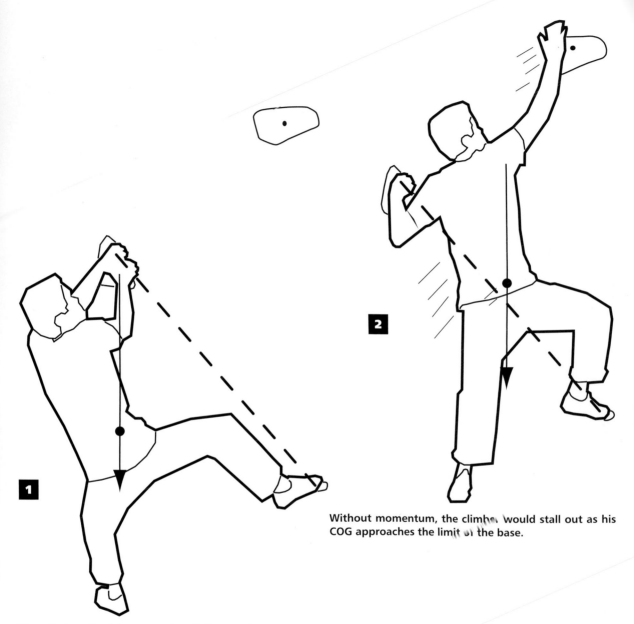

**2**

Without momentum, the climber would stall out as his COG approaches the limit of the base.

**1**

The third method for improving balance: use momentum. The climber starts low, allowing room to create momentum. Momentum is required to move the COG past the limit of the base.

**1**

**2**

Keep the body rigid to achieve stability and control of the center.

The fourth method for improving balance: Create body tension. These handholds are so poor that they will not allow dynamic movement.

The fourth method of dealing with poor balance is to create more body tension. Consider the example above, but imagine that the handholds are poorer slopers closer together. Now stabilizing the body in a position of offset balance is better than using momentum. In this case, the holds you are using are poor enough that if you did the move with any momentum, you would not be able to control it and would fall. You will need to have very precise control over the force you apply to the move and the center as it moves to the limit of the base. Keeping the body rigid during the reach helps stabilize the body and control the center.

These are just a few examples of the many ways that balance plays out in climbing moves. There are as many specific examples as there are individual moves, so you must apply the principles presented here to the moves that challenge you. These examples show that by analyzing movement in terms of balance, you will have a powerful and accurate tool for understanding what happens to your body in every move because you know the underlying structure of every move.

✔ Balance is the relationship between the center of gravity and the base of support. It is the defining and central aspect of all climbing movement.

✔ The center of gravity is the focal point of gravity's pull on the body.

✔ The base of support is defined by the size and shape of hand- and footholds as well as their orientation and position. The base of support encourages movement in some directions while inhibiting it in others.

✔ The orientation of the body to the line of gravity must be considered in order to understand the balance of a move.

✔ There are three types of balance: stable balance, where the center of gravity is well within the base of support; offset balance, where the center approaches the edge of the base of support; and dynamic balance, where the center passes outside of the base.

✔ Finding and using the best type of balance for each move is the central task for climbers.

✔ In climbing, you tend to experience balance through the amount of effort a movement requires, rather than as the sensation you feel when ice skating or walking a balance beam.

✔ Though balance may not be trainable in the same way as other aspects of climbing, the ability to "find center" is a good, learnable skill.

✔ The most common ways to improve balance are to broaden the base of support; alter the movement of the center of gravity to bring it more within the base of support; begin moves from the position that offers the best possible balance; use momentum when the center must pass outside the base of support; and create as much body tension as possible in positions of low-quality offset balance.

CHAPTER 2

# Establishing a Good Base of Support

In many sports, skill and efficiency of movement are more important than raw physical strength. Competitive swimmers are physically powerful athletes. Broad shoulders, stout legs, and solid abs are evidence of the swimmer's physical prowess. But no one would ever propose that the foundation of a swimmer's ability is muscular strength. Rather, it's an efficient stroke, a precise and practiced motion that applies muscle strength in the optimal way to produce speed and conserve energy. Simply having strong shoulders in no way equates to great swimming performance, and even skilled swimmers practice their strokes under the watchful eye of a coach.

For climbers, efficiency of movement rather than raw physical strength is the basis of effectiveness, and efficiency begins with learning to establish a strong base of support. At its root, a climber's base of support consists of where and how he contacts the rock surface, or in other words, how effectively he places and uses his hands and feet. Contact quality, in turn, is determined by proper hand and foot positioning and precise, swift placement. The relationship between the holds and the climber's center of gravity is also critical. Their size, shape, and orientation determine what directions of force can be resisted and thereby influence his choice of potential movements.

## Hand and Foot Positioning

Holds can be grouped into categories depending on their shape, position, and use. The following descriptions are of a basic, general nature and do not reflect the many varied ways that you can employ holds. If you are just getting started in climbing, however, these guidelines will give you a solid basic understanding of how to use the different categories of holds. Only face-climbing holds are described here, because there are many well-written texts available on crack climbing.

### Handholds

Handholds come in an infinite combination of shapes and sizes, but they are grouped into categories by hold characteristics and orientation. The combination of hold type and orientation determines, in large part, the most effective body position for that hold. The best body position in many cases determines whether a handhold is useful. In the following sections, pay special attention to not only how to grasp a particular type of handhold, but also to the most effective body position relative to that hold.

### Crimpers

A crimper is a flat (horizontal) or in-cut (sloping down from the outer lip to the back of the hold) edge one inch deep or less. To get the most out of a crimper, a climber often needs to hold his second knuckle at a 90-degree angle while pressing down and in on the hold with all of his fingertips. This position provides two advantages.

First, the 90-degree angle allows the fingertips the most contact with the hold, a positioning advantage

To maximize surface area contact on a crimper, hold the second knuckle at a 90-degree angle.

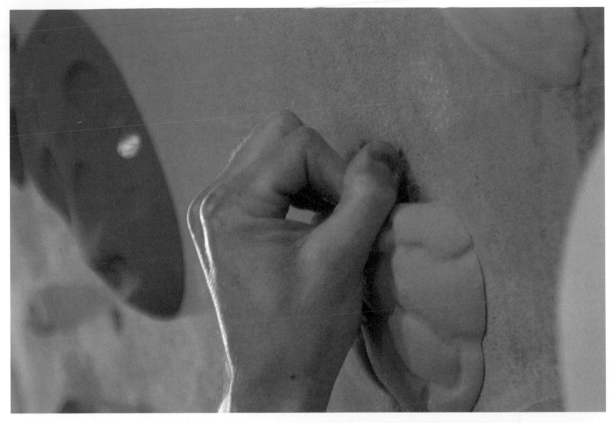

**Closing the thumb over the nail of the index finger increases the force you can exert on a hold.**

also seen with other hold types. Try this experiment: Find a crimper and position your hand with the second knuckle at 90 degrees. Feel how your fingertips make contact with the hold. Next, using the same crimper, drop the heel of your hand so that the second knuckle opens up to more than 90 degrees into an open-hand position (your little finger may slip off the hold). Note how your fingertips feel on the surface of the hold. Can you feel the difference? In the crimp position, your entire fingertip should be in contact with the hold. After increasing the angle at the second knuckle, the fingertips touch only the hold's outer lip. In some situations, it is necessary or more comfortable to use a crimp-type hold in this manner, but in general, a 90-degree joint angle will foster greater surface contact between fingers and hold.

Second, the 90-degree crimping position forces the fingertips down and in, making it less likely that the hand will slip backward off the hold. Try the same experiment as above, this time pulling outward on the hold. Did your hand feel more secure in the crimp position?

There are two crimping methods: open and closed. In an open crimp, the thumb is positioned away from the fingers. In a closed crimp, the thumb tip wraps over and presses on the nail of the index finger. Although somewhat painful, the closed crimp can be more powerful because the thumb is used along with the fingers.

The crimper is a type of hold that can be used with many body positions. Its multidirectional nature means that the position of the climber's center of gravity relative to the crimper is less of an issue than with other holds.

Beginners often rely heavily on crimping because climbers new to the sport tend to already have some natural crimping strength. But just because crimping feels natural and easy doesn't mean you should ignore the other types of holds.

*Slopers*

A sloper is a handhold that slopes from back to front. Effectively using a sloper involves maximizing surface area contact with the hold. Typically this means the hand is in the open position, with fingers extended and the second knuckle at greater than 90 degrees. Try the surface area experiment once again, this time on a large sloper. First apply a crimp position and note the contact area. Then let your hand conform to the hold by opening the angle at the second knuckle. Can you feel the difference in skin contact with the hold?

The effective use of slopers is dependent on the position of your center of gravity relative to the hold. Slopers work best when your center of gravity is close to the wall and directly below the hold. Try this: Find a large sloper about seven feet off the ground. Place both hands on the sloper and step off the ground. Position your feet so that you can move your center of gravity both toward and away from the wall. How does the hold feel as you move your hips away from the wall? You should feel less secure on the sloper as your center of gravity moves away from the wall. Now, keeping both hands on the sloper, move your center of gravity vertically. Can you feel the sloper becoming less secure as you move your hips higher and nearer to your hands? Body positions that encourage outward force will make a sloper more challenging to use.

A sloper is often a difficult hold for beginners and even some advanced climbers to master. Hand strength is dependent on position; the joint angles at the knuckles and wrist are static on any given hold, making the effort isometric in nature. Isometric means that the muscles involved remain the same length as they contract to resist a force. Isometric strength in the forearm is highly dependent on finger joint angle, and strength at one angle does not translate readily to other angles.

Maximizing surface area contact on a sloper requires an open-hand position.

**1**

When using a sloper, try to keep your COG close to the wall and directly below the hold. Your hips should be as low as possible.

With one hand on the sloper and both feet on holds, the range of motion is nonexistent. The climber can barely maintain his position, let alone move.

**2**

Moving your hips away from the wall will make a sloper more difficult to use.

Raising your COG relative to a sloper will also make the hold more difficult to use. Here, the range of motion is also limited.

**3**

**4**

**1**

This climber using an in-cut hold enjoys a large range of motion. Note how far away from the wall he can position his COG.

He also can move easily from side to side. Here he moves to the right.

**2**

The climber can stand up very easily. He has the full range of vertical motion.

Here he stretches to the left.

**3**

**4**

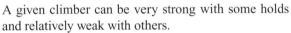
**5**

Here again the climber demonstrates side-to-side range of motion to the left.

**6**

And to the right.

A given climber can be very strong with some holds and relatively weak with others.

Sloper strength must be developed by climbing with an open hand. Many climbers, beginning and advanced, prefer to climb using their crimping strength, but if you want to advance to your potential, you'll have to master slopers. Working with climbers of all abilities, we've seen that a conscious training effort can turn a weak area into a strength.

### Pockets

A pocket is typically a hole in the rock where fewer than four fingers will fit. A pocket is recessed into the rock and usually small enough that it precludes a crimped hand position. As the hand closes from an open to a crimped position, the second knuckle usually makes contact with the outer edge of the pocket before a 90-degree joint angle can be attained. Thus an open-hand position is, by necessity, used most often. There are a variety of ways to hold pockets, however, depending on their depth, shape, and size. A cluster of pockets may be grabbed bowling ball style, or a shallow pocket with a lip may be crimped.

Pockets force us to use three, two, or even one finger, this last kind known as a mono-pocket, or mono for short. Because of the stresses on these isolated fingers, injuries are more frequent. Use care in working holds where fewer than three fingers are used.

Pockets can be used multidirectionally—that is, the best part of the hold can be on either side, on the top, or on the bottom of the pocket. Pocket hand positions are unique isometrically, and climbers must use or train in these positions to improve strength.

### Underclings

An undercling is any hold you pull up on rather than down or to the side. It can be any type of hold (crimper, sloper, pocket) as long as its orientation forces you to use it with your palm face up.

Using underclings effectively depends on the opposition of forces between the hands and feet. In order for an undercling hold to work well, there needs to be at least one opposing foothold. The hand pulls up and the feet press down, creating an opposing tension that glues the climber to the wall. You can feel this tension by locating a large, deep undercling on a vertical wall at four to

One, two, or three fingers and an open-hand position are required for pockets.

five feet above the ground. Make sure there are a couple good footholds just off the ground. Grab the undercling with both hands, step onto the footholds, and straighten your legs. Can you feel the opposing tension between your hands and feet? Your body feels like a coiled spring, with your arms, legs, and torso all under tension.

Although the specific demands of any given move are different and will dictate various body positions, in general an undercling will become easier to use as the center of gravity rises in relation to the hold and more difficult to use as the center of gravity sinks lower. Select a large undercling about seven feet above the ground on a vertical wall. You'll need a number of footholds at various heights under the undercling. Using low footholds and only the undercling as a handhold, step off the ground. Gradually move your feet to higher footholds while maintaining your grip on the undercling. As your center of gravity moves higher, can you feel the undercling becoming easier to hold?

### Sidepulls and gastons

Sidepulls and gastons are two different methods for using holds that are oriented vertically. Such holds are difficult to pull down or up; here the force must be applied to the side.

An undercling is any handhold used with the palm facing up. TOM ADAMS ON COP KILLER 5.13D/14A, AMERICAN FORK, UTAH.

**Involving the thumb by pinching the hold can improve its usefulness.**

A sidepull's effectiveness is often dependent on the climber's center of gravity being opposite the hold. In other words, if you have a sidepull with your right hand, moving your center of gravity to the left makes the hold easier to use. Moving your center of gravity to the right, toward the hold, makes it more difficult to use. Find a flat, right-facing sidepull at head height on a vertical wall, and grab it with your right hand. Stand on footholds slightly to the left of the sidepull. Begin by leaning to the left. Then move your body horizontally toward the sidepull. Do you feel the sidepull becoming increasingly difficult to use as your center of gravity approaches it? You should be able to feel your balance changing from stable to offset and the hold requiring more effort to grasp.

A gaston can be thought of as the opposite of a sidepull. Get back on the wall, but this time grab the right-facing sidepull with your left hand and position your feet slightly to the right of the hold. You should feel yourself pulling away from or across your body, instead of toward it as in a sidepull. Even though you use the hold with the left hand, your balance will be most stable when your center of gravity remains left of the hold. The classic gaston move is one where the center of gravity shifts away from the hold in the "wrong" direction, making the balance more offset and the hold more difficult to use.

### Pinches

A pinch is any hold the climber can use with thumb and fingers in opposition, thereby pinching the hold. Pinches can be any combination of crimper, sloper, and pocket, as long as the climber uses thumb and fingers in opposition. A pinch is less dependent on body position than most other holds, because the finger and thumb combination to some extent negates direction. For example, a

A right hand sidepull. Note that the climber's COG is positioned to the left of the hold.
DOUG HEINRICH ON DIMINISHED CAPACITY 5.12A, AMERICAN FORK, UTAH.

their hands and feet. The better climbers rarely miss their intended holds, and this accuracy contributes to that graceful look.

Simply understanding how to use holds is not enough; an effective climber must be able to find and evaluate holds, and then place his hand or foot quickly and accurately. Efficient climbing involves, in no small part, the precise, speedy placement of hand or foot in the optimal position.

## Precise Feet

Precise foot placement begins with a visual assessment of a hold and ends with weight being applied to it. Your first step is to select a hold to use and decide how to stand on it. Precision requires not only selecting a hold, but also choosing which portion of the hold to use. This is not a problem for the smallest holds, because they provide only one place on which to stand. Larger holds require more consideration. Choose a hold, and then decide which is the most advantageous foot position for the part of the hold you wish to use.

Step two is acquiring the hold in a swift, precise manner. Speed often leads to imprecision, so follow this simple rule of thumb: Move as fast as you can without losing the ability to put your foot in precisely the position you envisioned in step one. At first you need to move very slowly, but as you acquire skill, you can speed up the placement motion until you can quickly place your foot in the position desired.

Step three is a result of steps one and two, rather than a distinct and separate phase, but it deserves attention because of the feedback it will provide you in fine-tuning your footwork. An accurately placed foot does not require adjustment; so if, after executing steps one and two, you find a need to move or adjust your foot placement before putting weight on the foot, you have

**Heel up for maximum holding power on an edge.**

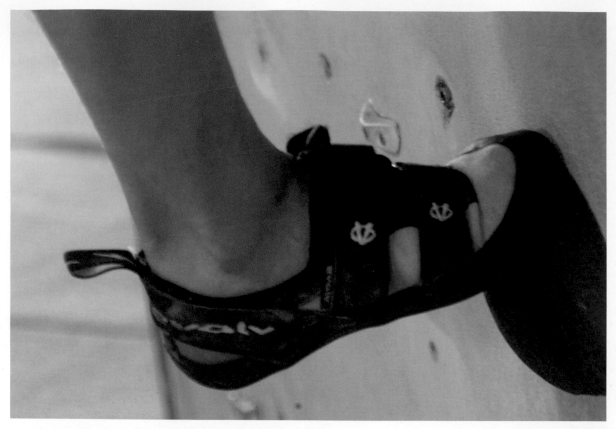

**Heel down improves surface area contact when using a smear.**

not achieved the precision desired. Strive to get your foot to the hold, place it where you want it, and put weight on the hold without having to adjust your foot.

*Activity 3: Silent Feet*

The classic exercise for learning precise foot placement is known as silent feet. On an easy vertical wall with large holds, step onto the rock and traverse, making as little noise with your feet as possible. Beginners should stand on their big toes, feet parallel to the wall, to learn this most basic of climbing foot placements well. More advanced climbers may also stand on the big toe with the foot at a 90-degree angle to the wall or in a back-step position. Simple, right? Maybe, until you know what we consider noise. Any bump, adjustment, or slight scrape is noise and should register with you as immediate feedback that you're not placing your feet as precisely as you should. The goal is to place the foot exactly where you want it every time you move. Not so simple now, is it?

Now it's time to try what you've learned so far. Get on an easy wall and traverse it several times, making as little noise as possible. Count the number of times you misstep in each traverse, and write that number down so you have a reference with which to judge your progress. Be honest with yourself. As you're traversing, ask yourself the following questions: What am I doing that helps me keep my feet silent? How have I changed my climbing to accomplish this goal?

There are several important components to mastering the silent feet exercise. The first is the speed at which you move your foot toward the next hold. A faster speed can result in less precision, so slow down and really try to get your big toe exactly where you want it on your first try. Traverse the wall several more times, slowing your movement way down. If you're still missing the hold, slow down even more, carefully placing your big toe on the part of the next hold on which you wish to stand.

Another component is planning ahead. You simply cannot be precise if you don't choose the exact place on a hold you wish to use before you move your foot. Look, evaluate, decide, and then move. Slowing down will provide you the time necessary to complete this step.

Finally, beginning climbers tend to concentrate their attention on what their hands are doing. This is natural, as we spend most of our lives working with our hands and not our feet. We focus on the hands, and it's hard to break that habit. Beginners often look away from the foot as it approaches the next hold but before it is firmly set. Attaining precision requires that you watch your foot all the way to the hold. You can accomplish this by placing weight on your foot before looking away.

Let's review the three steps to successfully performing the silent feet exercise: Locate the next foothold and evaluate where on the hold you wish to stand. Slowly move your foot toward the hold, aiming the big toe at the chosen target. Make contact with and put weight on the hold before looking away.

Now try the exercise again, incorporating the important elements and counting your missteps. Did you improve over your first few traverses? Keep up the practice and you will soon look as smooth and graceful as those good climbers you've envied. Doug once commented that, once learned, silent feet are a way of life. He practiced the exercise almost daily, even to the point of precisely placing his feet on the stairs at home. Be rigorous about this exercise; precise feet are that important.

## Precise Hands

Attaining hand precision, although usually less difficult than foot placement, is just as important. Climbers often have to move swiftly from one handhold to another, and a missed hold can result in a fall. Moving dynamically illustrates the importance of precise hand placement, but it is certainly not the only situation in which swift and precise placement is important. All misses and adjustments cost time and energy and result in less-than-

optimal performance, so the objective is to improve your accuracy in gaining handholds without having to adjust and compensate.

Efficient use of handholds begins with an evaluation of the next hold. You should determine not only the best hold to use, but also how best to use the hold and which part to grasp. Step two is the swift and precise movement to the targeted part of the hold. Step three is applying weight to move you in the direction desired.

*Activity 4: Glue Hands*

The best exercise for improving hand placement is known as glue hands. Find an easy wall to traverse, and imagine that your hands have been treated with a special glue. Once you touch a hold, regardless of where or how, the glue sticks and will not allow your hand to move. It's pretty tough to get anywhere with both hands glued to the wall, but, like we said, it's a special glue, so that when one hand touches a hold, the other hand can be released and moved to a new hold. Continue across the wall in this manner.

Traverse the wall several times, keeping in mind that once you touch a hold, you may not move your hand until the other hand moves to a new hold. If you need to adjust your hand's placement in order to stay on the wall or make the hold more useful, count one misplacement. Keep a count of the number of misplacements so you can gauge your progress.

As in the silent feet exercise, there is a three-step methodology for mastering this exercise. Begin by evaluating the holds. Choose one and target the exact surface you wish to contact. Step two is to move your hand slowly toward the chosen hold and contact it exactly as you envisioned in step one. Step three is to watch your hand all the way to the hold and put weight on it before you look away.

By combining both precision exercises, glue hands and silent feet, you are encouraged to concentrate on each hand and foot as it moves to a new hold. Your focus needs to be on the appendage that is moving. Concentrate on a single hand or foot movement using the three-step process, and transfer your attention only after weighting the hold.

Are you still using silent feet? Remember: It's a way of life!

## Practicing Precision

The silent feet and glue hands exercises are powerful tools to help you establish a strong base of support, but without the proper environment in which to practice, your efforts won't result in the desired effect. Seek to practice at first in a stress-free environment. Fatigue, physical stress, and fear all affect your ability to focus and perform. When, where, and how often to practice are all important criteria in creating a training regimen and should be carefully considered before you step off the ground.

Practice technique when you are physically rested. If you're tired, you won't be as coordinated or you won't be able to concentrate. You'll develop bad habits. If you practice poor technique, you can expect to acquire poor technique. The object here is to repeat and internalize good habits, not bad ones.

Practice in a safe environment. Fear is paralyzing and causes hesitation, impairing your ability to perform the exercise. Although we normally think about fear in a climbing context as arising from the possibility of being physically injured, fear can also be caused by the risk of being embarrassed by failing in front of others. It's important to eliminate both by practicing where falls are inconsequential and you are either alone or surrounded by others who are supportive.

Practice on easy climbing terrain. If you practice on easy routes or traverses, you'll minimize stress and keep physical exertion at a low level. If the climbing is difficult, you'll spend your physical and mental energy on simply staying on the wall and won't be able to put that effort into practicing.

An important step in gaining proficiency is measuring your progress over time. Keep a journal and note the number of misplacements you make in every practice session. Stay on easy terrain until you are making very few mistakes, say no more than one every fifty feet of climbing.

A new skill, once acquired in a safe environment, must be hardened in increasingly stressful situations for it to be useful in real climbing situations in which you may become physically or mentally stressed. Because stress can originate from physical exertion or fear, you need to stress-proof for both. This stress-proofing should be done gradually, and only when you're ready. Gain mastery of the skill at each slightly heightened stress level, and then increase the difficulty again.

You can create physical stress by moving to smaller holds or a steeper wall. You can create fear by leading or climbing under the watchful eyes of others. Gradually increase physical stress by incrementally reducing hold size or increasing the steepness of the wall. Gradually increase the level of fear by leading easy routes and then moving to more difficult problems, and by climbing in increasingly more populated locations or times. Count your mistakes, record your progress in a journal, and boost the stress after mastering each level, until you are able to perform the desired skill in most situations. You can practice movement training as often as you'd like. We recommend you practice some form during every climbing session and engage in targeted movement training sessions at least twice a week.

And one last thing: Are you still living the silent feet lifestyle?

## QUICK TICKS

✓ Efficiency of movement, rather than raw physical strength, is the basis of effectiveness, and efficiency begins with learning to establish a strong base of support.

✓ The best hand or foot position for a given type of hold is generally that which maximizes surface area contact.

✓ Look for ways to get your thumbs involved. Even a slight purchase by the thumb can hold the fingers in place just long enough to complete a move.

✓ Climbing efficiently means the precise, speedy placement of the hand or foot in its optimal position.

✓ Efficient use of any hold begins with an assessment of how best to use it, followed by the swift and accurate placement of your hand and foot.

✓ To master the silent feet or glue hands exercise, move slowly, plan ahead, and watch your hand or foot all the way to the hold.

✓ Practice movement skills when you are rested, in a safe environment, and on easy terrain.

✓ After reaching proficiency with a new skill, gradually increase stress by incrementally reducing hold size or increasing the steepness of the wall.

Keen perceptual awareness of the body is critical to learning movement. You can improve your climbing and succeed on more difficult routes by developing the ability to perceive and respond to ever more subtle information about how you are oriented in space, the quality of your balance, your muscular tension, and the position of your limbs. All this suggests what movements are available to you at any given moment. The ability to do this at a high level means you must know your body very well; it means having an excellent kinesthetic map of your body.

Kinesthesis is the means by which you perceive movement, the action of your muscles, and your orientation in space. Having a kinesthetic map of your body refers to your sensitivity and ability to respond to all the important information gathered from the central nervous system, the inner ear, and sensory organs located in your muscles and around your joints. Do we consciously or unconsciously know how to turn subtle kinesthetic cues from the body into efficient and enjoyable movement? This is the central question when considering body awareness in climbing.

Unfortunately, the way we tend to learn climbing is haphazard and inconsistent. As a result, our understanding of our bodies and the kinesthetic information we receive from them is incomplete and resembles the maps of the world produced in Europe during the Middle Ages. On these maps, trade routes, cities, and towns were drawn in great detail, but beyond these well-known areas were regions with almost no detail at all, marked "terra incognita," Latin for "unknown lands." This is an apt metaphor for how climbers understand their bodies. It's safe to say that most climbers have good kinesthetic maps of the arms, fingers, shoulders, and toes, and that many decisions about movement are made based on the kinesthetic information received from these areas. But how many climbers can sense kinesthetically, understand, and control with precision the movements of the spine, pelvis, and hip joints when climbing? This kind of awareness tends to be the hallmark of elite climbers, and the rest of us have vast areas of "terra incognita" on the perceptual maps of our bodies.

To determine how well developed your own map is, listen to the language you use to describe your climbing. When you are struggling to learn a new move on a boulder problem or redpoint project, how do you describe the challenges you face? What kind of solutions do you propose? You'll tend to look for solutions based on what you are most comfortable with and understand best about your body. Are you the climber who says, "I need to pull harder on that crimper," or would you be more likely to say, "I need to toe in hard with the left foot, arch my back, keep my arm straight, and turn"? Someone who says the latter obviously has the more developed map and an understanding of how each part of the body contributes to climbing movement. All climbers can develop the awareness and control that lead to improved movement, resulting in better efficiency.

## Some Muscles Used in Climbing

Creating a more complete map of the body is aided by knowledge of the muscles and bones that contribute to climbing movement. A few of the more obvious muscles of the upper body are well known to climbers, but many other muscles also make essential contributions to climbing movement.

Muscles work by contracting or pulling against their points of attachment; they are incapable of pushing. There are three types of muscular contractions: concentric, eccentric, and isometric. Concentric contractions occur when muscles shorten to move a body segment, such as the lift phase of a biceps curl. Eccentric contractions lengthen the muscle; in this case, the muscle is resisting movement of the body segment. Being the loser in an arm-wrestling contest provides a good example of eccentric contractions: The loser is trying to resist the force of his opponent, but as his arm is slowly forced down to the table, the muscles involved are being lengthened even while contracting. Both concentric and eccentric contractions are isotonic, or dynamic, in nature, in that the muscles are moving, either shortening or lengthening. In contrast, in isometric contractions, the muscle remains the same length.

When you grip a handhold, be it a pinch, crimper, or sloper, your fingers remain in the same position, resulting in muscles that are neither shortening nor lengthening despite what may be powerful contractions. This is because the force you apply to a handhold is exactly equal to the force trying to pry your hand off the hold, and this equalization of forces keeps the fingers—and muscles of the forearms—stationary.

When describing muscles, we will refer to their origins and their insertion points. The origin of a muscle is the part that attaches closest to the middle or midline of the body. The insertion is the attachment farthest from the middle of the body. The actions of muscles depend on the movements of joints. These movements are described in terms of flexion, bending a joint such as the elbow; extension, moving a joint from a flexed to a straighter position; hyperextension, moving a joint beyond a straight position; adduction, moving a limb closer to the center line of the body; abduction, moving a limb away from the center line of the body; and rotation, turning a body part.

Following is a list of muscles found in different regions of the body and a description of some ways you use them in climbing. The list is not complete, but it's a good start for understanding the reliance climbers place on many different parts of the body. See if you can feel these different muscles at work when you perform the various activities throughout the book. You can familiarize yourself with these muscles and their actions simply by placing your hand over the muscles being described and moving your body through the range of motion for each joint.

## The Trunk and Back

Trunk movements include bending forward, called flexion; bending to the side, called lateral flexion; straightening, called extension; bending backward, called hyperextension; and twisting from side to side, called rotation. Hyperextension simply refers to movements that extend the spine beyond simple extension and does not imply harm or danger.

### Erector spinae

This group of three overlapping muscles is found on either side of the spine. These muscles are responsible for extension and hyperextension of the spine and also help with its lateral flexion. On steep moves where you face the rock, depending on how your feet are positioned, the action of gravity will either flex the trunk slightly or extend it. Many steep moves require you to stabilize the trunk in an extended position or hyperextend the trunk to keep your feet on the rock, move your center toward the rock, and maximize your reach. The erector spinae muscles make all this possible. On steep moves where your side is in toward the rock, the action of gravity will either laterally flex the trunk away from the rock or extend the trunk. The erector spinae muscles help stabilize the spine and flex it in toward the rock. They are an essential element in all long moves and moves requiring body tension.

### Quadratus lumborum

This muscle's origin is at the top of the back crest of the pelvis, called the ilium. Its insertion is all the vertebrae of the lumbar spine and the twelfth rib. The quadratus lumborum also assists in lateral flexion of the spine, and it supports the lumbar spine through all other ranges of motion. The lumbar spine is of great importance in climbing, as it is involved in almost every move you make.

### Rectus abdominis

Commonly known as abs, these are the obvious muscles on the front of the body that look like a six-pack in well-developed individuals. Their origin is the pubic crest of the pelvis. Their insertion is the cartilage around the sternum and ribs. The main action of the abs is to flex the trunk forward. In many climbing situations, though, slight trunk flexion occurs without any effort on our part, and many moves require extension and hyperextension of the trunk. So why do climbers often have well-developed abs? The climber's trunk is flexed from side to side in a great many situations, a movement to which the abs contribute. The abs also are often used to stabilize the pelvis and trunk. In moves where you bring your feet up high, you often begin with your legs bent and your spine flexed slightly forward. As you stand up to reach for a hold, you extend your legs and spine, and although the abs don't contribute to this extension, they stabilize the pelvis and trunk through this range of motion. This support is critical.

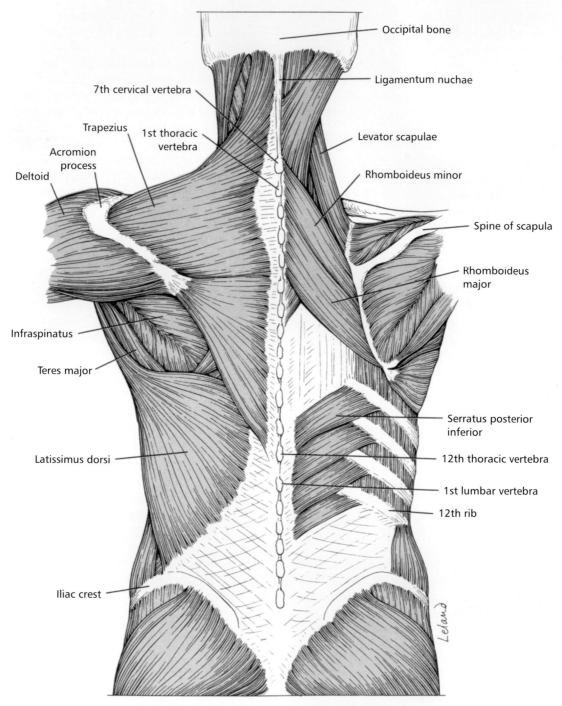

**Posterior muscles of the scapula, trunk, and shoulder**

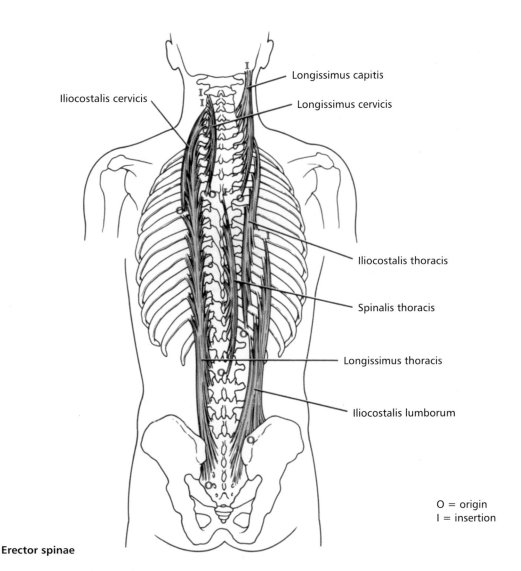

Iliocostalis cervicis

Longissimus capitis

Longissimus cervicis

Iliocostalis thoracis

Spinalis thoracis

Longissimus thoracis

Iliocostalis lumborum

O = origin
I = insertion

**Erector spinae**

## External obliques

These muscles run down from their origin on the lower eight ribs on a slight diagonal to their insertion on the front half of the ilium and the crest of the pubis. Their action when working together is flexion of the trunk. Working independent of each other, the external obliques assist with lateral flexion and rotation of the trunk. You routinely use these muscles and the internal obliques on steep moves to twist the trunk, such as in long cross-throughs, or to turn the side of your body in to the wall and stabilize the trunk.

## Internal obliques

These muscles run diagonally from their origin on the crest of the ilium to the linea alba (the vertical line of tissue that divides the abs) and the cartilage of the eighth, ninth, and tenth ribs. Their actions are flexion, lateral flexion, and rotation of the trunk.

There are many muscles that flex the trunk. In climbing, these muscles often work in an isometric manner, stabilizing and supporting the trunk without resulting in movement. Without this support, the body would become unstable, and steep moves would be far more difficult.

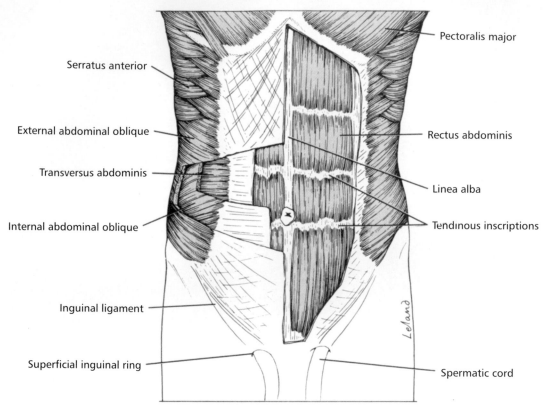

Serratus anterior

External abdominal oblique

Transversus abdominis

Internal abdominal oblique

Inguinal ligament

Superficial inguinal ring

Pectoralis major

Rectus abdominis

Linea alba

Tendinous inscriptions

Spermatic cord

Leland

**Abdominal muscles**

## The Hips

The main actions of the hip joints include allowing the femur, or thighbone, to move forward, called flexion; backward, called extension; in toward the body, called adduction; and laterally away from the body, called abduction. In addition, the femur can rotate in the hip joint. The number of muscles in this region is large. The following are those most important for climbing.

### Iliopsoas

This is a group of three muscles that have their origins on the sides of the lumbar vertebrae, the inner surface of the ilium, and the sacrum. They run in front of the hip joint to their insertion on the inside of the femur's shaft. These muscles, along with several others, are responsible for flexing the hip joint. The iliopsoas are important in climbing because when they are inflexible, they limit extension of the hip joint. Limited hip extension means

that there will be circumstances when you are unable to position your pelvis in the way that is most advantageous. Further, very tight iliopsoas can contribute to tilting the pelvis forward and can cause chronic hyperextension of the lumbar spine. Tight iliopsoas mean that extension and hyperextension of the hip joint force hyperextension of the lumbar spine. Although there is nothing inherently wrong with hyperextension of the lumbar spine, the prolonged, forced hyperextension caused by tight iliopsoas can contribute to back pain.

### Hip adductors

These muscles have their origin on the front of the pubis and insert along the inside shaft of the femur. Their main action is to pull the femur in toward the body or resist a force pulling the femur laterally away from the body. Climbers often use them to pull the knee down in drop knees or to stabilize the hip joint in back

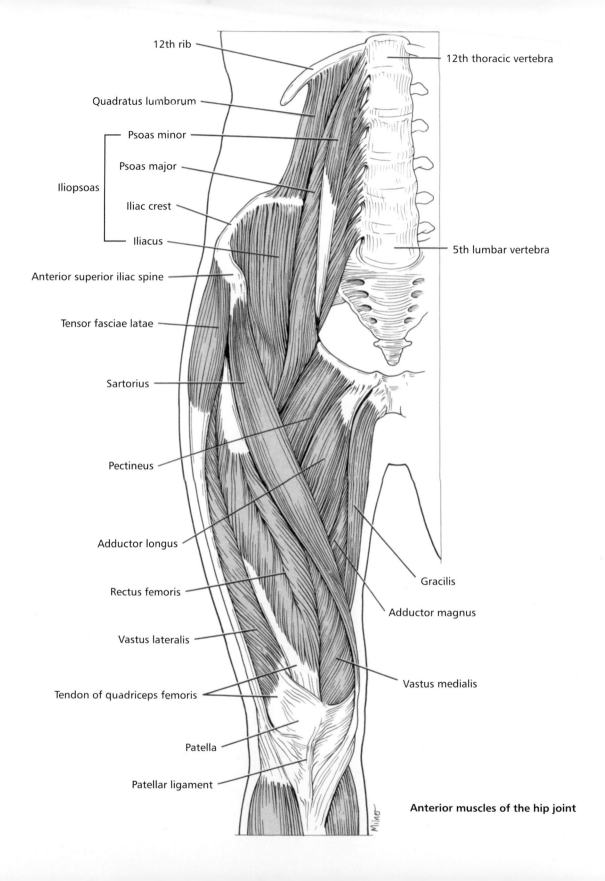

12th rib

Quadratus lumborum

Psoas minor

Psoas major

Iliopsoas

Iliac crest

Iliacus

Anterior superior iliac spine

Tensor fasciae latae

Sartorius

Pectineus

Adductor longus

Rectus femoris

Vastus lateralis

Tendon of quadriceps femoris

Patella

Patellar ligament

12th thoracic vertebra

5th lumbar vertebra

Gracilis

Adductor magnus

Vastus medialis

**Anterior muscles of the hip joint**

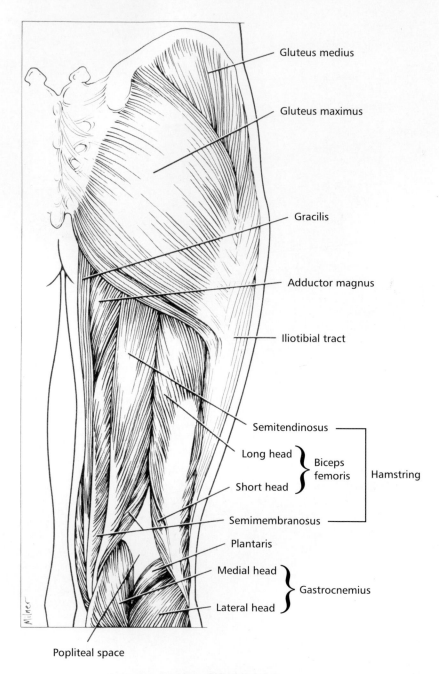

**Posterior muscles of the hip joint**

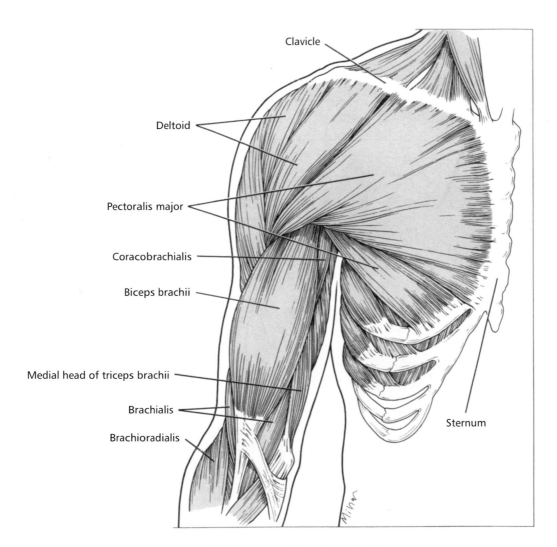

Clavicle

Deltoid

Pectoralis major

Coracobrachialis

Biceps brachii

Medial head of triceps brachii

Brachialis

Brachioradialis

Sternum

**Superficial muscles of the chest, shoulder, and anterior arm**

steps and many positions requiring body tension. In general, anytime you are on a steep move with the side of the body turned into the wall, the hip adductors play an important role.

### Rectus femoris

This muscle's origin is on the front of the ilium, and its insertion is the patella (kneecap) and tibia (shinbone). The rectus femoris muscle does double duty—it both flexes the hip joint and extends the knee. In climbing, you use this muscle every time you stand up on a

foothold. This muscle also helps stabilize the knee and hip joints in a variety of moves.

### Hamstring

The hamstring consists of three different muscles that have their origins at the bottom of the pelvis on a bone called the ischium. From there, these muscles run down the leg and insert at different places on the tibia. Just like the rectus femoris, the hamstring also crosses both the hip and knee joints. Its actions are to extend the hip joint and flex the knee. In situations of body tension, the hamstring works hard to extend and stabilize the hip joint while working with the rectus femoris to stabilize the knee.

### Gluteus maximus

The origin of the gluteus is on the crest of the ilium, and it inserts near the top of the femur. Like the hamstring, the gluteus extends the hip, and it also rotates the hip. The rotation of the hip joint is most important on vertical moves when you are facing the rock. In such situations, rotating the femurs outward allows the pelvis to move closer to the rock, improving balance. On steep moves, the role of the gluteus in hip extension is most

important. Extension of the spine and the hip is essential to body tension, especially at the end of a long move. The extensors of the hip joint are vital in such moves. When we try to do long body tension moves without using these muscles, the results are inconsistent and unstable.

## The Shoulders and Arms

### Latissimus dorsi

A well-known muscle among climbers, the latissimus dorsi's origins are the crest of the ilium, the sacrum, the vertebrae of the lumbar spine, and six of the thoracic vertebrae. Its insertion point is near the top of the shaft

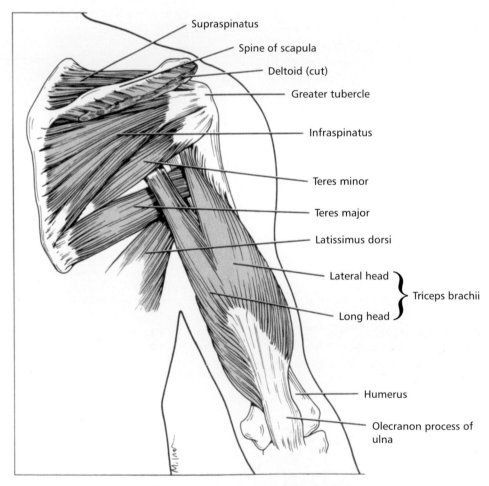

**Deep posterior muscles of the shoulder**

of the humerus bone. This large muscle is critical in adduction and extension of the arm and internal rotation of the humerus. You use your lats in a majority of moves; every time you pull down on a hold over your head, you are using your lats.

## Pectoralis major

Climbers are not generally known for having the well-developed chests that attract attention at the beach. Yet we do use the lower and middle sections of the pectoralis, commonly known as pecs, in many situations. The lower portion of the pecs has its origin on the sternum and cartilage of the first six ribs. It inserts on the outside of the humerus. This is one of the muscles you use when you turn in climbing; it helps turn your trunk in toward your arm. You also use the pecs when you have an arm extended and are pulling or pushing down on a hold.

## Deltoid

The deltoid has three sections. The origins of the deltoid are on the scapula and clavicle (collarbone). The insertion is on the humerus. In climbing, you use the middle section of the deltoid to raise an arm up over your head when reaching for a hold. The anterior and posterior sections also play a role in extending the arm, pulling the arm down and turning the body into the arm on moves such as a cross-through.

## Biceps brachii

The biceps are the easy-to-see muscles that run down the front of the upper arm. Their origin is on two parts of the scapula very close to the shoulder joint. Their insertion is on the radius of the forearm and a band of connective tissue called the bicipital aponeurosis. This means that the biceps brachii crosses both the shoulder and the elbow joints. In climbing, you use the biceps to flex your elbow and rotate your forearm, such as when you use an undercling.

## Brachialis

This muscle lies under the biceps. Its origin is at about the midpoint of the humerus, and its insertion is near the end of the ulna. It is often called the true flexor of the elbow.

## Triceps brachii

This is the prominent muscle on the back of the upper arm. The three parts of the triceps originate on the scapula and along the length of the humerus bone. The triceps insert on the ulna of the forearm. It crosses the shoulder and elbow joints. In climbing, you use the triceps to extend your elbow, such as when pushing down on a hold, something you do almost continuously. Most climbers have well-defined triceps.

## Flexors of the wrist and fingers

Despite their small size, these are muscles that climbers rely on in every move. Six muscles are primarily responsible for flexing the fingers and wrist: flexor carpi radialis, flexor carpi ulnaris, palmaris longus, flexor digitorum superficialis, flexor digitorum profundus, and flexor pollicis longus. Their origins are on the ulna, humerus, and radialis (forearm bones) close to the elbow. In the hand, the tendons of these muscles cross the wrist and finger joints to insert at various locations on each finger. In climbing, the main action of these muscles is to resist the forces attempting to pull you off your handholds. This is important to keep in mind, since there is little correlation between the strength developed in isotonic contractions found in many "hand grip" training devices, which move the fingers through a range of motion, and isometric contractions, which are involved in using handholds.

## Extensors of the wrist and fingers

Eight muscles are responsible for extending the wrist and fingers: extensor carpi radialis longus, extensor carpi radialis brevis, extensor carpi ulnaris, extensor digitorum communis, extensor indicis, extensor digiti minimi, extensor pollicis longus, extensor pollicis brevis, and extensor pollicis longus. Like the flexors of the fingers and wrists, their origins are at various points on the ulna, humerus, and radialis near the elbow, and their insertion points are at various locations in the hand and fingers. Some assume that climbers don't use these muscles much, but this is not the case. Climbers use them in hand and fist jams, which use wrist and finger extension to help the hand wedge into cracks.

The wrist extensors are also at work in other positions, such as on crimps. If you look at the position of

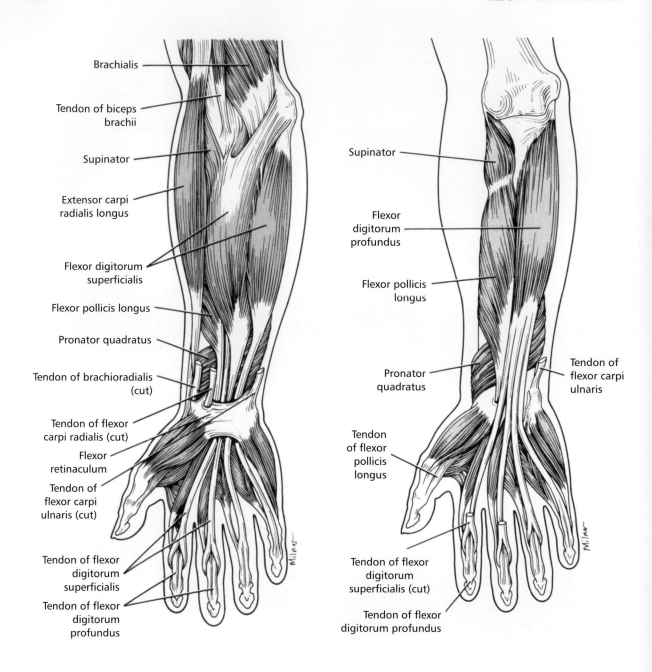

Brachialis

Tendon of biceps brachii

Supinator

Extensor carpi radialis longus

Flexor digitorum superficialis

Flexor pollicis longus

Pronator quadratus

Tendon of brachioradialis (cut)

Tendon of flexor carpi radialis (cut)

Flexor retinaculum

Tendon of flexor carpi ulnaris (cut)

Tendon of flexor digitorum superficialis

Tendon of flexor digitorum profundus

Supinator

Flexor digitorum profundus

Flexor pollicis longus

Tendon of flexor carpi ulnaris

Pronator quadratus

Tendon of flexor pollicis longus

Tendon of flexor digitorum superficialis (cut)

Tendon of flexor digitorum profundus

**Anterior muscles of the forearm: middle layer (left); deep layer (right)**

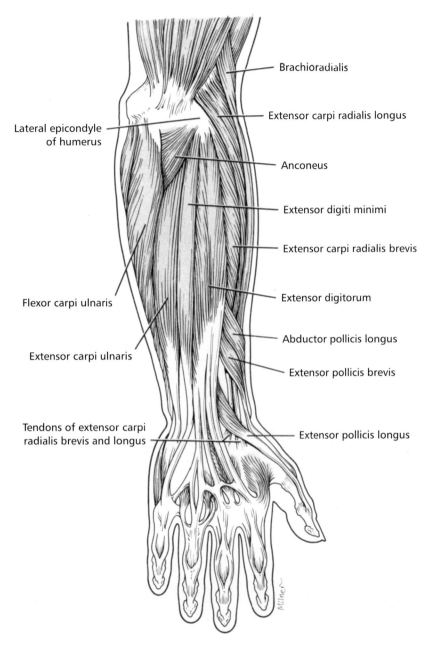

Brachioradialis

Extensor carpi radialis longus

Lateral epicondyle of humerus

Anconeus

Extensor digiti minimi

Extensor carpi radialis brevis

Extensor digitorum

Flexor carpi ulnaris

Abductor pollicis longus

Extensor pollicis brevis

Extensor carpi ulnaris

Tendons of extensor carpi radialis brevis and longus

Extensor pollicis longus

**Posterior muscles of the forearm: superficial layer**

the wrist and hand in many crimping situations, you will notice that the wrist is not straight; it is extended to a greater or lesser degree. One possible explanation for this is offered by climber and mechanical engineer Mike Anderson. Mike points out that extending the wrist brings it closer to the rock. In mechanics, the horizontal distance between your wrist joint and your finger's contact with the rock is called a moment of force. Bringing the wrist closer to the rock through extension shortens the moment of force, which reduces the forces acting on the hand and fingers, thus making it easier to use the hold. Since these muscles cross the elbow joint, they also play a role in flexing the elbow. It would be incorrect to think of these muscles simply as the antagonists of the wrist and finger flexors.

## Body Awareness Activities

The following activities will help you develop your kinesthetic map and find different ways of engaging your body in movement for increased control. They also encourage you to pay attention to balance and how various moves feel to you. You need to do these on easy territory so that you can pay attention to what is happening in your muscles and with your body.

### Activity 5: Blind Climbing: Finding Center

Climbers tend to rely a great deal on visual input. Eliminating that input will make it easier for you to pay attention to what's happening inside your body, perceive the movement of your joints and muscles, and be aware of the position of your center in space. The idea of finding

**Eliminating visual input will increase awareness of the position of your COG and the movement of your joints and muscles.**

center may be a little abstract for some, but basically it teaches the ability to feel where your center of gravity is and feel and understand slight changes in your balance.

In its simplest form, the rules for blind climbing are easy: Put on a blindfold and climb. To make this a better learning experience, climb indoors on a vertical wall with a large number of good holds, and use a top rope. Give yourself adequate time to overcome your initial awkwardness at not being able to see the holds. Once you have become acclimated, you will be able to pay attention to the inner world of your movement. As you climb, take the time in each different position to experiment with your range of motion. Push your body as far as you can to the right and left; move yourself close to the wall, and then move farther out from it. Do you feel your balance changing as you do this? You may be surprised—positions you didn't expect to be are actually stable. Examine how close you typically hold your pelvis and trunk to the wall. You may discover that you tend to hold them so far away from the wall that you are compromising your balance.

Is there anything that you naturally become more aware of as you move? Often climbers report that their attention is drawn to the movement of their hips, both the movement occurring at the hip joints and the orientation of the pelvis. Other climbers report being more comfortable on their footholds or being more aware of whether their arms are straight. These responses reflect the different ways that our attention can be focused inward. Don't just do this activity a few times and then discard it. You'll get more out of blind climbing if you try the activity often enough to be able to maintain an inward focus in your climbing even after the blindfold is removed and you can see the holds.

### Activity 6: No-Handed Climbing/Press Exercise Variations

This activity consists of a series of variations of no-handed climbing on a slab. In this case, "no hands" means that your hands can touch the wall but may not be used to grab any holds. This activity provides an opportunity to explore your lower body and look for patterns in how you use your legs.

This first version is best practiced with a top rope on a slab containing many large holds, preferably one to three per square foot. You can make do with fewer holds

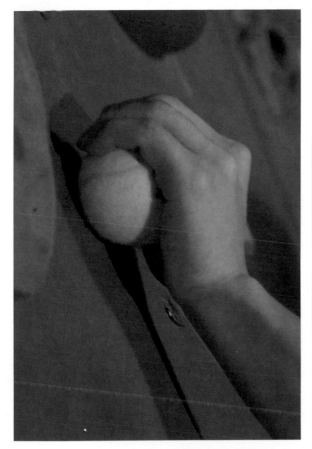

**Correct use of tennis balls for no-handed climbing. You may press the ball against the wall for balance.**

the moment when your center of gravity is positioned exactly over your toe? Try this with footholds of various sizes and shapes.

Because your hands will be of no help in getting you up the wall, you'll need to focus all your attention on your lower body. As you climb, pay attention to what you feel happening in your leg muscles. Every time you feel yourself generating significant tension or movement anywhere in your legs, say the word "pressing" out loud so that your belayer can hear you. Your belayer's job is to compare what he sees in your movement to what you say you are doing. If you don't feel anything happening in your legs, don't say anything. The goal here is only to report what is happening in the lower body; there is no right or wrong amount to be pressing. Pressing refers to more than pushing straight down on the holds; pulling

as long as you have several choices of where to place your foot for each step. Taking small steps is better at this stage. Do this activity in a gym, as it is often difficult to find climbs outside that have the combination of desired angle and enough holds. To prevent you from using your hands while climbing, make fists or hold a tennis ball in each hand. Don't allow yourself to hook the tennis balls or your fists on holds; they should only touch the surface of the wall.

The first time you do this exercise, do it as a finding center activity. At the end of each move, you will be in a position in which you are balanced over one foot, and even small changes in the position of your center will have a dramatic impact on your balance and how stable you feel. Experiment with leaning into the wall and out away from it. Move slightly side to side. Can you feel

**Do not hook tennis balls on holds. Your hands should only be used for balance and not to provide force for movement.**

into the wall with the toes, pushing sideways off a hold, or holding tension to stay on a small hold all count as pressing here. Top-rope the slab one or two times.

What muscles could you feel working? There is a wide range of responses to this question; try to identify where you felt yourself exerting effort. It does not matter how hard the muscles were working; the point is to recognize that your lower body is at work while you climb. Note how high in the body you felt your muscles working. Some climbers will say that the tension stopped at the knee; others will say the hamstring or the glutes. Keep this in mind for later.

How often did you press? The answer varies from climber to climber. Some press the entire time, others find very little pressing necessary, and still others press during upward movement but stop pressing between

**Shift your weight from side to side and front to back. Can you feel when your COG is directly over your foot?**

**Using tennis balls for no-handed climbing.**

steps. If there were times when you were not pressing, what were you doing instead? Were you completely relaxed? Were you actually pressing but didn't realize it? Were you using just enough tension to stay on the hold but not much else? Did you ever need to press as hard as you could, or did you barely feel your legs working? For more experienced climbers, the answer to these questions is often no, because of the easy angle of the wall and the size of the holds. For less experienced climbers, a no answer is often due to a lack of awareness. So how hard did you need to press?

These questions all address the same issue—that is, your level of awareness of the contribution to movement made by the lower body and the refinement of this knowledge. The questions are meant to encourage you to probe your experience and learn all you can about the movement generated by your lower body.

Do the press exercise a second time. If you didn't feel much happening in your legs the first time, take slightly larger steps and try to identify what muscles are working. If you did feel your legs at work, try to press as hard as you can this time for the entire time you are on the wall.

Did you like the way pressing harder felt? Climbers sometimes prefer pressing harder because they can feel it more, and because it feels like they are really taking charge of the activity. Did pressing harder change the way you moved? Often pressing harder makes climbers move faster. Was this harder, easier, or the same as doing no-hands climbing the first time? Often climbers will say that they put more overall effort into it, but this made individual moves feel easier.

At the end of the move, the climber maintains tension from the foot all the way up the spine by arching his back.

Say "press" if you feel tension in your lower body. The climber has shifted his COG to the left by leaning his upper body.

Pressing as hard as you can is not always necessary or desirable in climbing, but practicing this activity gives you an idea of just how much power resides in your legs. Additionally, the exercise should make it possible to take larger steps more smoothly and with greater control.

Now do the press exercise a third time, this time focusing on the end of each move as you balance on one foot. Your goal is to create a line of tension that runs from your foot up your body, as high as you can extend it. Focus on the end of each move. Can you create a line of tension from your toe that extends through your leg and into your lower back? Can you extend that line of tension from your toe up the back of your body? This line should link the efforts of your calf muscle, hamstrings, gluteus maximus, and erector spinae.

Creating a line of tension is important for a number of reasons. It helps develop awareness of various muscles, their contribution to movement, and how this feels. It is important to learn to create and control this tension in your body, since it is essential in many situations, from long moves on thin faces to offset balance moves and moves on steep faces.

As you formed these lines of tension, what muscles did you feel working? Which muscles were not working? Climbers who have difficulty holding tension lines typically are not engaging the appropriate muscles, such as the glutes or the erector spinae. Flexing the glutes at the top of the move is a great way to connect the tension of the leg to the trunk and upper body, which is important on any moves requiring body tension.

### Activity 7: Press Exercise on Steeper Walls

Now that you have spent a significant amount of time working without your hands, try the press exercise on vertical routes using your hands. Keep the wall angle mostly vertical or slightly overhanging; getting on a roof or a really steep face is off-limits. Use a route that you consider moderate, one that you can always do and that doesn't require much effort. If you are a 5.13 climber, choose an easy 5.11. If you are a 5.10 climber, use a 5.8.

In this variation of the press exercise, you'll be examining the relationship between your upper and lower body. Perform the press exercise on your chosen route, and as you climb, address two issues in each move: How hard you are pressing, and whether there are times when you are not pressing. Repeat the activity on at least two moderate routes.

On each move, how hard were you pressing with your legs as opposed to pulling with your arms? Less experienced climbers typically use their legs to "fill in the gaps." That is, they don't drive the body upward from the lower body so much as they pull the body up from the arms and let the legs make up for what the arms can't do. More experienced climbers tend to recognize that even if they use their legs well, there is a degree of complacency in their movement; they aren't actually getting all they could from the lower body.

Were there times when you were not pressing as much as the move called for? Climbers of all abilities usually discover that as the hand approaches and grabs the next hold, they tend to stop pressing and in some

**Climbing with straight arms helps encourage movement in the shoulders, hips, trunk, and knees.**

cases even relax their bodies, dropping body tension and simply hanging from the new handhold. If you didn't notice yourself doing this, go back and do the press exercise on another moderate route, this time paying close attention to what happens in your legs and trunk as your hand reaches the next hold. You may find that you stop pressing but were not aware of it.

This habit of dropping tension, pressing less, and hanging, to a greater or lesser degree, from each new hold is so common that most climbers are safe in assuming that they are committing this error. It is inefficient and wastes a great deal of energy by placing more of the movement effort required on the arms.

To correct this problem, get back on one of the moderate routes that you did earlier, this time trying to produce the lines of tension that you created at the end of each move on the slab. Keep tension running from your toes all the way up your body to your shoulders as you attain the next handhold. Climbers practicing this exercise frequently report that the moves feel easier while taking pressure off their arms. We are not encouraging you to climb with a lot of excess tension in your body; this would be wasteful. We are encouraging you to experiment with using tension at moments when you are prone to relax and to assess the difference this makes. You can't change a well-ingrained habit such as this in one day. You'll need to practice pressing and holding tension every day as part of your climbing warmup and on moderate routes.

*Activity 8: Straight-Arm Climbing*

We include climbing with straight arms as a variation of a number of activities in this book, but it also has value when done on its own. The goal of this activity is to make you aware of how much you are currently using your arms in movement and to help you learn ways to translate this dependence on the arms into movement in other parts of the body. With a little work, a great deal of inefficient pulling with the arms can be replaced with movement of the shoulders, hips, trunk, and knees. There are many situations when the arms need to bend, but the point of this

activity is to reduce the amount of work you are doing with your arms.

Start by top-roping a vertical wall with many good holds. Your goal is to never bend your elbows, so pretend that your arms are in plaster casts from just below the shoulder to just above the wrist. At first you may not even notice when you are bending your elbows, so your belayer should let you know when he sees you bending an arm. Whenever you find yourself bending an arm, try to see what alternatives are available by changing your footholds or body orientation or using your shoulders, hips, and knees. This may take a great deal of practice before you can do straight-arm climbing on actual sequences. This is fine—practice on any holds as long as necessary. If this activity still feels difficult, the skills in the next chapter should help make it easier.

For new and less experienced climbers, gaining an awareness of the possibilities residing in the lower body and learning to maximize the contribution to movement made by the legs and trunk are critical steps in developing as an athlete. Experienced and knowledgeable climbers who are already quite familiar with using their legs tend to find that there are many subtleties to how the lower body contributes to movement. While doing the activities, you may discover bad habits, the effects of which can be felt in every move.

**QUICK TICKS**

✓ Kinesthetic perception is the means by which we sense movement, the action of our muscles, and our orientation in space.

✓ Every climbing move uses many muscles throughout the body working in concert. The stereotype of climbing as relying only on the upper body is incorrect.

✓ Developing a better kinesthetic map of your body will help you to better enjoy and control what you do in each move.

✓ We all have patterns of tension and relaxation in our movements; some are helpful, but others may be inefficient. Becoming aware of them is the first step in controlling or changing them.

ELLEN POWICK ON PUMP-O-RAMA 5.12D, RIFLE, COLORADO. PHOTO: NATHAN SMITH

This chapter groups together a number of moves that climbers usually think of as being independent and distinct, including drop knees, flags, and back steps. Although these movements look different, they serve the same basic mechanical function: They are all ways of bringing the center of gravity closer to the base of support in positions of offset balance.

Turning is one of the first movement skills we teach new climbers. Many climbing movements rely on the ability to turn, and without it, a great deal of climbing terrain is functionally off-limits. Learning to turn properly fosters good movement habits and is often a breakthrough for less experienced climbers. It can be the first time a climber experiences the precision and finesse in his own movement that he recognizes in advanced climbers. This is significant because the aesthetic and emotional values of movement are important motivators when it comes to learning new movement patterns and developing one's self-image as a climber. Further, turns allow climbers to apply their individual style with great personal flair. A turn in climbing can be just as fun, powerful, and dramatic as a turn in dance.

Among experienced climbers, such as those working at the 5.12 level and above, well-executed twists, turns, flags, and drop knees are common, but few climbers are knowledgeable and skilled enough to employ the entire range of flagging and turning opportunities present on steep climbs. Climbers at this level often have one or two favorite moves that they attempt to apply to all situations.

## Turning

From subtle twists on vertical cross-throughs to huge drop knees on steep cave routes to inside flags on gently overhanging faces, all movements that turn a side of the body into the rock achieve specific mechanical advantages. First, turning improves the stability of your balance. When you turn the body, you are moving your center of gravity closer to the rock and toward the center of the base of support. This improves the stability of your balance, thereby reducing the amount of force necessary to reach the next hold.

The second benefit is that turning fosters mechanical efficiency in both your upper and lower body by shifting the effort of movement from smaller muscles in the appendages to larger muscles close to the center of the body. Your bones and joints are levers and fulcrums that are moved by your muscles. Most joints are third-class levers, like a crane, favoring range of motion and speed over the production of force. Turning

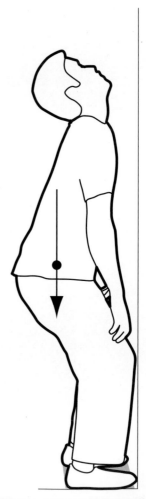

Try to squat with your toes touching a wall. As you squat, your COG moves away from the wall, eventually pulling you backward.

improves efficiency because it helps you keep your arms straighter, thereby allowing the shoulder rather than the elbow to act as the primary fulcrum that moves your trunk, a job for which the shoulder is better suited.

When turning, the forces created by your legs are easily applied to move the center up and in toward the rock. Since your knees cannot bend from side to side (the knee joints cannot abduct or adduct), turning in to the wall provides a distinct mechanical advantage. In a frontal position, efforts initiated from the legs may move the body up, but they may also push the center of gravity out from the rock, necessitating additional counteracting force to be applied by the arms. With the legs turned to the side, it is far easier to generate upward movement by extending the knees and inward movement by adducting the hip joints. A quick demonstration is in order: Stand facing a wall with your toes touching the wall. Attempt to squat, and you'll find yourself falling over backward because your center of gravity is forced away from the wall. Now turn 90 degrees, with one hip touching the wall. Attempting to squat in this position is relatively easy, as is standing up again, because you are able to keep your center of gravity over your base.

In short, turning improves the stability of your balance by positioning your center of gravity closer to the rock and to the center of your base of support. Turning creates a mechanical advantage by allowing your arms and legs to be more effective levers. Finally, turning allows for more effective application of the forces created by pushing with the legs.

So how do you improve your ability to turn? What follows is a sequence of activities specifically designed to teach turning to less experienced climbers. Anyone

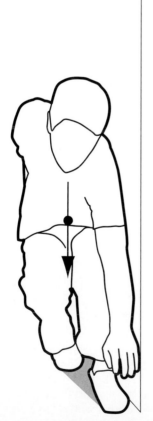

**Squat with your hip touching a wall. Your COG remains over your base, allowing you to squat and stand up easily.**

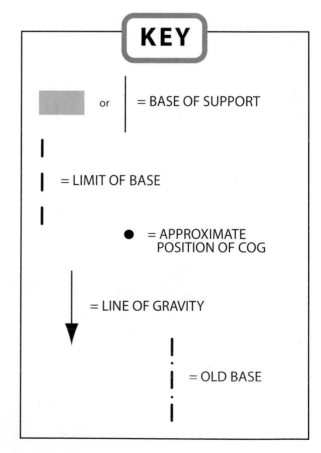

**KEY**

or = BASE OF SUPPORT

= LIMIT OF BASE

● = APPROXIMATE POSITION OF COG

= LINE OF GRAVITY

= OLD BASE

In the backward traverse, you face away from your direction of movement.

The climber is facing to the right and moving left. His toes are pointed to the right.

Move your hands and feet as much as you like, but keep the same hip in to the wall and toes pointed in the opposite direction of movement.

climbing under 5.12 should, at the very least, attempt activities 12, 13, and 14 as a way of checking themselves for this particular skill. Activities for experienced climbers are given in the flagging section.

Perform the activities on a vertical wall in a gym. The wall should have a great many comfortably large hand- and footholds, with at least two large footholds per horizontal foot of wall. These activities do not work on a wall that has few holds or is less than vertical. All should be done with a partner, and each will require about an hour. Take a light approach; being too serious and focused on getting the exercise right will limit your creativity and prevent you from noticing when you really feel the advantages described above. Each activity may seem awkward initially and require a great deal of effort, but with repetition you will feel yourself moving more fluidly and with greater confidence. The feeling generated by each move matters, so your goal is to discover what you find aesthetically rewarding in each activity. Refer to the DVD for demonstrations of the following activities.

*Activity 9: The Backward Traverse*

In this traverse, you won't actually do any turns, but it's an important first step to turning. The rules for this exercise are simple: Keep your toes pointed away from the direction in which you are moving. In addition, try to keep your hip into the wall as you move. This will effectively maintain your body at 90 degrees to the wall. Do the traverse two times, first moving from right to left and then from left to right. As you do, ask yourself whether it's easier to move your right or left hand. In our classes, new climbers find that as they climb to the left, moving the left arm is slightly more comfortable, and when climbing to the right, moving the right arm feels more natural and comfortable. This is because of the body alignment forced by the backward traverse. Having the left side in facilitates moving the left arm, and vice versa. This principle holds true in most climbing situations, which makes learning this pattern important. This traverse keeps you in the same body position for each move. The position is referred to as a back step, in which you stand on the outside edge of one foot and the inside edge of the other with all your toes pointed in the same direction.

*Activity 10: Pivoting*

Another important preliminary skill is to learn how to pivot your foot on a single hold. The goal is to seamlessly turn your foot, without losing contact, from standing on the big toe to weighting the little toe and back again.

Stand up on a couple of low footholds a bit wider than shoulder width, facing the wall. Now turn both feet and your hips so that your toes point to the right and your left hip is in to the wall. Both feet should pivot on their holds simultaneously. You should be facing right, having turned approximately 90 degrees. Leave enough room between the front points of your shoes and the wall so that pivoting won't lever your feet off the holds. Now pivot again, turning your hips so that you face in the opposite direction, being mindful to pivot your feet at the same rate at which your hips turn. If a foot comes off a hold, it's likely you didn't leave enough room between your toes and the wall to allow for the pivot. Repeat the turns until you can fluidly face one direction and then the other.

*Activity 11: Same-Side-In Traverse*

This traverse is a natural next step from the backward traverse and pivoting exercises. This time it's not necessary to keep your toes pointing continuously in the same direction, but every time you want to move your right hand, you must first turn your right side in to the wall, and vice versa—hence the name same-side-in traverse. In order to accomplish this, you must turn your body 180 degrees between each hand move. Your goal is to turn smoothly, focusing on positioning your body.

When pivoting, it is necessary to leave a little room between your toes and the wall.

Turn 180 degrees so the opposite hip is in to the wall. At the same time, pivot your feet so that your toes point in the opposite direction.

Don't worry about what hold you will reach for or how many times you must reposition your feet; by turning and getting into a good position, holds will become available to you. The first few times, this traverse may feel awkward and uncomfortable. Newer climbers may need to move their feet more than they are used to between hand moves. This exercise also requires pivoting on your toes as you learned in activity 10.

Avoid the classic error that climbers often make while practicing this traverse: Some climbers get out of

A common error in the same-side-in traverse. The climber is moving his right hand when his left hip is in to the wall.

Same-side-in traverse. The climber is facing right with his left hip in to the wall and is moving his left hand.

The climber reaches his chosen left handhold.

He now begins his turn to get the right hip in to the wall.

The climber steps through to a new right foothold. Note that he has turned and his toes now point left.

The completed turn with right hip in to the wall and toes pointed left. He is now ready to move his right hand.

Activity 13 on top rope. The left hip is in, toes are pointed right as the climber reaches a new left handhold.

Maintaining straight arms requires pivoting around the right handhold. The lower body provides most of the upward movement.

The right hip is in, toes are pointed left after the climber completes his reach for a new right handhold.

The climber pivots out away from the wall instead of to the side.

sync and try to move the left hand when the right side is in to the wall and the right hand when the left side is in to the wall. This feels terrible and is mechanically a mess. To move your right hand, you must have your right hip in to the wall, and vice versa.

Do the same-side-in traverse as many times as you need to make it feel smooth and comfortable. As you climb, you should feel a rhythm emerging; your movement becomes a little smoother and more confident, and you don't have to think about every hand and foot placement. Now try to combine the same-side-in traverse with silent feet. If you can do this well, you are ready to move on to the next exercise; if not, keep practicing. It can take anywhere from minutes to days to feel comfortable with this activity, depending on your experience level, so don't get frustrated. Relax, have fun, and don't be hard on yourself if success comes slowly. Go back and compare your movements to the examples on the DVD.

### Activity 12: Same-Side-In Top Rope

The rules for this exercise are the same as those for the same-side-in traverse, except that instead of moving sideways, you'll be going up the wall. Don't stick to a route; use all hand- and footholds available. The wall should be at a more or less constant angle of vertical to slightly overhanging. A roof, inside corner, slab, or arête will not work.

If you find that things are going well on top rope and it doesn't take all your attention to do the activity, combine it with the press exercise (activity 6) or silent feet. Try to create a rhythm in which you turn, press, reach, step up, and repeat. This activity ends up forcing every move to be the same, in that as you reach for your next handhold, you are always in some variation of the backstep position.

### Activity 13: Same-Side-In Traverse with Straight Arms

This exercise puts both parts of the formula together, turning the hips and keeping the arms straight so they function as long levers connected to the trunk. Traverse as before, turning your left side in before moving your left hand, and vice versa. Don't run these movements together; complete each turn before you reach for the next handhold. Imagine transferring all

the movement and effort that would have occurred in your elbows to other joints in the body, such as the shoulders, hips, and knees.

Don't worry about getting it right the first few times; the key to all these activities is to relax and experiment with movement. It will take a few tries to figure out what to do with your body to keep your arms straight, and that's okay. But take the idea of keeping your arms straight seriously; imagine your arms in casts or think of them as cranes. Repeat the activity four more times. When you can perform it smoothly, try it on top rope for another three or four laps, using the same rhythm you developed in activity 12. If this goes well, apply the exercise to a variety of wall angles, but don't try to apply it to individual climbs yet. Spend the next several climbing days learning and ingraining this movement pattern. Combine it with other activities such as silent feet, glue hands, and the variations on the press exercise. A good goal is to use this activity on thirty or more pitches in the next several days.

Even though you're practicing this exercise with straight arms, there are many climbing movements in which the arms must bend. The point of this activity is to eliminate unnecessary work by the arms, to learn the full range of movement of which your body is capable, and to let your arms bend as a result of the action of the entire body rather than trying to initiate movement in the arms.

### Activity 14: Straight Arms Variation (Turn from the Knees)

It can help to realize that a specific part of the body can do a great deal of the work of turning. After you are comfortable with the straight-arms version of the same-side-in traverse, perform it with a concentrated effort to use your knees to turn your body. For each turn, can you move your body by turning your knee inward first and letting this motion naturally lead your pelvis and trunk into turning?

## Flagging

Flags are the mechanical wonders of overhanging movement. They feel great, look good, and do a fabulous job stabilizing your balance. The moves most readily identified as flags—the inside, outside, and back-step flags— all serve the same basic purpose of bringing the center of gravity more in line with its base of support.

Inside and outside flags occur when your points of contact with the rock are on the same side of your body: left hand and left foot or right hand and right foot. Your choice of footholds makes a big difference as to which type of flag is optimal. As a guide, your foothold will often be directly below the handhold you are using.

Inside and outside flags can sometimes be used for the same situations; the decision of which to choose is often determined by the height of the available footholds. Inside flags become more difficult with footholds that are high relative to the handhold, leaving little room to rotate the body inward. In these situations, outside flags are more advantageous. However, outside flags will tend to force the center of gravity farther from the rock, because the pelvis does not naturally turn in to the wall in this move. You can turn the pelvis in to the wall in some outside flags, but it takes conscious effort. Additionally, the relative height of the foothold will change an outside flag: With the foot high, the flagging leg has a greater range of motion; with the foot low, the flagging leg will cross subtly behind the foot on the wall.

One very important difference between inside and outside flags is that inside flags often provide greater reach, because they bring the center of gravity higher and closer to the wall. Outside flags are often used as static positions that keep the center of gravity low in relation to the base, whereas inside flags can be done in moves where the climber is standing up, extending the leg, and raising the center.

All flags are by definition moves of offset balance, since the base of support is the thin line between the handhold and foothold. If you are in a flagging position with your center of gravity directly on this line, you will feel fairly stable. You will not need to press your flagging leg into the wall to counter your body's tendency to rotate outward, commonly known as barn-dooring, because with your center on the line, there is no rotational force. As you try to move your center of gravity away from the base, however, either you'll find the movement impossible unless you press your flagging leg into the wall, or you'll find that you can move a little but

An outside flag used to improve balance during a clip. The climber has just reached his left handhold.

He begins to flag by bringing his right leg behind his left leg.

Having used the right leg flag to shift his COG under his left hand, he begins to clip.

The climber completes his clip.

Chris Lindner using an outside flag on a long move on the Big R 5.14a/b, Smith Rocks.

The high left foothold precludes use of an inside flag.

The right foot flag shifts Chris's COG under his left hand, allowing him to release his right hand.

Chris uses his right foot to press against the wall to gain additional height and prevent a barn door.

Right handhold attained, Chris begins to move his right foot to its next position.

it becomes difficult as your body begins to rotate. At this point, pressing the flagging leg in to the wall becomes essential. This outward rotation, or barn-dooring, is a result of the physical principle that states that the farther away a force is applied from the center of gravity, the more likely rotational movement is to occur. On steep moves, this happens very fast, and moving the center just slightly away from the line will result in a powerful rotational force that will try to pull you off the wall.

Back-step flags are simply back steps with one foot off the wall. They differ from outside and inside flags in that the points of contact are on opposite sides of your body: left hand and right foot or right hand and left foot. Despite this difference, back-step flags still position the side of the pelvis in to the wall, and the flagging leg pulls the center of gravity closer to the base of support.

Climber moving into a back-step flag. Contact points are on opposite sides of his body (right hand and left foot).

Try the following exercises as a means of developing your flagging skills. These activities are more challenging than those for turning. Regardless of how hard you climb, these skills should be learned on a vertical wall with many hand- and footholds. Later, you can try them on a variety of wall angles.

### Activity 15: Line and Flag
*(One-Foot-Off Traverse and Top Rope)*

In this exercise, you climb in the same fashion as in the same-side-in traverse, but with only one foot on the wall when you reach for each new handhold. You can take as many foot moves as you like between hand moves, but when it comes time to move a hand, you may have only one foot on the wall. This rule forces you to inside, outside, or back-step flag for every hand move.

Knowing where to place your foot makes this exercise much easier. You can determine this by "drawing the line." The idea is simple: As soon as you reach your next handhold, but before you move a foot, imagine a line extending straight down the wall from your new handhold. The footholds that fall closest to this imaginary line will provide the best balance for the next move. Holds farther away from the line will offer less stable balance and make the move more difficult. The movement pattern looks like this: 1) reach to hold; 2) draw the line to find a foothold; 3) turn and place your foot on the hold; 4) do whatever flag feels best; 5) reach for a new hold.

Practice this traverse as many times as necessary to get the hang of it. Don't worry if it feels strange or takes a lot of thought in the beginning. With repetition (four or five traverses), you should start to develop a rhythm and the ability to perform good flags on many moves. As you repeat the traverse, monitor which flags you are doing most often, either by memory or, better yet, by videotape. Do you find that you favor one type of flag over the others? If so, you are not alone; many climbers prefer one type of flag, with a majority leaning toward the back-step version. If you find yourself favoring the back-step flag, the next traverse will force you to explore other possibilities.

### Activity 16: Line and Flag Variation

This variation really helps climbers to start turning and flagging well. It requires two changes to the previous activity. Try the traverse again, but this time use only points of contact on the same side of your body: right hand and right foot, or left hand and left foot. In addition, you may make only one foot move for each hand move. This forces you to stay in a pattern that requires an outside or inside flag for each move. The process goes like this: 1) as you step onto the wall, make contact with either your right hand and right foot or left hand and left foot; 2) flag and reach for a new hold; 3) draw an imaginary line down from your new handhold; 4) turn your body to move your free foot to a hold on the line. Starting in this manner and following the one-foot move rule will keep you in the right pattern for the entire traverse. This takes a lot of thinking and will take several repetitions before you understand the pattern and the movements involved. Pay attention to what

**1**

Line and flag activity. Reach to a new handhold and draw a line straight down from your hand to find the foothold with the best balance.

Reach to the new right handhold and again imagine a line straight down from your hand.

**2**

Flag and look for a new handhold.

Find a foothold on the line and step to it.

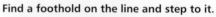

**3**

**4**

**5** Turn and flag by weighting the new left foothold and flagging the right leg.

**6** Complete the turn and repeat the process by reaching for a new handhold.

works and what does not. After doing this as a traverse, also do it as a top rope.

## Variations on Flags

There are a few other important applications of inside and outside flags that are not commonly used. These often occur when the body is in a horizontal orientation. Here are two examples.

### Inside flag while the body is horizontal

When you need to make a long reach at the lip of a roof, an inside flag can sometimes help twist the body higher and stabilize balance. In this case, both the hand and the foot are at the lip of a roof. In this situation, an outside flag alone would not bring the body high enough to complete the move (see page 80).

### Inside flag on a roof

Here you are in the middle of a roof rather than at the lip, but a similar mechanical advantage is achieved, in that the flagging leg pulls the center of gravity closer

to the base of support and extends your reach. An outside flag in the same situation would not provide this advantage (see page 79).

## Drop Knees

The popularizing of the drop knee in the 1980s and '90s proved to be something of a minor revolution in climbing. As sport climbers ventured onto overhung face climbs in areas such as American Fork, Utah; the New River Gorge, West Virginia; Rifle Mountain Park, Colorado; and Logan Canyon, Utah, drop knees proved to be useful on many of the steepest and hardest routes. Drop knees dramatically improve the quality of balance by widening the base of support and lowering the center of gravity within the base. The drop knee puts into practice the basic balance principle that a body with a lower center of gravity and broader base of support is more stable. Drop knees also position the legs so that the pelvis is turned and pulled closer to the rock with far less effort than would otherwise be required from the

**1**

Line and flag variation with contact on the same side of the body (left foot and left hand). The right foot is flagged.

After reaching a new left handhold, the climber steps through with his left foot to a new hold on the line and flags his right foot.

**2**

After reaching the new right handhold, the climber steps through with his right foot to a new hold on the line. His left foot is flagged.

**3**

arms. Behind this remarkable leverage are the hip rotator and adductor muscles, which pull the body closer to the wall. Because the hips are in such close proximity to the body's center, these muscles provide the potential for large forces to be applied directly to the center. Drop knees can thus provide more stable balance in situations that would otherwise involve offset or dynamic balance, and they transfer the muscular effort of positioning the center to muscles that are better suited for the job. For these reasons, dropping a knee remains one of the most common and useful moves on steep climbs.

The drop knee is used in the same situations as flags. Which move will be more efficient depends on the sit-

Use of an inside flag on a roof.

As the climber moves onto the roof, he realizes his next handhold will require a long reach.

As he flags and extends, the climber's body and COG are lifted toward his base.

The flagged left leg provides leverage as well as a good position for the COG, making the reach as efficient as possible.

uation. In theory, if a foothold is available, a drop knee will be more stable than a flag because it broadens the base of support. But the size of the foothold, its exact position, the steepness of the move, and the direction of movement are variables you must address before deciding on a drop knee or a flag.

*Activity 17: Practicing Drop Knees*

Repeat the same-side-in, one-foot-off top rope exercise (activity 15) on a slightly overhanging wall with lots of large hand- and footholds, but this time use both feet. If you want to reach with the right hand, first place the left foot on a low hold, and then bring the right foot to a hold that is at knee level or slightly higher. Turn the

knee so it points to the left or down toward the ground. Keeping your left arm as straight as possible, twist your right hip in to the wall using the large muscles of your torso and upper legs, and then, only after completing all these steps, reach for the next right handhold. Repeat for a left-hand reach.

Continue up the wall in this manner. You may move your feet around as much as you like between reaches, but do not move a hand until the appropriate knee is turned down and the correct hip is turned in to the wall. Climbers new to this exercise frequently reach before setting both feet and turning a hip in to the wall—make sure you complete the lower body movements before moving a hand. Remember to keep your arms straight.

A dynamic inside flag used to lift the body at the lip of a roof. The climber prepares to kick his left leg inside the right.

Throwing the leg has created two advantages: momentum to carry the climber upward and a powerful turn with the COG near the base of support.

As you move up the wall, get a feel for the powerful leverage developed by the drop-knee position. Try a reach by facing frontally in frog position with both feet pointed out and standing on the big toes. Repeat the same move using a drop knee, and you should feel that the reach takes less upper-body effort.

## Back Steps

Besides being a prerequisite to turning, back steps have two important functions. First, they do a great job of holding the body in to the rock all the way through a move and allow the powerful muscles of the upper leg and hip to initiate and control movement. Second, with the legs positioned below and in front of the body, back steps provide you with the ability to apply force directly

to the center of gravity and in the desired direction. Back steps are common, and most climbers don't seem to have any difficulty identifying situations in which they are appropriate. However, many climbers have not mastered the many ways to initiate back-step movements. See chapter 5 for a number of ways to initiate movement from a back step.

*Activity 18: Passing Your Farthest Point*

This activity is a good barometer of how well you have learned your turning and balance. In this exercise, each time you move a limb, you must move it beyond your farthest point of contact. For example, let's say you are traversing to the left, and your left foot is the part of your body that is currently extended farthest to the left. In this situation, you may move

A drop knee broadens the base of support and holds the center in. The climber brings his left foot high to prepare to drop the knee.

Having also moved his right foot higher, he begins the turn into drop knee position.

Left hip turned to the wall, his torso provides powerful leverage for his left hand reach.

The passing your farthest point traverse. The farthest point of contact here is the climber's left foot.

The climber has passed his left foot with his left hand. The dotted line represents the previous farthest point, while the solid line shows the new farthest point.

He now passes his left hand with his right foot.

Practicing drop knees. The climber has raised her left foot and is beginning to turn.

A drop knee position of stable balance. Notice the triangular base of support and the COG positioned well within it. She is now ready to reach with her left hand.

Left hand reach is complete. She will now need to bring her right foot high for the next move.

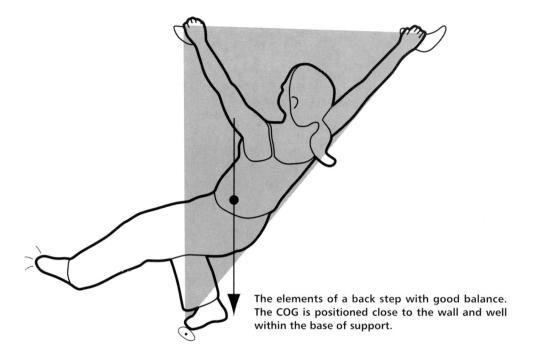

The elements of a back step with good balance. The COG is positioned close to the wall and well within the base of support.

either hand or your right foot farther left than your left foot. This will establish a new leftmost limit, which you will pass in your next move. Begin by making small reaches and steps; the longer the moves, the more difficult the traverse. Repeat this a number of times on a variety of wall angles. The key to this exercise is the turning and flagging skills you just learned.

As you traverse, you'll be constantly battling offset balance. Turning and flagging, in their many forms, will help you counter the inevitable barn doors that will result from this activity. If you can control your balance during this traverse and make the moves feel good, it's a safe bet that you are doing well in terms of turning and flagging.

## QUICK TICKS

✔ Turning the body in to the rock is an essential skill that helps create more stable balance by moving the center of gravity closer to the base of support.

✔ Turning makes moves more mechanically efficient by allowing the arms to remain straighter and the legs to push the center of gravity in the desired direction.

✔ There are three main types of flags: inside, outside, and back-step flags.

✔ All flags are moves of offset balance.

✔ Flags move the center of gravity closer to the base of support.

✔ Drop knees are used in similar situations as flags but keep both feet on holds, which widens the base of support and lowers the center of gravity within the base.

# CHAPTER 5

# Controlling Force: Movement Initiation and Movement Centers

Every move has an origin in the body, as specific muscles and joints begin to work first and set everything else in motion. Being able to control how moves are initiated means controlling the force necessary to do the moves. A move's initiation determines how it will develop, from which muscles will be used to the move's timing and overall effectiveness. In climbing, movement initiation is an important topic, as you typically have two, three, or four points of contact with the rock at the start of each move, providing you with a number of possible movement origins. Unfortunately, climbers tend to leave the initiation of movement up to chance or old habits, which may or may not be advantageous. Some climbers are naturally skilled at initiating and controlling movement without even realizing they are doing it. For the rest of us, learning to use different parts of the body to control movement takes practice. Whatever your abilities, the activities in this chapter provide opportunities to gain a kinesthetic and intellectual understanding of what it means to control movement centers and initiation in order to create more efficient, precise, and aesthetic moves.

Movement centering is defined as the ability to place physical, emotional, and cognitive focus at key points in the body in order to aid in the execution of movement. Movement centers can be points of initiation, but they can also define points in the body that are used to control a move at any time in its development. True efficiency, control, and precision cannot be achieved without being in command of movement initiation and centering.

In a general way, climbers are already familiar with the importance of movement initiation and movement centers. When someone shouts, "Use your feet" to a less-experienced climber, he's acknowledging that there is a choice about how and where to create movement in the body, as well as what muscles to use. Unfortunately, the encouragement to use one's feet is vague and does not address how you might actually go about doing it.

In addition, climbers often unknowingly focus emotional energy on specific aspects of a move that cannot help them. Almost any hand- or foothold you do not like will become the emotional focus of a move as you concentrate on gripping the hold with greater force or worry about slipping off a bad foothold. Holds make very poor movement centers, though, often inhibiting your movement rather than helping it. The goal of this chapter is to provide a method for creating the most advantageous physical and emotional centers for each move you do.

Although climbing is not considered a high-speed sport, individual climbing moves do tend to be rapid and often take a mere fraction of a second to complete. Within that brief time, there is a story, an intricate narrative in the body with a beginning, middle, and end. The beginning is the movement's initiation: what muscles are recruited, what joints begin to move first. The middle is what events follow as a result of the initiation—how the move develops and is controlled, and what path the body takes through space. A move ends when the objective is either attained or missed, when the forces created in the move dissipate or are redirected, transferred into the next move.

As in any classic novel or film, great things can happen within the narrative of a single climbing move. A single move can include radical changes in the positioning of the center of gravity, may use more than one type of balance, and might employ many joints and muscles working together in concert. This narrative requires precise timing among different body parts. In this context, a move is more than a body position, like a drop knee or stem, performed in a particular manner, such as dynamically or statically. Here we're concerned with the inner workings of a move, and we consider a movement initiated from the shoulder to be completely different from one begun with the knee, even if both moves use the same holds and body position. This is not merely an academic distinction. In very practical terms, moves with different points of initiation will have different timing, use different muscles, have diverse paths through space, and may even use dissimilar balance. By the criteria central to our understanding of movement, the moves are completely different even though they may look almost exactly the same to the untrained eye.

## A Brief History

How you conceptualize movement plays a central role in shaping the quality of your movement. The ideas behind movement initiation and movement centers have a rich history. Examining this history will encourage climbers to expand and challenge their thinking about climbing movement and its ultimate potential.

In the eighteenth and nineteenth centuries, the arts, including classical dance, were viewed in a more theological light. At this time, some commentators based their opinions of a dancer's movement on what they perceived to be the dancer's use of her soul during a performance. The belief was that dancers had the ability to move and position their souls within their bodies in a way that would both enhance the dramatic content of the dance and aid in the physical performance of each movement. Dancers were praised for applying their souls well and criticized for using their souls inappropriately. In fact, one writer in 1810 suggested that marionettes had more movement potential than humans, because they have no souls marked by original sin.

No doubt such ideas are alien, if not downright comical, to contemporary climbers, yet there are some interesting concepts at work here. First is the idea that movements have physical, emotional, and even spiritual centers, and that people have precise control over these centers. Second is that there are both good and bad centers. Good or well-chosen centers make moves more aesthetic and efficient, whereas poorly chosen centers make a move more difficult and less pleasing. Finally, the acknowledgment of the power and value of movement is evident. There can be no such thing as "just another move" if you believe that each move compels the investment of your body and soul, including your physical, emotional, and spiritual self. If

climbers had a similar commitment to movement, there would be far fewer flailing their way up routes, doing little more than groping for holds.

In the twentieth century, the legendary dance choreographer Rudolf Van Laban advanced his idea of the kinesphere, an invisible sphere or shell surrounding the body, where every point on the sphere is connected by a line to the body's physical center. Think of a dandelion, which is made up of a large number of individual seeds all attached to a central point. Since the seeds are the same length, they form a sphere in space around their central point. For Laban, the relationship between center and shell was absolute. One can never leave the kinesphere, and moving the body in space requires transporting the kinesphere with it. The remarkable aspect of this idea is that the structure of the kinesphere necessitates that all movements originate in the body's center, radiate outward along the lines that connect the center to the kinesphere, and as a result, affect the rest of the body.

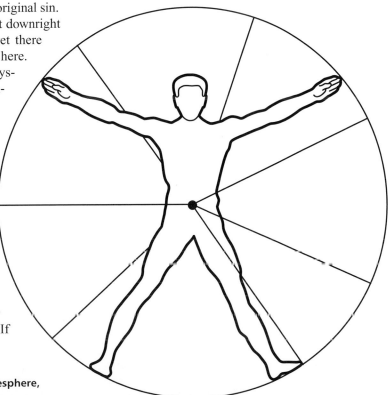

**Laban advanced the notion of the kinesphere, with its center at the center of the body.**

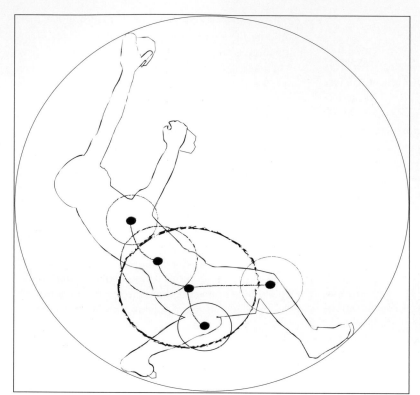

Forsythe suggested that movements have multiple kinespheric centers.

over movement, as it keeps their attention focused inward and allows them to select the best center for every stage of a move's development. A move may have one or multiple movement centers, based on the athlete's skill and the demands of each move.

From these ideas, we can extract a number of productive concepts for climbers. First, it is possible to be deeply invested in movement. More than simply getting from hold *a* to hold *b*, your movement contains a great deal of expressive potential. For example, the manner in which you move on a climb reveals your emotional state. You can easily describe the differences you might see in the movement of a confident climber versus one who is frightened. But beyond exposing your emotions of the moment, movement can also be an expression of your ideals about what climbing is or should be. Certainly the movement of climbers renowned for their grace, creativity, or physical power is a direct reflection of both their skills and beliefs. To think of movement in these terms is to have respect for each move and confidence in the intrinsic value of movement, characteristics common to those who find success in climbing.

Conceptualizing the soul of a move, the kinesphere, and movement centers are all creative ways of engaging the basic physical fact of movement: All movements have points of origin in the body, and in each move you have the ability to control these origins. The use of a center may be intentional or unintentional, well matched or poorly suited to the needs of a given move. Poorly chosen centers make movements more difficult, inconsistent, and less efficient. Well-chosen centers create precision, efficiency, and a sense of mastery and control.

What makes this construct appealing is not just its creative imagery, but also its real effectiveness for creating movement. Considering the importance of balance in movement, you can appreciate in Laban's method the significance of initiating all movement from the body's center as a way of creating stability and power.

During the latter half of the twentieth century, other dancers expanded on Laban's ideas. William Forsythe suggested that movement need not have a single fixed origin in the body. Forsythe suggested that a movement could be initiated from any number of points in the body, not just the center, and therefore complex movements may be made up of multiple smaller kinespheres, each being centered on a different point in the body. Forsythe replaced the model of a single fixed center with a dynamic model of multiple emerging centers capable of interacting with one another throughout the body. Forsythe's model of multiple and dynamic kinespheres is well suited to the demands of the complex, often asymmetrical movement found in modern dance. Using this model, athletes can gain remarkable control

## Initiating Movement from Centers in the Lower Body

The activities in this section will foster impressive improvements in movement quality. To obtain the best results, practice them when you have sufficient time to examine the details of your movement. You will be exploring the link between body and mind and between ideas and physical movement, so have fun and don't try to force a result. If you are not in the mood or attempt to rush, they will provide you with little benefit.

For this set of activities, you will be on a slab, on top rope, doing a variation of no-handed climbing. Choose a slab with many large, comfortable footholds. Your hands can rest against the wall for balance, but do not touch the holds with them or use them in any way to

**Activity 19: Experiment with the range of motion. This climber is shown at his left- and right-most limits.**

make upward progress. Before you start the exercises, make sure the climbing on the slab is easy for you. You should not have to struggle at all, and there should be many foothold choices at all times.

Each of the activities requires you to center your movement in a different joint. To accomplish this, you need to prepare for each move by doing the following. First, experiment with the range of motion of the specified movement center. This means testing how far you can move that joint in all directions; get to know the full range of possibilities, only then deciding on the best position from which to begin the move. As you move, the rest of your body will naturally follow along. Don't worry about the rest of your body; focus on the range of motion in your chosen center. Second, consider the speed of the move. Will it need to be fast or slow? Will you explode or glide? Third, concentrate exclusively on that joint. A good way to do this is to close your eyes as you play with the range of motion of the joint, and visualize its movement through space. Now perform the move, remaining fully focused on the initiating joint. Repeat this process on each move to the top of the slab.

Initially, this process may take a lot of effort. Think of these activities as play or experimentation with movement; you don't need to do them perfectly. With practice, they will become easier, more automatic and more fluid.

### Activity 19: The Higher Knee

The goal of this activity is to initiate movement from the knee. Get on the wall with your left foot higher than your right. Your left knee will be the point of initiation for the first move. For every move, begin with both feet on the wall, and end balanced on what began as your upper foot. Then put your free foot back on the wall a little higher than the foot you were balancing on and try another step. This pattern will be the same for the next several exercises. Take medium-size steps so you can focus all your attention on the point of initiation. Use your hands for balance only, and not to help in any way with your upward movement.

Before performing each move, take a moment to focus on the higher knee. Experiment with the range of motion and really feel the knee moving. How far can you bend it? What is the most comfortable starting point for this move? How fast or slow will you need to move in order to initiate movement from the knee? After you

Centering a move in the upper knee. Focus on the higher knee and test the range of motion.

Now, while fully focused on the upper knee, perform the move.

have answered these questions, and all your physical and cognitive energy is focused on your knee, try the move. Keep proceeding in this manner to the top of the wall.

How successful were you at initiating movement from your higher knee? How did initiating from the knee feel? Did it feel familiar or strange? If this movement center felt familiar, it's because this is the way we commonly ascend stairs. It is also a common way to initiate stepping up in climbing. To find the limits of initiating movement in the higher knee, get back on the wall and take a larger step—one in which your higher foot is much higher than the lower foot. Again focus on the knee, making it the sole point of initiation for the move. What happened? Depending on the size of the step, the move is either difficult or impossible.

*Activity 20: The Lower Knee*

Now shift the point of initiation to the knee of the lower leg. Go through the same process you followed in the previous exercise, again looking critically at the range

of motion. How fast will you need to move? Where is the best starting point? Focus all your physical and mental energy on the lower knee. Initiating movement from the lower knee may be more difficult. If so, try imagining that as you bend down into your knee, you are compressing a powerful spring. When you are ready to move, release the compressed spring and ride it upward. Try taking different-size steps and note what happens. Top-rope the slab, focusing on the lower knee at least three times before moving on.

How successful were you at initiating movement in the lower knee? How did these movements feel to you? Was initiating from the lower knee better for some steps than others? The answer is usually yes. Climbers often report that small and medium steps work well when done from the lower knee, but on high steps, it is difficult to get all the way up when centering only in the lower knee.

Centering a move in the lower knee. Focus on the lower knee and test the range of motion. Bending down into the lower knee helps begin movement initiation.

This is fine; one movement center often can't do it all. For now, you just want to get familiar with using different movement centers. As you practice movement initiation from the lower knee, several problems may arise:

- *Initiating movement from the upper knee despite attempting to use the lower knee.* Often initiating moves from the upper knee is a well-established habit and thus hard to change. Practicing repeatedly with the image of the spring may help you switch from upper to lower knee.

- *Moving too slowly to force the body to follow.* If you try to initiate a medium or large step from the lower knee and do it slowly, you will default to initiating the move from the upper knee. Practice with the image of the spring, or try exploding from the lower knee. When done right, it feels like you're gliding.

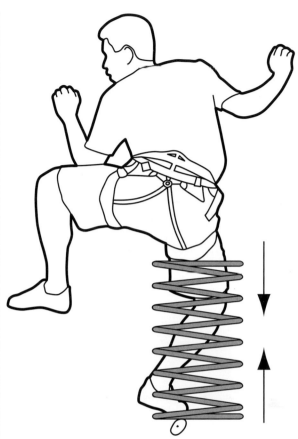

**Imagine your body compressing like a powerful spring to help initiate movement from the lower knee.**

**2**

**Concentrating all your physical and mental energy in the lower knee, complete the move.**

- *Rushing each step and not fully centering your attention on the lower knee before moving.* Doing these activities presents real challenges: They ask you to think about movement in different ways. They ask you to invest great concentration on the simplest features of movement. Doing these things takes patience and time. Don't rush, and don't worry that you look silly working so hard on a slab. Remember, this is an exploration.

*Activity 21: Both Knees Together*

This activity is based on Forsythe's notion of multiple interactive centers. Here you initiate movement from the knee of the lower leg and finish the move with the knee of the upper leg. Again, put some thought into the

**Using two movement centers to step up. Bend down to begin the move in the lower knee.**

**Finish the move by focusing on the upper knee. Note the tension in the muscles of the upper leg as the climber shifts emphasis from lower to upper leg.**

range of motion, speed, and style of each move before each step up. Also work on differentiation between your legs, starting with one and finishing with the other. Can your partner see what you are doing in each move? Are both knees really participating in the move? Practice this on at least three top-rope runs before moving on.

How successful were you? How fast did you need to move and why? What kind of steps did this work on? Climbers often find that using both knees provides more control and allows much larger steps. The lower leg is in a better position to initiate a step up, and the upper leg is in a better position to finish the move. Using multiple movement centers should have made the moves far easier than using only one. You can apply this way of moving to many other situations in which you would rely on your arms to pull through a large high step. If using both knees as movement centers felt

good and powerful to you, move on to the next activity. If not, keep practicing until you get the timing right and it starts to feel natural.

### Activity 22: The Hips and Pelvis

This activity is based on Laban's concept of the kinesphere, wherein moves originate in the center of the body and move outward. Again, rest your hands on the wall for balance only, position one foot a bit higher than the other, and find the potential range of motion and optimal speed for each move prior to stepping up.

With your eyes closed, move your pelvis slowly from side to side while visualizing the movement. Feel your hips moving smoothly in their sockets, and see in your mind's eye your center moving back and forth. How far can you move to the left and right? After feeling your range of motion and focusing your attention

1

Initiating movement from the center. Notice the effect this has on the climber's spine. He has coiled his center like a spring.

The movement of the center to the left has carried the climber through the move. Note continued tension in the arched back.

2

As the move progresses, the climber arches his back and effectively throws his center to the left.

on the pelvis, try the move. Begin each move with both feet on the wall, one above the other, and finish balanced on what began as your upper foot.

How does focusing on the pelvis feel compared with the knees? Is the pelvis a good center for some moves but not others? Climbers tend to feel that centering movement in the pelvis is smoother and does a good job of tying everything together, with the rest of the body easily following along. If it didn't feel this way to you, practice it a few more times before moving on. The pelvis may be the single most important movement center, so keep practicing with it, throwing it with different amounts of force on both smaller and larger steps.

*Activity 23: Switching It Up*

Top-rope the slab again, this time trying to choose the center that will be best for each step. After each move, see if your partner can tell what center you used to initiate the movement. If you are focusing well, your partner will easily be able to tell what center you chose,

3

Using different centers has a dramatic effect on how the body moves. Here the climber uses his upper leg.

The arched back is evidence of movement initiated in the climber's center.

In this instance, the climber has initiated movement from his lower leg.

because each move will look different. If your partner can't tell, take a look at the examples on the DVD and compare them to your own movements.

## Movement Initiation on Vertical and Steep Terrain

The next step in learning to control movement initiation is to try moves that involve the upper body along with the lower body. For this exercise, find an easy vertical wall with many holds at a grade far below your current ability.

### Activity 24: Back-Step Top Rope

In this exercise, you'll perform the same-side-in traverse (as in activity 11) by initiating each upward movement from the knee of the leg directly under you. The same-side exercise requires you to turn your right side in to the wall before moving your right arm, and vice versa, so that each move is a back step. It is the inside, or back-stepped leg from which you initiate movement. While

Activity 24: Begin the exercise in the back-step position.

Focus on the knee of the back-stepped leg.

Initiate movement in the knee. Experiment with different starting positions and speeds.

in your starting position, consider the range of motion, best starting point, and speed at which you should move. Play with this by starting in different positions; have fun and compare what you are feeling to what your partner sees. Repeat several times. The goal is to find the best speed and starting point in each move. You want to find

the starting position for each move that allows you to create a powerful movement center in the knee, giving you the feeling that the center is doing all the work and you are gliding up the wall.

After some practice, perform a variation of the exercise, this time keeping your arms straight. This should make the feeling of initiating from the knee more dramatic. While performing the original exercise, you may have been initiating some of the movement from your arms without knowing it. Keeping the arms straight makes it very difficult to initiate from the arms, so this version will reveal how good you are at initiating from the knee.

Now perform another variation, this time initiating the movement from your hips. Because of the orientation of your body and the angle of the wall, you will experience a much different range of motion and feel than when working on a slab. Try to sag down and slightly out from the wall before initiating the move; this will create some space for you to work within. If you are close in to the wall and already standing up, any movement will be minimal.

## Using Imagery to Assist Movement Initiation

Imagery is a powerful tool, not just in terms of previsualizing a sequence before a redpoint or on-sight attempt, but also for controlling how you perform individual moves. In truth, all the activities presented in this chapter thus far have relied on a general type of imagery: In every exercise, you were asked to imagine that the movement was centered around specific points in your body. You likely found that this changed the way you moved, suggesting that imagery is indeed a powerful movement tool.

By using the concept of a point in your body as the center of a move or imagining your leg as a spring, you can achieve precise control over the development of individual moves. In fact, the subdiscipline of kinesiology known as ideokinesis is dedicated to studying the use of imagery for body alignment and the execution of movement. In the remaining activities in this chapter, you will use different images to control movement initiation and discover the power that visualization has to improve your climbing.

1

The same-side-in exercise with straight arms. Keeping your arms straight prevents you from initiating movement in the arms.

The climber's arched back suggests he has initiated this move from his center.

2

Observe the tension in the climber's legs as he reaches for a higher right handhold.

Using the left handhold as a pivot, he moves away from the wall to rotate upward. Movement initiation in the legs was necessary to complete this move.

3

4

**To initiate movement, imagine your spine being stretched like taffy. Let the image of your spine being lengthened carry you to the next hold.**

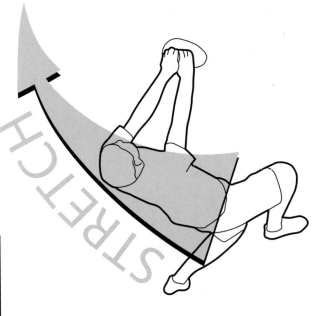

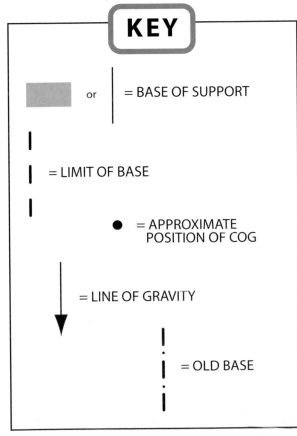

## KEY

| | |
|---|---|
| ▮ or │ | = BASE OF SUPPORT |

│ = LIMIT OF BASE

● = APPROXIMATE POSITION OF COG

↓ = LINE OF GRAVITY

┊ = OLD BASE

*Activity 25: Lengthening the Spine*

Start with the same-side-in traverse (activity 11), but this time focus on your spine during the phase of movement when your center of gravity is rising and your hand is moving toward the next hold. Initiate the movement by lengthening your spine as if it were a piece of taffy being stretched. Rather than focusing on the reach, let the image of your spine being lengthened carry you to the next hold. You want to visualize your spine lengthening and feel it being gently stretched. Repeat the move using this image until you can both visualize and feel your spine lengthening.

This image, like most, will be more effective on some moves than others. Make a point of trying it on long and short reaches. Where is it most effective for you? What happens as you initiate movement this way, and how is it different from just reaching for the next hold? Not surprisingly, this image works well for a variety of long moves. It often does a good job of helping the legs and trunk work together on moves.

A climber sags in preparation to initiate movement from her hips on an overhanging route.

The climber has thrown her hips upward, carrying the rest of her body with them.

The momentum created by her hips allows the climber to reach the next hold.

Initiating movement by arching the back and focusing on the center.

### Activity 26: Arching the Back

Like lengthening the spine, this method of initiation is easiest to learn in a back-step position. It is applicable in many situations, but a simple back step gives you enough room to learn the move. Find an easy back step on a slightly overhanging wall and position yourself very low, with your back relaxed, even sagging a little. Initiate the move by arching your back. Imagine this arch rising up and carrying your body with it; let it pull your body through the move. Practice the move with this image several times, arching your back at different speeds and with different amounts of force. For learning purposes, it is often best to exaggerate the move as much as you can to get the feel of it.

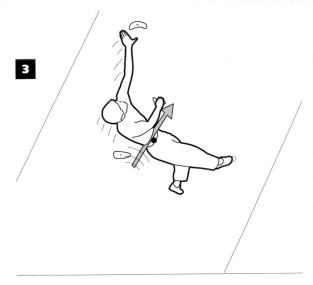

**3**

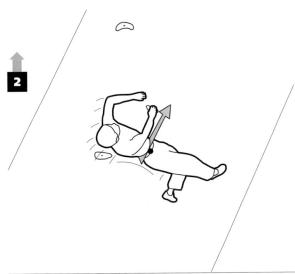

**2**

**1**

What changes did you notice in your movement when you initiated by arching your back? How did the rest of your body respond, especially your legs? The lower back is of great importance in climbing, and many climbing moves are initiated with some degree of back extension. In addition, body tension is dependent upon the lower back. As a consequence, you should continue to practice initiating movement from the pelvis and lower back each day. A well-initiated movement from the lower back should feel as if you are being lifted. You will often feel like you are pulling much less from the arm and your body is more stable than usual. Spend some time watching more accomplished climbers, and note how often and in what patterns you see them arching their lumbar spine.

*Activity 27: Applied Bouldering*

The next step is to apply what you've learned to real climbing. Find a steep boulder problem with large holds three V grades or more below your current bouldering level. Your goal is to break down this problem move for move and decide on the best method of initiation for each move. The activities thus far have not explored all the possible movement directions or ranges of motion for each movement center. You are going to need to use different ranges of motion and different combinations of centers to be successful on each move. Figuring out how to do this takes patience and effort. Perhaps the simplest way to approach this boulder problem is to climb it one time and determine how much of the effort of your movement came from your upper body. As you then experiment with each move, your goal will be to transfer that effort to the movement centers you deem best for the move.

There can be a good deal of individual variation in how movement centers are applied. We all have different preferences; some centers feel better than others, so as you practice, note which moves work best for you. The descriptions that follow are guidelines, but they do not describe the full range of possibilities.

**Initiating a reach by arching the back. Begin in a back step with your back relaxed. Initiate the move by arching your back and letting it pull you through the move.**

- Arching the lower back: Moves requiring a lot of body tension, back steps on steep climbs, very thin moves at any angle.

- Stretching the spine: Any long reach, especially reaches in which covering the last few inches to the next hold is very difficult or moves that start out in stable balance and become low-quality offset balance as your center rises and your hand approaches the next hold.

- Throwing the pelvis: Dynos and any move on steep rock. The smaller the holds or the steeper the rock, the more important throwing the pelvis becomes. Always keep in mind that timing is critical on such moves. If your pelvis reaches its most inward posi-

tion too early or too late, it will make the move more difficult. The pelvis must reach its most inward and upward position at the same time your hand reaches the next hold.

- Knees: Stepping up on any angle, almost any back step, drop knees, and any turn where the footholds are good enough to pivot on. When learning to center moves in the knees, it's best to practice on moves with large footholds that allow for significant pivoting. When learning to center a drop knee in the knee, it's best to do so on dynamic drop knees; that is, any drop knee in which you can throw your knee down with some real force so you can feel the effects this has on the rest of the body. Also use both knees together for high steps.

The real power of controlling movement centers will become apparent only when you learn to use them in combination (similar to Forsythe's ideas about moves having multiple emerging kinespheres), such as initiating a long turning move in the knees, then throwing the pelvis, and finishing by arching the back. If you can master this type of patterning, you will discover that you can repeat a challenging move the same way again and again. In fact, one of the most powerful uses for movement centers and initiation is prescribing specific centers for redpoint crux moves. Being able to repeat a crux sequence precisely will keep you efficient even when you tire.

## The Shape and Path of Moves Through Space

Just as every move has one or more points of origin in the body, each move also has a path through space. Another powerful way to approach movement initiation is to visualize how the body needs to move in space: Visualize a specific shape or path, and then initiate the move in an attempt to make the movement of the center conform to the path you visualized. The path of a move in space is both a physical and perceptual fact. The path, or position of the center of gravity, is a result of all the forces working on it during a move, so knowing and controlling the path of a move can tell us a lot about how well we are executing it. Since the center is not a fixed point in the body, it is somewhat difficult to

**The light approximates the path of the center through space. The path is a result of all the forces working on the COG.**

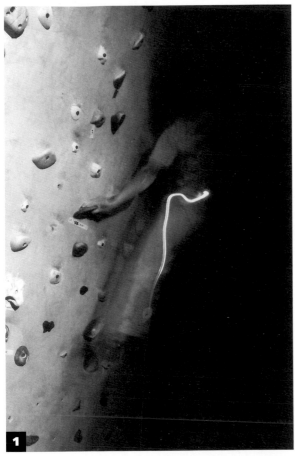

Two different attempts on the same dynamic move: The first attempt has little control. The path of the body is more straight up during the move and out from the wall at the end of the move.

In the second attempt, the path through space is diagonal up and in to the wall. The center does not fall out from the wall at the end of the move.

calculate its position during movement. We will refer to moving the pelvis through space, since its position in the body is constant, and the center of gravity remains fairly close to the pelvis in most situations.

On the perceptual level, climbers have talked about the shapes of moves for years, especially when describing dynos. It is often said that well-executed dynos can be created by throwing the body into an outward C-shape arc. In casual observations, dynos sometimes appear to have an outward arc shape, but when more rigorous observational methods are used, we no longer see an outward arc but rather diagonal lines and inward curves. This makes sense because setting the center of

gravity in motion away from the rock is, without question, mechanically inefficient. When contact with the rock is broken on long dynos, the body will move in a straight line until acted upon by another force. If you were to execute a long dyno via an outward arc, you would need to find some other force to bring you back in to the rock, which does not happen.

In some situations, though, a small outward arc is visible, but this does not contribute to the move's efficiency, nor is it something a climber can intentionally create. When a climber is facing the rock straight on, the feet are at the same level, relatively high at the start of the move. A small outward arc of the pelvis is a result

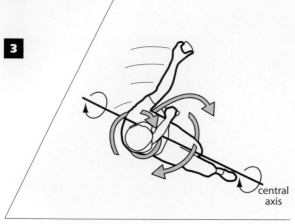

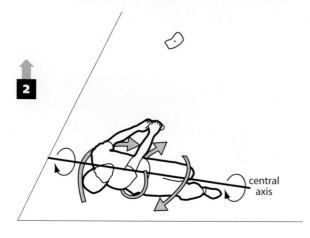

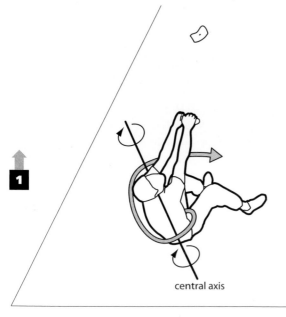

of the climber pushing down with the feet as the femur rotates around the axis of the knee joint the way the hands of a clock rotate around a central point. In this position, the knee is unable to move inward because the rock blocks this movement. In short, the arc of the pelvis is a result of where the knee is in space but not an inherent characteristic of an efficient dyno.

The path of the pelvis has many variations, especially at the beginning and end of moves, but there are some common features among the forces at work in different moves, which lead to similarities in what we want to visualize. Most, if not all, climbing moves involve forces at work to move the center upward and inward toward the rock. Newton's third law states that for every action there is an equal and opposite reaction, which reminds us that creating a force to move the body inward and upward is achieved by applying outward and downward forces to footholds and handholds. The timing of these forces is influenced by the size and shape of the holds.

Challenging moves on slopers require that the outward force be applied to the handholds very early in the move, since slopers have little ability to resist outward force. You can feel this when attempting to down-climb a difficult sloper move. The start of the move, when you release the higher handhold, is most difficult, and as your center moves lower, the move gets easier. The only time a sloper will be able to resist significant outward force is when your center of gravity is sufficiently lower than the hold itself, so on difficult sloper moves, inward movement must be initiated first, before the center of gravity rises and the mechanical advantage of the handhold is lost. In moves such as this, the path of the pelvis may take the shape of a slight inward arc, which makes mechanical sense because the center will begin to move inward just before it begins to rise.

**When a move involves turning, the path of the pelvis can take on a twisting, corkscrew shape.**

On moves with positive hand- and footholds, the path of the pelvis will be different. Since positive hand- and footholds can resist outward force throughout the move, climbers often apply outward and downward forces equally throughout the move, meaning the path of the pelvis will be a diagonal line. In other situations, such as a long move that transitions from an overhang to a slab, the path of the pelvis may be a more or less straight vertical line, since no inward movement of the center is necessary. In moves involving turning, the path of the pelvis can take a twisting path similar to that of a corkscrew. Use the activities that follow to practice initiating movement according to the shape you want it to have.

### Activity 28: Creating Inward and Outward Arcs

On a wall that is either vertical or slightly overhanging, find two large sloping handholds close together that you can use comfortably without pinching them. With your body facing the wall, attempt a small two-handed dyno to positive holds from these slopers. Make the target holds within what you could reach statically, about a foot or two above the slopers. Try the move one or two times to see if it's easy enough for you and to get a feel for where your feet need to be placed. Then try the move by visualizing and using an outward arc for the path of your pelvis. Take a moment to visualize this outward arc, and then throw your pelvis into the arc to execute the move. What happens? This provides a dramatic demonstration of why an outward arc does not work in climbing. You may have found it impossible to create an outward arc, or the outward arc may have thrown you off the wall. Either possibility is likely, since slopers are able to resist only a very small amount of outward force. You could create an outward arc using in-cut jugs for your hands, but again, since the final position of the pelvis will be up and in to the rock, initiating movement by throwing the pelvis away from the rock will not be mechanically efficient.

Try the double dyno from the slopers again, but this time visualize an inward arc as the path of your pelvis. When you can imagine this inward arc clearly, throw your pelvis into it to initiate the move. This time you should have been able to do the move. Practice the move a number of times, experimenting with how much force you put into creating the inward arc. How does creating the inward arc feel? If it feels awkward, try to figure out

An outward arc requires that an outward force be applied to the handholds. Since this is not possible on a poor sloper, an outward arc cannot be achieved.

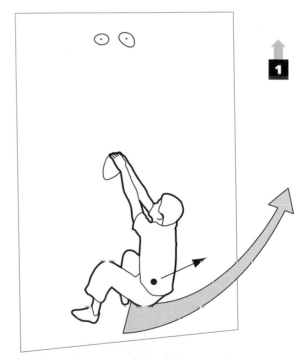

Starting position for a two-handed dyno from a poor sloper. Attempting to create an outward arc.

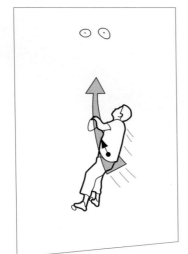

if it is because this type of movement is new to you or if there is something about the size of your handholds and the positioning of your feet that makes it so. The amount of force you put into creating the path matters a great deal. Some moves require that you throw your center into the arc, while on other moves the same amount of force would destabilize your body and lead to a fall. Practice this move a number of times, and then try it on easy boulder problems.

*Activity 29: Two-Handed Dynos*

Two-handed dynos are good for learning to use a specific path through space and to integrate the path with what is learned through the press exercise. This activity should be done on a very easy wall or route with many holds. You are going to do several small, easy two-handed dynos in a row. We need to emphasize that they must be very easy. The challenge should never be getting to the next holds; it should be creating a specific path through space and using tension.

Set up for each dyno with one foot slightly higher than the other and both hands at the same level. Look for two positive holds at the same level, one or two feet above your current handholds. Position yourself low, and in this starting position, visualize the path you want your center to take. Do you want to move in an inward arc, a diagonal line, or just straight in? Make a decision, and when you have a strong image of what this will look like, do the dyno. Repeat the dyno several times using different images, comparing what works and what doesn't. Do this on several different two-handed dynos.

**Activity 29: Try the two-handed dyno again, this time by initiating movement with an inward arc. Since less outward force is required on the handholds, the move has a greater possibility of completion.**

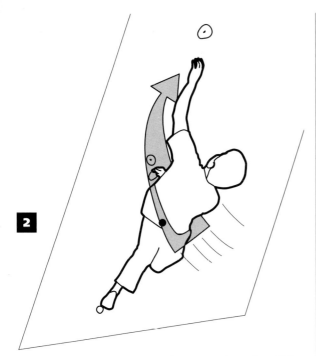

Create an inward and upward arc. Practice using different amounts of force to reach the next hold.

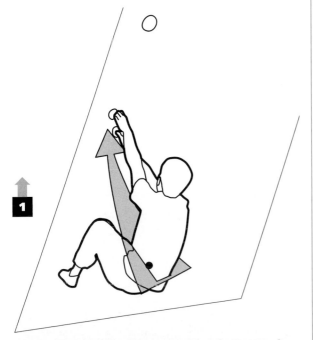

Activity 31: To begin, relax your core and sag away from the rock.

*Activity 30: Variation on Two-Handed Dynos*

This time, make the dynos longer. They should still be very easy, but you should have to fully extend all the way on your upper leg to reach your target holds. This time, see how much hang time you can create before you grab your target holds. You should be able to "float" in front of the holds for a moment before grabbing them.

The best way to do this is to initiate the move faster but also to use a strong line of tension in the second half of the move. As your hands are approaching the next holds, you should create a strong line of tension from your toes up into your back. Your leg and back should be extended and tight. Experiment with the move by doing it with tension, then without tension, then with tension again, or with varying degrees of tension. What do you like, what don't you like, and why? Repeat the dyno several times or do a number of different dynos. Have fun and experiment!

*Activity 31: Movement Path with the Side of the Body in to the Wall*

Find an easy back step on a slightly overhanging wall. From this position, reach for a hold that is high and slightly behind you using the inward and upward arc, but this time trace the arc with the side of your pelvis in to the wall. To begin each move, relax your core muscles, letting your body sag slightly away from the rock, and then create the inward and upward arc. Practice this several times using different amounts of force, but always visualize the arc first. Do not start the move until you can see and feel the shape of the arc in space.

Other common paths are

- Straight in: On thin vertical moves or steep moves that consist of a short reach where the center of gravity does not need to rise in order to attain the next hold, visualize the path of the pelvis as a straight line in to the rock. Sag out a little at the start of the move to create some room, and then throw your center straight in toward the rock. On the steeper moves, this will be more dramatic, on vertical moves, more subtle.

Throw your center straight in toward the rock and let your momentum carry you to the next hold. As you latch the hold, hold the tension in your core to prevent your center from sagging.

On shorter reaches, you can imagine a path that moves the pelvis straight in to the rock. To start, let your body sag slightly.

**Initiating a move by imagining a line that moves the body straight up.**

• Straight upward: This image can be helpful on any long move of offset balance to a very bad hold, especially a sloper. In such moves, any outward force at the end of the move is likely to destabilize your body and pull you off the hold. All the forces working on the center must be perfectly balanced at the end of the move so the center remains stable as you attain the new hold. Visualizing the straight line is a good way to create the balanced forces that these moves need.

• Corkscrew: Use this image on dramatic turns, such as dynamic drop knees, when your starting position has you facing the rock and you are dramatically rotated by the end of the move. This image is not literal, but it does help in getting climbers to twist and turn further than they normally would in a move.

When learning and practicing the application of these movement paths, the key is to focus your energy on creating the specific path through space. Make sure the moves are easy and don't worry about hand- and footholds or how hard you are pulling. The key is to practice each one as often as you can and try to apply them to moves on moderate boulder problems and routes until you know them well enough and are comfortable enough to use them on more difficult moves.

## QUICK TICKS

✓ All movements have one or more points of origin in the body.

✓ These points of origin control what muscles are at work, the body's path through space, and the timing of the move. In short, they control how force is applied to a move.

✓ You can learn to have conscious control of where movements are initiated and centered in the body.

✓ Controlling movement initiation is essential for creating precise, efficient, and aesthetic movements.

Motor learning is the process you undergo to acquire the skills involved in climbing—from tying knots, using holds, flagging, placing gear, clipping, and so on. You never stop motor learning, no matter how long you climb or how good you get. The work an elite climber puts into memorizing and refining sequences to maximize efficiency on a new test piece is no more or less significant than the effort that a brand new climber applies to learning to grasp holds of different shapes or an average climber puts into becoming skilled at everything from applying maximum force to footholds to dynos. Motor learning is at the heart of climbing at all levels of difficulty and experience. Over the course of your climbing career, whether you realize it or not, you will put more time into learning moves and movement than anything else.

## Information Processing

Information processing precedes, and is essential to, motor learning. While you are climbing, your brain is bombarded with information from both outside and inside your body. External information includes the size, shape, and orientation of the holds; the quality of the rock; your distance above your last protection; your assessment of the climbing just above you; the weather conditions; and the attentiveness of your belayer or spotter. Internal information includes the quality of your balance; the position of your body in space; the speed at which you are moving; your level of fatigue; how you feel emotionally; and the tenderness of the skin on your fingers. You process a huge amount of information when climbing, and it is your brain's first job to sort out and prioritize this information to create effective movement.

Cognitive scientists break information processing into three stages: stimulus identification, response selection, and response programming. In the stimulus identification stage, you gather information and identify what is most important to you. Your ability to prioritize is affected by your emotional state. Thus high-pressure situations, such as a long run out or competition attempt, may result in a different type or qual-

ity of movement than less stressful situations, such as doing an easy endurance workout. Your ability to process information will be different in each case. The more pressure or more emotional stress you feel, the more likely it is that you will be aware of only a limited number of stimuli, and those stimuli may not be the most important in terms of creating effective movement. Research suggests that your experience influences what stimuli you consider most important. For example, researchers A. M. Williams and K. Davids, studying how soccer players process information, reported that players with only a few years' experience spend more time looking at their opponents' feet and the ball, while players with more than ten years' experience pay more attention to the hips of the opponent with the ball, which allows them to anticipate where the ball will go next. As we gain experience, we undergo many changes in how we perform an activity and what stimuli we consider most important to the task. Experienced athletes are likely to be cognizant of more subtle yet important information, whereas newer athletes perceive only the most obvious stimuli.

In the response selection stage, you assess the stimuli and decide what action to take. For example, a boulderer may need to decide whether to step off a problem in control or try a move that may lead to an awkward fall. A climber attempting an on-sight may have to choose between a large foothold that feels out of place and a smaller one that is better positioned. There are many aspects to how and why you make these decisions, but what's important is that the decision precedes any action on your part. The body does not move until the brain has made a decision.

During the learning process, response selection changes over time from being consciously controlled to being more automatic. Controlled response selection requires cognitive attention and tends to be slower, as when new climbers find it relatively difficult to choose the next hand- or foothold on even the easiest gym traverse. In addition, their body position does not change appreciably based on the holds they use. Experienced climbers, on the other hand, show evidence of auto-

# Information Processing

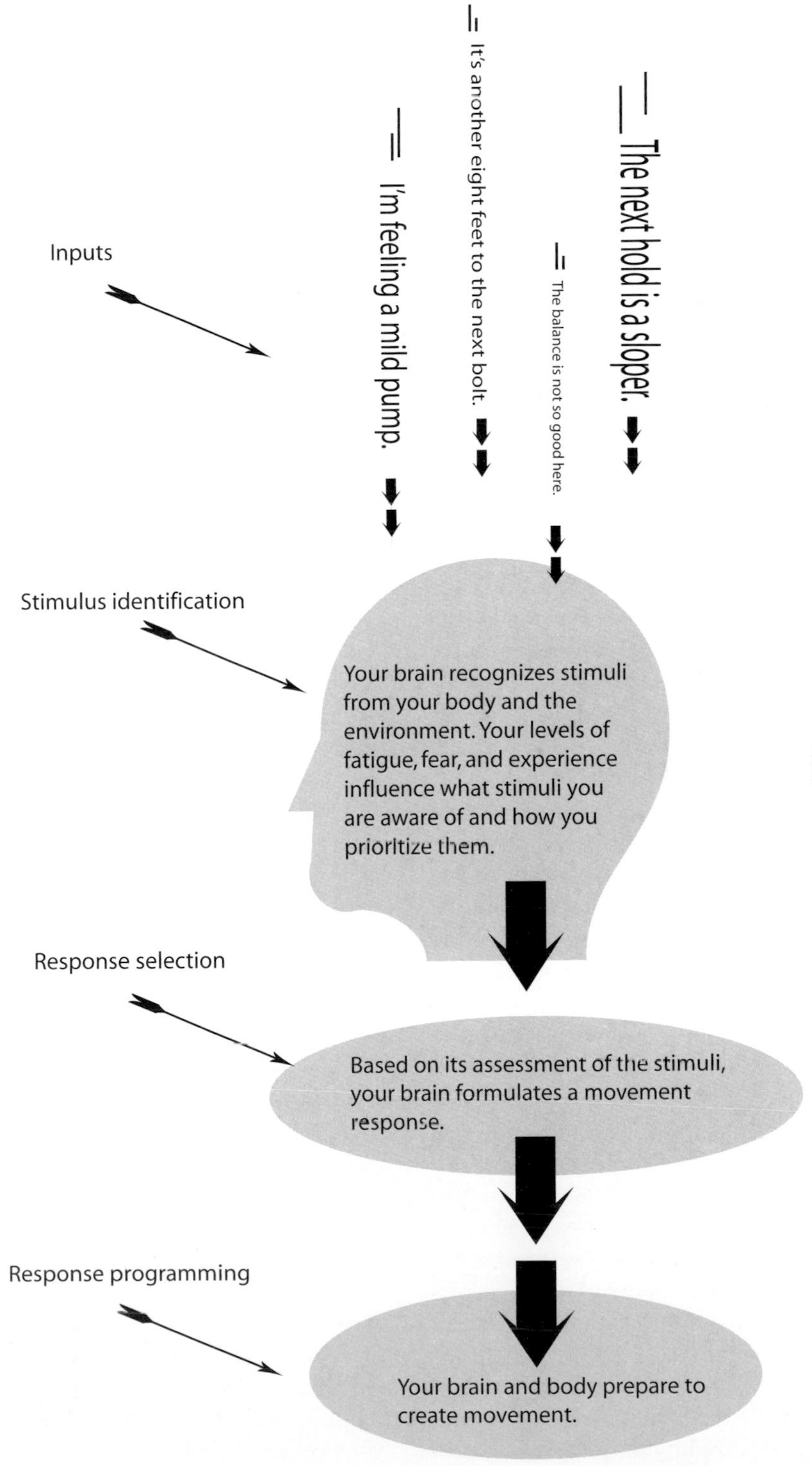

Inputs

I'm feeling a mild pump.

It's another eight feet to the next bolt.

The balance is not so good here.

The next hold is a sloper.

Stimulus identification

Your brain recognizes stimuli from your body and the environment. Your levels of fatigue, fear, and experience influence what stimuli you are aware of and how you prioritize them.

Response selection

Based on its assessment of the stimuli, your brain formulates a movement response.

Response programming

Your brain and body prepare to create movement.

matic response selection as they drop their bodies down low when they encounter a sloper or lean sideways on a sidepull. These decisions require less and less conscious effort as climbers gain experience. As a result, experienced climbers can focus their conscious attention on higher-order issues, such as examining the sequence to come or considering how to initiate the next move.

In the response programming stage, the motor system is organized to produce the output of the decision in the form of movement. Though scientists describe information processing as occurring in three distinct stages, it often occurs so rapidly that an observer cannot distinguish among them. They are easier to discern in beginners or climbers working difficult problems, but they are far more difficult to observe in a climber who is moving quickly or is on a climb he knows well. As an exercise, the next time you go climbing, watch a few climbers and see if you can distinguish the stages of their information processing. Do they show signs of controlled or automatic response selection, or both?

Information processing is important when doing the activities in this book, because many of them work by manipulating how you process information. The silent feet exercise, for example, makes a rapid and dramatic difference in improving the foot placement and smoothing out the movement of new climbers. But why does climbing with silent feet do this? One explanation is that it helps climbers process information by telling them in advance what stimulus is most important. On easy terrain, new climbers are able to focus on the important visual and auditory aspects of their foot placement and ignore less significant stimulus that would otherwise slow down their processing.

Numerous theories have been developed to explain how we learn, become fluent in, and execute movement, but the most prominent theory is that of motor programs. In the sense germane to climbing, most of our movements are probably controlled by generalized motor programs, which you can think of as templates or basic patterns for movements. No two climbing moves are exactly alike: Every flag or high step is both similar to and different from all the other flags and high steps you have done in the past. Rather than storing a large amount of specific information about each and every movement, generalized motor programs store a few key elements about a move, and the rest of the information is provided by feedback received from the body and the environment.

## Closed- and Open-Loop Control Systems

Both new and experienced climbers alike are often able to control and change their movements based on information received from their bodies or the environment. Yet there are other times when they are unable to alter their movements after they have been initiated. Scientists postulate two different types of motor control governing these situations, known as closed-loop and open-loop control systems.

Closed-loop control applies to any movement you can change based on feedback. Let's say a climber is placing his foot on a small hold and feels the hold start to crumble under his weight. Based on this feedback, he can take his foot off the hold and place it on another one nearby. The climber was able to receive tactile feedback from the environment and change his movement accordingly. The majority of climbing movements may use this closed-loop control. Watch an on-sight attempt, and you will see the climber making many changes in his movement based on internal and external feedback.

Open-loop control applies when feedback cannot be used to alter a move. This is the case for rapid movement, such as dynos. Once the climber has launched for the next hold, it is unlikely that he would be able to change the move based on new information received while in motion. The reason for this is the duration of his reaction time. Dynos are very rapid movements, and the climber may be in motion for only a few hundredths of a second. If new information comes in when the climber is in the air, his brain will not have time to receive and process the new input before the end of the move.

As these examples suggest, climbing uses both open- and closed-loop control. Unlike an Olympic diver, whose moves are performed at very high speed and therefore must be executed via open-loop control, climbers retain a degree of conscious control over their movements in most situations. This allows you to respond to what you learn from your body and the environment, and also to craft and enjoy your movements as you perform them.

# Closed-Loop Control

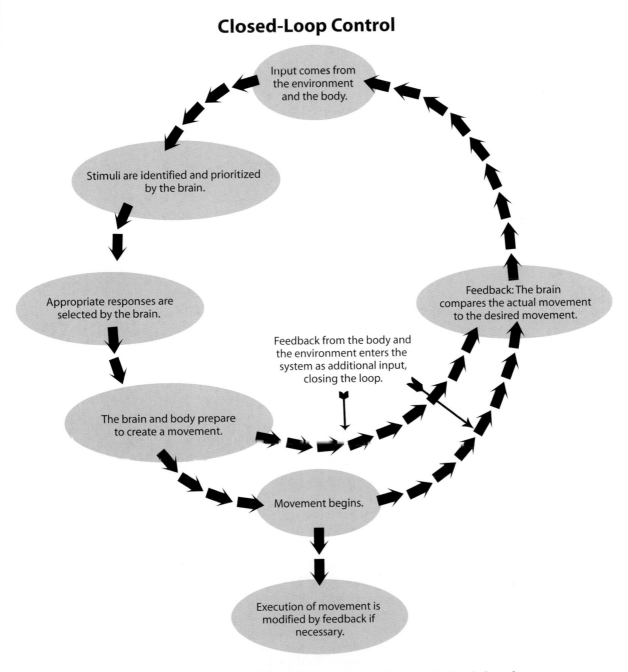

Input comes from the environment and the body.

Stimuli are identified and prioritized by the brain.

Appropriate responses are selected by the brain.

Feedback from the body and the environment enters the system as additional input, closing the loop.

Feedback: The brain compares the actual movement to the desired movement.

The brain and body prepare to create a movement.

Movement begins.

Execution of movement is modified by feedback if necessary.

**After a response is programmed and movement begins, the brain has the ability to monitor and change the move based on feedback. This ability to receive and incorporate feedback into a move gives this system the name closed-loop control.**

# Open-Loop Control

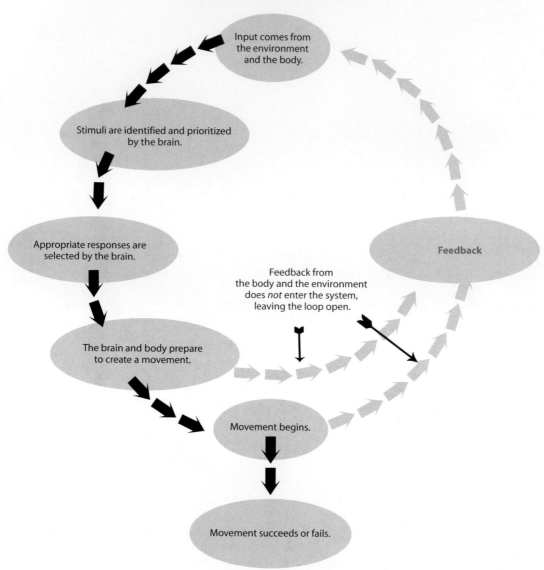

Input comes from the environment and the body.

Stimuli are identified and prioritized by the brain.

Appropriate responses are selected by the brain.

Feedback from the body and the environment does *not* enter the system, leaving the loop open.

Feedback

The brain and body prepare to create a movement.

Movement begins.

Movement succeeds or fails.

**In faster movements, there is no time for feedback to be processed and used to make changes in the move. In these cases, movement production occurs through a process called open-loop control.**

Having conscious control over movement means that a climber in the middle of a redpoint burn can make a mistake such as "z" clipping, reverse it, and keep climbing. An on-sight climber can accidentally reverse a hand sequence and find a match or cross-through later to correct the previous sequencing error. A climber in a gym can decide to skip the last hold of a boulder problem and finish it with an improvised dyno to the top. A competition climber can find a rest that no other competitor noticed and win because of it. These are all examples of how climbers with well-learned movement skills can alter their movements based on feedback from their bodies or the environment, or on their own ideas and desires about what they want their movements to be like.

## The Stages of Motor Learning

Cognitive scientists divide the movement learning process into three rough stages: verbal/cognitive, motor or diversification, and autonomous. In the verbal/cognitive stage, the student acquires a general feel for the skill, learning its most basic elements along with how and when to use it. The new skill requires a great deal of cognitive attention, and learners often engage in self-talk and spend a good deal of time thinking about and planning how to apply the skill or perform the movement. Despite the name of this phase, not all aspects of a movement skill rise to the threshold of cognitive recognition at this level. When acquiring silent feet, for instance, climbers are very aware of looking at their feet and attempting to produce little sound, but not how and why this activity makes their movement more fluid. Further, the verbal component varies a great deal from climber to climber both in the amount of self-talk they do and how well they are able to receive and integrate verbal instructions. This is true for activities as diverse as learning to tie a figure-eight knot and learning to dyno.

The duration of this stage also varies a great deal among climbers and from skill to skill. It may last only a matter of hours for some skills, but days or even weeks for others. Learning tends to be rapid during this phase, however, and you may see significant gains in just one climbing session. You can recognize when you're approaching the end of this stage, as the initial tension that comes with trying a new movement pattern begins to fade. You start to feel that you know what you're doing, and you get good results with less concentration or energy focused on the basic aspects of the task. But you will be able to apply the skill only in a limited number of contexts and on moves well below your current performance level. This is to be expected. Keep in mind as you learn a new skill that you are looking for the increased comfort with the skill that signals you are ready for an increase in the intensity level.

The motor stage or, more appropriately to climbing, the diversification stage can last from weeks to months or even years, depending on the frequency and quality of your practice. Since this stage is long, you'll have a variety of different experiences with the movement skills you are attempting to acquire. The stage begins as you develop more control over the skill and, most important, as you recognize more opportunities to apply the skill to your climbing, both on different angles and at higher levels of difficulty. On the other hand, you may not be able to apply the skill in on-sight situations because you won't see its possible application. You may not see opportunities for the skill when reading sequences, and you may be able to use it on harder moves only after trying other movements first. In situations of physical or emotional stress, you will revert to skills you know better.

In the autonomous stage, you have a broad ability to apply the new movement skill in a variety of situations. You can apply it well at your current performance level, use it in on-sight attempts, see opportunities for it when reading sequences, and employ it even in situations of physical and emotional stress. At this point, you have a large degree of conscious control over the skill—you can perform it with great precision exactly as you want. Unfortunately, not all your movement skills will develop to this level.

This description of the stages of learning runs the risk of making motor learning look tidier than it actually is. Besides specific types of moves, such as back steps and flags, movement skills also include making good contact with hand- and footholds as well as elements of individual moves, such as how they are initiated in the body.

Because most climbers learn movement in stressful environments, they often practice and learn things that may be detrimental to effective movement, such as overgripping or frequently initiating movement from the arms. If you're not brand new to climbing, your approach to movement learning needs to include the correction of those memorized patterns that hinder your performance in addition to the acquisition of new skills. For instance, climbers with a great deal of experience climbing cracks or granite tend to develop a very frontal movement style. These climbers don't know how to turn despite years of climbing experience, and the lack of this skill does not impede their climbing until they attempt a different type of climbing movement, such as that found on steep face climbs.

At any point in time, your various movement skills are spread over all three stages of learning, with most skills falling somewhere in the diversification stage. Naturally, your goal is to get as many skills to the autonomous stage as possible. This may be an important difference between elite and average climbers, with elite climbers having a much higher number of movement skills in the autonomous stage.

## Motor Learning and Movement Practice

Frequent, high-quality practice is at the heart of motor learning. Getting this practice is simple in some ways and more difficult in others. In climbing, expert performance of a skill at one level of difficulty or in one context does not mean that the skill can be performed with the same expertise in different contexts or at higher levels of difficulty. The pressures of climbing can be so great that it is easy to find settings in which skilled performance deteriorates, and it's a rare climber who exhibits equal skill in dramatically different situations.

How many climbers are as skilled on challenging moves in a gym, on a chossy sport route, or two thousand feet up a big wall? And how many can perform equally well on different types of rock or at different climbing areas? The demands made of a climber in Utah's Little Cotton Wood Canyon, the Gunks in New York, and the Verdun Gorge of France are so different that it's hard to imagine one climber doing well in all three areas without significant time spent adjusting to each. It's equally unlikely that someone who is well versed at flags, drop knees, and back steps on

V2s will be able to identify situations where these moves are necessary and execute them with the same skill at the V4 level. Even though the basic patterns may be similar, the significant differences in balance and the subtlety of the cues the climber uses to identify situations where these moves are effective are so great that the climber may appear relatively unskilled only a few grades above his current experience level. More important, it is nearly unheard of for a V2 or even a V4 climber to be well versed and highly skilled in these moves.

This raises one of the most important points about how we learn to climb. In the United States, the pursuit of difficulty eclipses all else. Movement is learned in a haphazard manner and in contexts that are too difficult or stressful to foster high-quality learning. Climbers rarely set out to learn and master a variety of skills and develop fitness at one grade before moving on to the next. Daily, in gyms across the country, climbers who have succeeded on one or two V3s throw themselves at V4s. Brand new climbers are put on V1s and V2s, where they flail, producing low-quality movement, when they should be starting on problems easier than V0 so they have a chance of producing repeatable higher-quality movement. This emphasis on attaining difficulty as quickly as possible is pursued largely at the expense of learning and developing skills. This explains why so many climbers can now boulder V6 or harder at their favorite gyms but are hard-pressed to climb V4 or even 5.10 at a different gym or outdoors. Low-quality learning experiences are counterproductive. Practicing poor movement on climbs that are too difficult or too frightening leads to inconsistent and highly variable climbing performances, as does being too narrowly focused on one type of climbing. In the end, the point is simple: When it comes to climbing, you are what you practice, and you are practicing every time you climb.

It is important to incorporate deliberate practice into each day of climbing in order to work on your movement skills. Set dedicated time aside in each session to learn, correct, or refine various movement skills and habits. The practice specifics depend on what stage of learning you are in for each skill and whether you have bad habits that need correcting.

# Movement Learning and Movement Practice

## STAGES OF LEARNING

→

## STAGES OF PRACTICE

### Cognitive Stage

**Length:** Days, if practice is consistent.

**Characteristics:** You get a general feel for the skill. This stage is defined by the need to think about and work through the basic elements of the skill and where it can be applied.

### Stage of General Patterning

**Intensity:** Very low.

Practice in the gym or on climbs with so many holds that following specific sequences is not necessary.

**Early Practice:** Can feel awkward or difficult, and your attention will be fully involved with the skill. Using the skill may feel wrong, even if you are doing it correctly.

**Later Practice:** Will feel significantly better than early efforts but will still require conscious attention to the basic aspects of the skill.

### Diversification Stage

**Length:** Weeks to months, with consistent practice.

**Characteristics:** You develop more control over the skill and will recognize more opportunities to use it. You will gain the ability to use the skill in different situations, but won't have complete freedom with it.

### Stage of Basic Application

**Intensity:** Low.

You will be practicing at a level well below your current performance level, but you will practice the skill on specific sequences and in different contexts. Emphasis should be placed on creating a large volume of high-quality movements.

**Early Practice:** The amount of conscious attention needed to produce each movement will continue to diminish, but you may find situations that require more thought and more effort.

### Stage of Submaximal Application

**Intensity:** Moderate.

At this point you practice the application of the new skill in fairly challenging situations and in many contexts. You will develop an understanding of the modifications that are necessary to apply the skill on different angles and types of rock close to your performance level.

**Later Practice:** Emphasize practice in a wide variety of contexts. You may feel you know it quite well, but some opportunities to apply it will still elude you.

### Autonomous Stage

**Length:** Years.

**Characteristics:** At this point you have a broad ability to apply the movement skill in a wide variety of contexts. You will be able to apply and control it at your current performance level, use it in on-sight attempts, see opportunities to use the skill when reading sequences, and employ it in situations of physical and emotional stress.

### Stage of Performance Application

**Intensity:** High.

At this level you will be practicing and applying the skill on moves at your current performance level and continuing to refine it through hard bouldering. This stage is about refinement and learning just how much control over the skill you have.

## The Learning Environment

Your practice environment needs to be diverse in some ways and relatively stable in others. It's important to learn both indoors and out, on comfortable leads, bouldering, and on as many different types of climbs as possible. An activity such as silent feet plays out differently in a gym, on a granite crack, or on a steep face, even though the goal is always the same. Context matters, and doing all your deliberate movement practice in one environment is far less effective than doing it everywhere you climb.

Another aspect of the learning environment is whom you choose to work with. Select partners who are supportive, fun, and who share your interest in moving well.

## Your Emotional State

It's important to avoid fear and other stimuli that draw your attention away from the task of learning. Being on top rope or a comfortable lead is better than being fifteen feet above your last bolt. Working in a quiet section of the gym is better than practicing movement in front of climbers you want to impress. In either case, fear is a distraction, when your attention needs to be focused on learning. Either you'll be unable to learn well, or you'll learn low-quality movement. Your emotional state should be relaxed and unhurried, willing and able to focus your attention on learning. Any distractions, especially fear, quickly become crippling. This has special meaning for climbers who deal with fear regularly. Almost any climbing situation offers different reasons to be afraid: an inattentive spotter or belayer, bad weather, a long run out, poor rock quality, or social pressure. A calm, quiet learning environment free of fear and distractions should be your top priority.

## Intensity Level

The intensity or grade level at which you learn is also critical. If the intensity at which you practice is too high, the quality of your movement will be compromised, and you will likely take longer to learn the skill and gain conscious control over how and when to apply it. You may learn the movement incorrectly or retain patterns that are inefficient or unnecessary.

## Practice Sequence

As coaches and instructors, we have found that the following is a good general sequence for practicing movement skills in climbing:

1. *Level of general patterning.* This is the starting point for skills that are brand new to you or for correcting movement habits that hamper your performance. This practice level is equated with the verbal/cognitive stage of learning. Practice should be on terrain that is far below your current performance level. The rock or wall should be easily climbable without using a specific sequence, and you should be able to repeatedly ascend the wall without any physical fatigue. Simple skills such as silent feet may require only limited practice at this level. For more complex skills such as turning and flagging, you may need several days to a few weeks of practice, with each session lasting thirty minutes or more. Your initial efforts will often be awkward and not feel very good. Though it's true that progress at this level is often rapid, you need patience to get beyond early frustrating efforts that may be disappointing simply because of awkwardness. When you can perform the skill well without having it take most of your attention, it has started to make sense to you, and you feel your body getting used to it, you are ready to move to the next level.

2. *Level of basic application.* At this stage, practice the skill on routes or boulder problems that are still far below your current performance level but require following a simple sequence. This level is consistent with the transition from the verbal/cognitive to the early diversification stage of learning. Perform the skill in as many situations as possible, varying the wall angle, types of holds, and rock type, and get in a large number of repetitions. Practice on top rope, very comfortable and easy leads, and safe, comfortable bouldering.

3. *Level of submaximal application.* This level of practice is equated with skills solidly in the diversification stage. Work on climbs that are one or two number grades below your current redpoint performance level. You might work a route at your consistent

on-sight level as you would a redpoint project, trying to apply a specific skill to all appropriate moves on the route. If you are a 5.12 climber practicing movement initiation, for example, use a 5.10 or 5.11 and attempt to find the best possible movement centers for every move. Then climb the route by perfectly applying all these movement centers in one continuous effort. You may need to take several tries to do all the moves on an easy route exactly as you want to. Repeat the route as many times as you need to. This phase of learning may be the most important because you are beginning to learn a skill well enough for it to become relevant to your performance.

4. *Level of performance application.* This is the type of movement practice that climbers tend to unknowingly engage in most often, but practicing skills only at this level often results in incorrect learning. This level is for skills far enough along in the diversification stage that they can be applied to a variety of challenging situations. Diversity remains important: applying the skill in a wide range of contexts is an essential element of this level of practice. Working the moves on a challenging redpoint project or boulder problem are examples of this type of practice. The difference between simply working a boulder problem and using the problem as movement practice is that in using the route for practice, there is no pressure to complete it. You approach the route looking for ways to apply specific skills, such as finding the best method of initiation for each move, or looking for skills that are best performed in a specific manner, such as inside flags. As a result, you can move from climb to climb using only the moves on each that meet the specific demands of your practice for that day.

There will be some fluidity among these categories and in the way climbers practice movement. When working a hard boulder problem, you are going to apply numerous skills at the performance level, regardless of your degree of competence with each. Understanding and using the stages of learning and the process of practicing at different levels will speed up your learning, make you competent in a variety of contexts, and move as many skills as possible to the autonomous level of learning. And because it can be a challenge to evaluate your own ability and gauge your own progress, using this practice progression will allow you to measure your learning as you see your movement skills advancing from one level to the next.

## Scheduling

The more you practice, the faster you will learn and the sooner your climbing performance will reap the benefits of improved movement. Fitting movement practice into your daily climbing is easy. It should take up at least the first hour of your actual climbing time. This does not include the time it takes to put on your shoes or belay your partner; measure practice time in terms of time spent moving. Fatigue is another form of stress you need to avoid while working with new movement patterns, so do your movement practice early in a climbing session, as your warmup or directly following. Movement skills that you need to practice at the general patterning or basic application level can be done as your warmup. Movement skills that you need to practice at the submaximal level should come after warming up. After some time working at this level, you should be ready to practice skills at the level of performance application.

At each level, you'll have more than one skill to practice. Give each skill roughly equal time, practice them in any order you like, and mix them up each day. Since you may need to practice on the slab angles and easier walls in your gym, avoid times when you know those sections will be busy.

Ultimately, the frequency and quality of your practice will determine how quickly you learn movement skills and improve your overall performance level. Taking time each day to practice movement skills at appropriate levels of intensity will foster high-quality learning and push more of your skills to the autonomous level.

✔ The aspects of motor learning of most concern to climbers are information processing, moving through the stages of motor learning, the nature of the learning environment, and the frequency and quality of practice.

✔ The frequency and quality of practice is the most important factor in how well you learn movement.

✔ Movement learning has three main stages: verbal/cognitive, diversification, and autonomous.

✔ Movement practice has four main levels: general practice, basic application, submaximal application, and performance application.

✔ Movement learning works best when it is practiced every day in a stress-free, relaxing, and supportive environment; at the proper level of difficulty; and with the goal of moving skills from the cognitive stage through to the autonomous stage.

# Improving Your Redpoint and On-Sight Tactics

Performance is the result of more than simply acquiring skills and building physical conditioning. The tactics you employ in attempting to redpoint or on-sight a route are also important and can determine your success. Efficient redpoint tactics can help you send a route in fewer tries, and an advantageous approach to an on-sight can mean the difference between success and failure.

## Redpointing

Your choice of which routes to redpoint is highly personal. Climbers have a tendency to choose routes that are too difficult. Beginners should start with a grade one level higher than their most difficult on-sight.

Your initial goal is to evaluate all the individual moves in the route. If you've chosen a route grade within your abilities, you should be able to reach the top, even if you have to hang on every bolt. In fact, the first attempt or two should be in a bolt-to-bolt fashion; your goal is to learn the required movements and not to link sections together.

Difficult sections may require multiple attempts to figure out the most effective sequences. Use your belayer and the rope to help position your body and provide rest between tries. Don't be afraid to ask your belayer for tension, help in positioning you exactly where you want to start, rests whenever you need them, and a good dose of patience. Working a redpoint route requires a strong effort on the part of the climber and the belayer, so choose someone with whom you can reciprocate. Your task at this stage is to figure out each move from the bottom to the top of the route so that you have a set of disconnected sequences for the entire climb. Each move can simply stand on its own, without considering what comes before or after it.

For this move-by-move work, you will eventually run into a piece of a climb that defies all your efforts to ascend it. After exhausting the possibilities, try the inch-by-inch method. Begin with your hand on the hold that has eluded you. Now place your feet and your other hand on holds that would allow the reach.

Get a feel for the position. Weight the rope and have your belayer lower you an inch so that your hand just comes off the farthest hold. Then try to move the last inch on your own. If you're successful, lower another inch and try again, repeating until you can do the move from its beginning.

Once you have a workable sequence for each short section, you can begin to link the moves together. Begin at the top of the route and lower to the last bolt. Climb to the anchors on the top rope. If successful, lower to the next to last bolt and climb to the top. Repeat until you can do virtually the entire route. Linking in this manner means that when you eventually attempt the redpoint, you will have learned the last bits of the route best. This is important because you'll be most fatigued toward the end, which impairs your judgment. If you've learned the last sequences best, there is a higher likelihood you'll be able to execute them when weary.

Sounds simple, right? Just figure out the moves, work the route from the top, and send. If you were lucky and all the moves you worked out flow together, your linking efforts will be minimal. Typically, however, linking adds complication to the individual sequences. You may have figured out the best way to do a particular move, only to learn that the end position won't allow you to progress into the next sequence. Your left hand may be on the hold your right hand needs, or you may be turned in the wrong direction. In this stage, you need to work out all the linking issues. This may necessitate finding different sequences than those you initially thought would work.

Additionally, you may discover that what you thought was the crux actually is not. Many times the hardest move, or technical crux, is not the move that prevents the redpoint. A separate redpoint crux, if present, is typically somewhere above the technical crux and exists as a result of cumulative fatigue. This makes your next task, finding all the rests, that much more important. Recovering while in the middle of a redpoint attempt is sometimes the difference between success and failure.

Recovery while climbing can be painful and seemingly counterproductive, because one hand usually must maintain a grip while the other is resting. The result of the grip-then-rest rotation is an average intensity that, if the average is below the anaerobic threshold, results in recovery, albeit slower than if you could drop both hands. Because the average intensity has not been reduced to zero, it can seem as if no recovery is occurring. To draw a running analogy, if you run too fast and begin to fatigue, you can slow your pace, thereby reducing the intensity, and recover. Should you stop running and walk, your recovery would be much faster than if you continue to run. Find and persevere at the rests; they can provide you the means to continue and triumph over redpoint cruxes.

While you're working the route, rest points may not seem important. You're focused on finding effective single sequences and resting on the rope between attempts at a small number of moves, but when you begin to link sections together, you will often find that recovering between difficult sequences is important to the redpoint effort as a whole. Finding these effective rests requires the same studiousness as discovering the best sequences, so you'll need to experiment at crucial points as you did with the movements.

A sport-climbing rest typically will relieve pressure on the fingers so the forearms can recover. Try wrapping your thumb around the holds, pushing with the heel of the hand, knee barring, stemming, or anything else that might help you take weight off your fingers. Finger fatigue is somewhat position dependent; for example, if you can open-hand the holds, you'll preserve some crimping strength. If you need that crimp strength for a crux high on a climb, try to do the easier sections below using an open-hand position.

You also need to pay special attention to any other sections that can result in failure. Climbing through the crux is important, but if you haven't paid much attention to the less difficult section just beyond it, you may find yourself falling at an unexpected point. Any difficult section can cause trouble, so don't ignore everything except the technical crux.

Following are some redpointing tips:

- *Go from bolt to bolt.* Force yourself to stop at every bolt to rest and review what you just climbed. After reviewing your sequence, you can lower down and work that section again, looking for a more efficient sequence, or, if you're confident about that sequence, begin work on the next section.

- *Go straight in.* When you hang at a bolt, take the strain off your belayer by using a quickdraw clipped between your belay loop and the bolt so that you are hanging directly from the bolt. Your belayer need not keep tension on the rope until you are ready to climb again.

- *Advance the rope.* After getting straight in, place a draw on the next bolt by leveraging off the draw at your waist, pull up slack in your rope, and clip it into a higher draw. This little process will help you get the draws up faster and work the next section on top rope. If you are unable to reach the next bolt, you can lower a loop of slack and pull up a stick clip.

- *Boinging.* Falling off a steep route while on lead often leaves the climber hanging in midair. Getting back to the rock typically requires the climber to attain the last bolt clipped, a difficult task with nothing but air to leverage. To regain the rock, first have your belayer jump up and simultaneously pull in the slack as he does so. This will leave him free-hanging a few feet off the ground. Now grab the rope above your head with both hands and pull down so a bit of slack appears between your tie-in knot and hands. At this point, you suddenly let go, and the momentary lack of tension from your end of the rope causes the belayer to fall a few inches and you to end up a few inches higher. Several boings later, you should be able to reach the rock.

- *Don't lose your high point.* Rather than falling and losing ground that you would have to climb again or boing, have your belayer keep you at your high point by instructing him to "take" at the appropriate time. Your belayer should take a few powerful steps backward, pulling as hard as possible with his body, to pull you tight before you let go.

- *Belaying.* Efficient redpoint preparation requires a responsive and attentive belayer. Your belayer should stand so that he can quickly take in or feed out slack as well as respond to your needs. When you say "take," you want to stay at your current height. Allowing even a small fall or slide makes your job as the climber more difficult. A belayer's job is to support the climber and make his work as easy as possible.

- *Preplace all the draws on rappel.* By eliminating a redpoint run to put up the draws, you can conserve energy. While rappelling, brush crucial holds to remove any buildup of chalk and shoe rubber, which can make them less useful. Use a light rope for redpoint attempts and carry only those things required for the route, leaving your belay device, daisy chain, tape, brush, and draws behind.

## On-sighting

On-sighting is defined as ascending a route the first time it's attempted without any information other than what the climber can gain by viewing the route with his own eyes. This means you can't watch someone on the route, listen to someone describe the route, or read a guidebook description that provides any clues whatsoever. You're on your own, with no help from anyone, and you won't know for sure, as you do with a worked redpoint, that a given preplanned sequence will actually work.

In evaluating a route for an on-sight attempt, you need to locate possible crux sections, rests, and holds from which you can clip or chalk. Sequence cruxes before you leave the ground with both a primary and a backup plan so that if your first choice fails to get you through the moves, you have an alternative to try. Rests allow you to recover and consider what comes next; scout these in advance. Where you clip and chalk determines your efficiency, so try to plan these in advance as well.

Once off the ground, you're in uncharted territory where uncertainty can impair your judgment. Will the climb become more difficult? What happens if this pump gets worse? I think that's a good hold, but what if it isn't? Questions like these can cause you to second-guess or even discard your plans. Uncertainty is a part of the game, and the ability to cope with it is often the deciding skill of a successful on-sighter. Some of the uncertainty will dissipate when you come to realize that it's okay not to know exactly what's ahead and that you can climb with a pump.

It is often difficult to commit to a move on an on-sight attempt, because once begun, it may not be reversible, and if it's the wrong choice, it can lead to a fall. The paralysis generated by uncertainty can prevent you from fully committing to a planned sequence. Trying and reversing a sequence and then attempting a different set of moves can help get you through tough sections, but when push comes to shove, you eventually must commit. The critical decision point of determining where you stop trying alternative sequences and pick one to fully implement can be learned only through experience.

Just as an understanding of balance is essential to grasping the essence of movement, a working knowledge of physiology is necessary to the study of physical conditioning. The components of physical conditioning are muscle physiology, aerobic and anaerobic energy, strength and power, and the basic principles of training.

## Energy Production in Muscle

The energy that allows muscles to contract and exert force is created by a chemical reaction in which a phosphate molecule group is stripped from the chemical compound adenosine triphosphate (ATP). The reaction produces adenosine diphosphate (ADP) and usable energy. Before more energy can be produced, the ADP must be recombined with the phosphate group to re-create ATP. The regeneration of ATP from ADP produces waste in the form of lactic acid, the quantity of which varies depending on the regeneration process used. ATP acts like stored energy and, once created, is available for immediate use. A limited amount of ATP exists within muscle, and once used and converted to ADP, the ATP can be re-formed by two different processes—one that requires oxygen (aerobic) and one that does not (anaerobic). The re-forming of ATP and not its breakdown into ADP and energy is the limiting factor in producing muscle energy and is therefore of greater concern to the athlete.

Think of a spring in a windup toy. In its unwound state, with all the energy spent, the spring cannot move the toy. The unwound spring represents ADP. The process of winding the spring is the ATP re-formation process. ATP is like the fully wound spring, its energy ready to move the toy once the spring is released. Note that in its wound state, the spring is ready to fire at any time. So too with ATP; once formed, it's available for the muscle to use.

Muscles have a small amount of stored energy in the form of ATP ready for immediate use. In fact, only eight to ten seconds' worth is available while a muscle is at rest. When demand is placed on the muscle, the stored ATP is used first. After that, the ATP must be re-formed through a combination of anaerobic and aerobic processes for the muscle to continue contracting.

Anaerobic restoration of ATP, known as glycolysis because of its breakdown of glucose, is a relatively inefficient source of energy and can sustain ATP production on its own for only one to three minutes. Glycolysis is, however, very useful in supplying sizable amounts of energy during intense activity. Its inherent inefficiency results in an accumulation of lactic acid, which inhibits muscle function and the ATP restoration process. Accumulating lactic acid results in the burning sensation commonly encountered in highly intensive exercise.

Aerobic energy production uses oxygen to efficiently produce ATP and can do so for an indefinite period of time. It is thirteen to sixty times more efficient than glycolysis, and although it cannot supply enough energy to sustain highly intense activity, oxidative energy is ideal for protracted, less intense exercise. The result, at a steady-state level of submaximal exercise, is the continuous production of energy and removal of waste, which can be sustained for long periods.

### Duration and Uses of Muscle Energy Sources

| Energy source | Duration | Best use |
| --- | --- | --- |
| stored ATP | < 30 seconds | initial high-intensity bursts |
| anaerobic system | 1–3 minutes | moderate to high intensity |
| aerobic system | indefinite | low to moderate intensity |

The three sources of energy—stored ATP, glycolysis (anaerobic), and oxidative (aerobic)—do not operate exclusively at any given level of exertion. Each contributes energy based on the demands of the moment, and there is no clear point at which one stops production and another begins. The intensity of the exercise determines, to a large extent, the contribution from each source. If activity is prolonged at a less demanding level, energy will be primarily derived from the

Energy for motion is stored in ATP. The breakdown of ATP results in ADP, energy and waste products. The ADP is re-formed into ATP by either aerobic or anaerobic processes. TJ URIONA ON DOUBLE DYNO V2, LITTLE COTTONWOOD CANYON, UTAH. PHOTOS: NATHAN SMITH

oxidative system; as exercise intensity increases, gly-colysis will provide a larger and larger share of the ATP. Depending on the demands of various segments of a route and your conditioning, you'll access all three energy sources in different proportions. For example, if you're a 5.12 climber on a 5.10, you're likely to derive a large percentage of your energy from the aerobic system, perhaps drawing substantially from the anaerobic system only at the crux. If, however, you were on a 5.12 route, your anaerobic system would contribute more heavily throughout. Understanding this concept is important in developing an effective training regimen.

### Relative Efficiencies of Muscle Energy Systems

| Energy source | ATP produced from 1 source molecule |
| --- | --- |
| stored ATP | NA |
| anaerobic system | 2 to 3 |
| aerobic system | 38 to 129 |

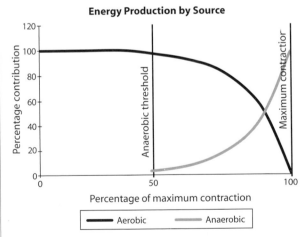

The proportion of ATP produced by the aerobic system decreases as movement intensity increases above the anaerobic threshold.

## The Aerobic Energy Production System

At lower levels of exercise intensity, the more efficient aerobic system is the primary source of the re-formed ATP necessary for continued activity. Its ability to use stored carbohydrates and fat and produce large amounts of ATP relative to by-product waste enables the aerobic energy system to function over long periods.

But the aerobic system has its limitations. As exercise intensity increases, so does the amount of oxygen the body needs, at least up to a point. The body can acquire, transport, and use only a limited amount of oxygen; this upper limit of oxygen use is known as the maximum steady state. To sustain a workload that demands more than the maximum steady state requires the anaerobic energy system. For example, as a 5.12 climber, you can sustain activity at the relatively low-intensity 5.10 level by using your aerobic system almost exclusively. The intensity is low enough that you rarely push through your maximum steady state. But at the increased workload of 5.12, your aerobic system would be incapable of producing all the ATP demanded by your muscles. You would cross through the maximum steady state on a regular basis and would therefore need to supply some ATP through anaerobic production.

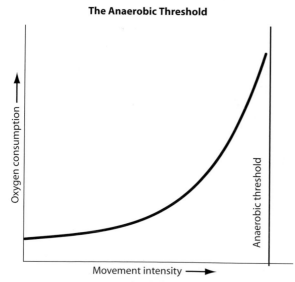

**The Anaerobic Threshold**

As movement intensity increases, so does oxygen consumption. The upper limit of oxygen consumption is called the maximum steady state or the anaerobic threshold.

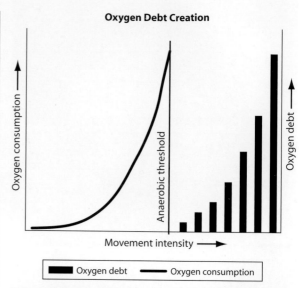

**Oxygen Debt Creation**

Oxygen debts are created at movement intensities above the anaerobic threshold.

The maximum steady state is also known as the anaerobic threshold. When you exercise above your anaerobic threshold, your body incurs an oxygen debt. As the anaerobic system produces the energy required, this debt occurs because the anaerobic system also produces large quantities of performance-limiting lactic acid. The greater the exercise intensity, the more rapidly the waste accumulates, until the muscle no longer functions. To clear lactic acid and remove the oxygen debt, you must lower your exercise intensity below the threshold and allow the more efficient aerobic system to remove the waste. Over its length, a climb can vary considerably in the intensity required, and you may move above and below the threshold several times in one ascent, both creating and then relieving an oxygen debt. This is why it's so important for climbers to have ample aerobic and anaerobic endurance. In climbing, however, oxygen debt occurs only in terms of specific muscles, such as those of the forearms, and not the entire body. It's rare for a climber to incur the same kind of systemic oxygen debt that a miler may experience at the end of a race.

Climbing at your physical limit requires a great contribution of energy from your anaerobic system. The higher intensity levels you reach are made possible by your anaerobic energy system. Your anaerobic threshold, however, is not static and can be improved with endurance and strength training. Endurance training for climbing focuses on increasing the capillary density in the muscles of the upper body, particularly the forearms. Capillaries are the tiny blood vessels that transmit nutrients and oxygen to the cells and remove waste products. The denser the capillary network, the higher the intensity of the workload that can be aerobically sustained. Additionally, endurance training can reduce the amount of time required to recover from an oxygen debt, both during and after a climb. Endurance or aerobic training works by increasing the maximum steady state, thereby delaying the onset of the inefficient anaerobic system and its resulting oxygen debt.

Strength also plays a role in determining your anaerobic threshold. Increasing your strength can effectively reduce the intensity of a given activity. In other words, the stronger you are, the less effort you must use to grasp a given hold, and less effort means that your body has to work less intensely. Compare yourself to a much stronger climber. A given handhold requires roughly the same force applied by each climber to sustain the grip, but the stronger climber uses less of his total potential or maximum strength. Using less of his total than you do means that he is working at a lower intensity level, and sometimes this is the difference between being below and above the anaerobic threshold. You might pump out on a hold he considers a rest.

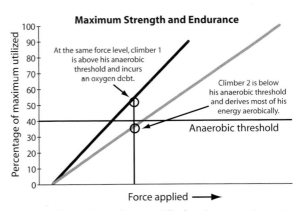

**Maximum Strength and Endurance**

At the same force level, climber 1 is above his anaerobic threshold and incurs an oxygen debt.

Climber 2 is below his anaerobic threshold and derives most of his energy aerobically.

Anaerobic threshold

A comparison of two climbers: Climber 2 can exert greater force on a given hold. At the force level marked by the vertical line, climber 2 can climb using primarily his aerobic system, while climber 1 must rely on the time-sensitive anaerobic system.

# The Anaerobic Energy Production System

As increasing intensity takes a muscle above the anaerobic threshold, the aerobic energy production system can no longer fully fuel the muscle's contractions. Although it continues to provide energy, the aerobic system must be supplemented by the anaerobic system.

In using stored glucose to re-form ATP, the anaerobic system generates higher quantities of lactic acid relative to the energy produced, thereby impairing the chemical process by which ATP is re-formed. Additionally, intense contractions pinch off the active muscle's blood supply, further restricting the ability of the aerobic system to contribute energy. The result is a rapidly deteriorating capacity to sustain activity.

The amount of usable energy generated by the anaerobic system depends on your tolerance for lactic acid accumulation. Every athlete can bear only a certain level of lactic acid, called the lactic acid reservoir. Think of the reservoir as a container that fills as the anaerobic system produces lactic acid in quantities that cannot be cleared by the aerobic system and empties as the exercise intensity decreases. As the reservoir fills, muscle contractions become increasingly impaired, and as the reservoir nears full, contractions cease completely. The rate at which the reservoir fills depends on the intensity of the activity. The more intense the activ-

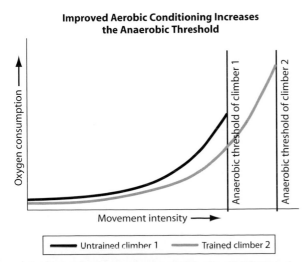

**Improved Aerobic Conditioning Increases the Anaerobic Threshold**

Oxygen consumption

Movement intensity

Anaerobic threshold of climber 1

Anaerobic threshold of climber 2

Untrained climber 1       Trained climber 2

Training can increase your anaerobic threshold, thereby delaying the onset of a pump.

Interval training for climbers is designed to increase your anaerobic reservoir so that you can climb longer after crossing the anaerobic threshold. CLIMBER: ANGELO GHIGLIERI

ity, the faster the fill rate, and the faster fatigue sets in. Fortunately, your lactic acid reservoir can be improved with training.

As you continue climbing above your anaerobic threshold, performance deteriorates in three ways. Motor reflexes (your ability to effectively contract muscles) are impaired. You become less coordinated, making it more difficult to generate precise contact with the holds and execute movements. You also experience a

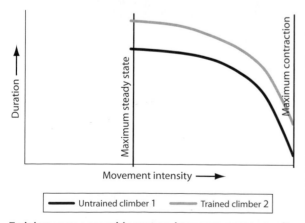

**Increased Anaerobic Capacity Increases Duration**

Training your anaerobic system increases your capacity to sustain higher movement intensities.

loss of judgment, which makes it less likely that you will choose the correct movements and holds. The result is that at the point of fatigue, when you need to be most efficient, lactic acid buildup causes a breakdown in your ability to concentrate, apply force, and execute movement.

The purpose of training your anaerobic energy production system is to increase the capacity of the anaerobic reservoir. Greater capacity means that you can sustain activity at higher concentrations of lactic acid and extend the time you can climb after exceeding the anaerobic threshold.

In climbing, then, you have two measures of endurance. First is aerobic endurance, the limits of which are defined by your anaerobic threshold. The threshold is the most difficult climbing you can sustain without getting a pump. The second is your anaerobic reservoir, which determines the volume and intensity of the climbing you can sustain once you have crossed the anaerobic threshold and are relying more heavily on the anaerobic system. Improvement involves a different training program for each.

## Strength and Power

Climbers typically use the words *strength* and *power* interchangeably, meaning the ability to apply force to a hold. But these words have two distinct definitions: Strength is indeed the force that is applied, whereas power is force times speed. Strength is solely dependent on the force a muscle generates, no matter how long it takes to reach that force. In fact, more force can be applied during a slow or even static (isometric) muscle contraction. Power, on the other hand, is a measure of strength and muscle contraction speed. A basketball player who can leg-press enormous weight, impressive as that might be, will never excel at his sport unless he can jump. Leg presses, which contract the muscles at relatively slow speeds, develop strength, whereas jumping, which requires a rapid contraction of the same muscles, depends on power.

In most sports, power is a key ingredient for success. Throwing, jumping, and sprinting, for instance, require rapid acceleration. To climbers, both strength and power are critical, and the distinction between them is important to your training. Using small handholds

## Force and Power vs. Velocity

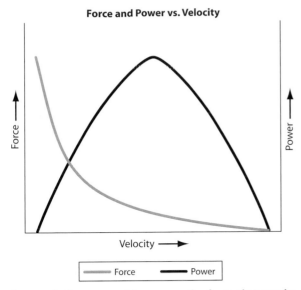

As speed of movement increases, the force that can be applied decreases. Power, which is force times velocity, increases to a maximum, then decreases as velocity increases.

while making slow or static moves depends on strength. Being able to move quickly to a new hold, contact it, and rapidly apply the force necessary to hold on depends on power.

Force, speed, and power are interrelated. As speed increases, force decreases. Force is maximized when the muscle is in a static, or isometric, position. Power, on the other hand, increases with velocity to approximately 30 percent of maximum contraction speed and then falls off, according to Knuttgen and Kraemer's "Terminology and Measurement in Exercise Performance," published in the 1987 *Journal of Applied Sports Science Research*. (For further discussion of strength and power, see chapter 10.)

## Principles of Training

There are several basic training principles related to physiology.

### Performance

Climbers need an objective way of measuring the physical demands for a given route or boulder problem, competition, or specific grade level. Having an objective measure allows you to target your training to meet the demands of your desired performance. You can measure these demands with this formula: performance equals movement intensity times duration, or $P = MI \times D$. Performance is defined as successfully completing a route, boulder problem, or climbs in a competition. Movement intensity is the difficulty of each section of the climb, as measured on the V or YDS scale. Duration is the amount of time the climb, or each of its sections, will take.

Using this formula to analyze the demands of your desired performance provides you with a precise structure for your training. This is an important concept. Many training activities in climbing lack a direct relation to performance goals, so their effectiveness cannot easily be anticipated. By conceptualizing training through the performance formula, you are able to set

**Tom Adams on a severe overhang on Whole Shot 5.14a Maple Canyon, Utah.**

Performance is a direct result of movement intensity and duration. If movement intensity is increased, duration must be decreased to keep performance constant.

specific and measurable training goals. This helps ensure that your training will be efficient and that you will have reasonable performance expectations for your current level.

There are many different types of routes at each grade, from one-move wonders to long-sustained routes with no rests. But even at these extremes you can determine the physical requirements. For example, on a 5.12d that is a true one-move wonder, the crux will be about V5+ or V6– with the duration of an average boulder problem, or about fifteen to forty-five seconds. On a long and sustained 5.12d you may have to climb 5.10+ or 5.11 for several minutes with little rest, and then do a V3 or V4– crux. On a short, intense sport route you may need to climb for one to three minutes on many individual moves between V2+ and V4.

Though these examples do not cover all the possibilities, two points should be clear: First, the demands of specific climbs and grades can be measured; and second, successful and efficient training must be targeted and measured in relation to the performance demands you anticipate.

## Specificity

The principle of specificity stipulates that muscles adapt specifically to the type of stimulus they encounter. For example, if a runner wished to be faster in a hundred-meter sprint, he would train by sprinting, not using long, slow runs. In other words, it is important to train those muscles needed for performance in the way they will be used.

## Overload

Living organisms are remarkably adaptive. Stress, as long as it doesn't cause traumatic injury, elicits a compensating adaptation that enables the organism to better control its environment. Nowhere is this more evident than in muscle. Provide an overload stimulus to muscle at frequent intervals by lifting weights, for instance, and it will react by gradually becoming stronger. Likewise, over time, jogging will stimulate the formation of additional capillaries in the leg muscles, a stronger heart, and better oxygen uptake in the lungs.

## Progression

To take advantage of the overload principle and be able to continuously improve, you need to adjust the exercise intensity or duration as adaptation occurs. For example, once you can perform a bouldering pyramid that tops out at V4, you need to bump the grades up to increase intensity or add more problems to increase duration in order to overload the muscles and continue improving. (See chapter 9 for a description of bouldering pyramids.)

## Individuality

Genetics, desire, the availability of resources, and other factors affect your response to training stimulus. One training prescription does not fill all needs. Even if you see others improving more rapidly, gauge your progress against a stable measure and your own goals, not someone else's successes.

## Diminishing Returns

Simply put, the longer you train, the smaller the gains you can expect. Beginning climbers progress rapidly, whereas those with years of training experience may see little or no gain as they bump up against the demands of career and family, limits of desire, and their genetic potential.

## Reversibility

The opposite of the overload principle, reversibility occurs when exercise stimulus is reduced or removed. Gains from prior training will gradually disappear. For example, Hakkinen et al., in their article "Neuromuscular Adaptations and Hormone Balance in Strength Athletes," published in the 1989 *Proceedings of XII International Congress of Biomechanics*, found that a two-week layoff produced a 3 percent decrease in isometric knee extensions. It does appear, however, that muscle and aerobic adaptations to exercise stimuli diminish at a much faster rate than anaerobic changes, and this may have some training application for climbers. In other words, layoffs from training as a result of injury, work, or family will cause your maximum steady state to drop at a more rapid rate than your anaerobic reservoir.

Energy to sustain muscle contractions is derived from two primary sources: the aerobic and the anaerobic systems. Aerobic energy production is efficient and can be continued over long durations but has an upper intensity limit known as the anaerobic threshold. At exercise intensities above the threshold, your muscles must rely more heavily on the anaerobic system. Although neither energy production system operates alone, the proportion of energy produced by each depends on the demands of the activity. At lower intensity levels, the aerobic system prevails. As intensity rises above the

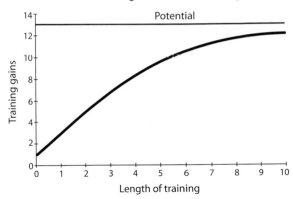

**Diminishing Returns from Training**

Over time, incremental gains from training become smaller and smaller.

anaerobic threshold, the anaerobic system produces an ever greater share of the energy. The anaerobic system is far less efficient, producing large quantities of lactic acid, which impair and can ultimately cause the cessation of muscle activity. The limit of anaerobic energy production is known as the anaerobic reservoir.

Strength is the slow application of force, whereas power involves rapid contractions. The force you can exert on a hold is highest when you move slowly or not at all; power is at its peak somewhere shy of the maximum speed at which you can move. Strength is important for static climbing movements, and power for the rapid contractions found in dynamic movement.

The basic principles of training are performance, specificity, overload, progression, individuality, diminishing returns, and reversibility. You can quantify performance demands by using this formula: performance equals movement intensity times duration. As either intensity or duration increases, the performance demands increase. The formula provides a method to gauge the demands of your goals and then tailor your training to more closely match those demands.

**QUICK TICKS**

✓ The anaerobic threshold, also known as the maximum steady state, is the maximum limit of energy the body can supply by way of the aerobic energy system.

✓ At exercise intensities below the anaerobic threshold, the aerobic system is the primary source of energy production. Above the threshold, the anaerobic system produces a greater and greater proportion of the energy needed as exercise intensity rises.

✓ Aerobic energy production is thirteen to sixty times more efficient than anaerobic energy production. You can increase your anaerobic threshold, thereby delaying the use of anaerobically produced energy, by training your aerobic system.

✓ The amount of usable energy generated by the anaerobic system depends on your tolerance for lactic acid accumulation. The maximum limit of your tolerance is called the anaerobic reservoir.

✓ You can increase your anaerobic reservoir, thereby increasing the length of time you can climb at intensities above your anaerobic threshold, by training your anaerobic system.

✓ Strength is the force that is applied, and power is force times speed.

✓ Performance equals movement intensity times duration. Performance is defined as successfully completing a route, boulder problem, or climb in competition.

In 1960, a little-known track coach from New Zealand named Arthur Lydiard took his country's middle-distance team to the summer Olympics in Rome. At that time, New Zealand had a population of 2.5 million, roughly the equivalent of today's Boston. His team consisted of five middle- and long-distance runners who had been trained in a manner that was unusual for the time. The team came away from Rome with two gold medals and one bronze. How did runners from such a small population pool do so well in these events?

Prior to Lydiard, coaches trained middle-distance runners using intervals. This technique consisted of relatively short, fast runs with timed rests, or intervals, between the sprints. Interval training is a wonderful way to train the anaerobic system, but it does little to enhance the sustainable production of aerobic energy. In the 1950s, Lydiard, dissatisfied with his own conditioning, began experimenting with programs that eventually led to his revolutionary training regimen. Lydiard discovered that improving the aerobic system through long-distance runs at an exertion level just below the anaerobic threshold significantly improved his performance as a middle- and long-distance runner. He began to use what he had learned in his own training with others, and their times began to drop.

Today the benefits of aerobic training are well known, and many believe the foundation for most athletic pursuits is the aerobic energy production system. This training method is popular because the aerobic energy system efficiently moves oxygen and nutrients to the muscles, restores ATP, and removes waste. A difficult redpoint is a lot like a middle-distance event, taking from two to ten minutes and requiring significant contributions from both the aerobic and anaerobic systems. Both middle-distance running and redpointing have an intensity level that is relatively high combined with a similar duration. But there are differences, primarily because of the general nature of aerobic conditioning needed by runners versus the local endurance prized by climbers.

General endurance sports stress both individual muscles and the cardiopulmonary system. Running is a general endurance sport in that your muscles, heart, and lungs all are taxed. Local endurance sports, on the other hand, stress the specific muscles engaged but don't put much pressure on the cardiopulmonary system. In climbing, it's typical that only the muscles of the forearms reach their aerobic limit. These muscles are small in comparison to those of the legs, so reaching their limit does not require a response from the entire system. If you run at a fast pace until your legs burn from lactic acid accumulation, it's likely that you'll be breathing heavily and have a high heart rate. You can pump your forearms until they are a solid mass, however, and not elicit a similar cardiopulmonary response.

The anaerobic threshold of your forearms directly affects your performance. The higher the intensity of climbing you can sustain aerobically, the less you will rely on the inefficient anaerobic system. Having this kind of endurance means more than delaying the onset of a pump. Your anaerobic threshold level also plays an important role in determining the time it takes you to recover both within a route and between routes, your on-sight level, how much climbing you can do in a day, and how well you do at competitions.

## Benefits

Training your aerobic energy system has one performance goal: to raise your anaerobic threshold. This refers to the most intense level of exercise that can be sustained indefinitely by the aerobic process. Raise your exertion level above this threshold and the anaerobic system kicks in, causing lactic acid, with its associated pump, to accumulate. For runners, the pace, slope of the course, and conditioning determine how much energy is derived from the aerobic and anaerobic systems. The factors affecting climbers are similar: pace, difficulty of the moves, and fitness. Climbing pace is different from that in running, however, because up to a point, moving slower tends to push climbers into the anaerobic range faster by increasing the amount of time muscles are contracted on holds.

Sustained routes that lack difficult cruxes, such as Survival of the Fittest (5.12d) in the Gunks, New York, or The Beast (5.12d) in Rifle, Colorado, highlight the importance of the climber's anaerobic threshold. Climbers who can pull many consecutive V2 moves without getting pumped remain below the anaerobic threshold longer, relying more on aerobic energy, and therefore find these routes relatively easy, as they don't get much of a pump. Climbers for whom steep V2 moves are above the anaerobic threshold tend to find these routes much harder, because lactic acid begins building as soon as they step off the ground. They must climb most of the route on anaerobic energy alone. Division (5.11d) in American Fork, Utah, features sustained V0 climbing up to a crux at the end of the route. Climbers who can sustain many V0 moves below their anaerobic threshold will have plenty of strength left for Division's technical and strenuous crux. Climbers with a lower anaerobic threshold must use anaerobic energy on the V0 and V1 moves below the crux and will face the added difficulty of having to ascend the most difficult part of the route with a good pump.

Climbs have many different combinations of cruxes, rests, and sustained sections, but the same point holds for all routes: The more climbing you can do below your anaerobic threshold, the better off you will be. This is especially true for competitions and on-sights.

Several studies have clearly proven the efficacy of raising the anaerobic threshold through aerobic training. Davis et al., in their 1979 article "Anaerobic Threshold Alterations Caused by Endurance Training in Middle-aged Men," in the *Journal of Applied Physiology,* found that the anaerobic threshold in untrained individuals is roughly 55 percent of maximum oxygen intake. Martin and Coe in *Better Training for Distance Runners,* second edition, found that trained athletes can have anaerobic thresholds as high as 80 to 90 percent of maximum oxygen intake. Training effectively lifts the anaerobic threshold, thereby delaying the anaerobic system from kicking in as well as decreasing the recovery time from an oxygen debt. These studies focused on systemic aerobic training such as a runner might pursue. Climbers, on the other hand, have an acute interest in the local endurance of their forearms. But the benefits of aerobic training, for runners and climbers alike, extend beyond the cardiopulmonary system to include improving circulation and aiding in the formation of enzymes that enhance aerobic energy production.

Increasing your maximum steady state, or anaerobic threshold, increases the time you can spend on a route.
PHOTO: LESLIE RIEHL

Several physiological changes important to climbers result from aerobic endurance training. First and foremost, the capillary network is enlarged. Aerobic energy production is dependent on the transport of oxygen, nutrients, and waste by the blood. The more blood that can flow to and from the muscles, the higher your anaerobic threshold. Second, endurance training increases the amount of oxidative enzymes present in your muscles.

**Aerobically Untrained Climber**

Maximum duration at any given intensity level

Duration →

Anaerobic threshold

Maximum contraction

0  10  20  30  40  50  60  70  80  90  100

Movement intensity as percent of maximum

**Aerobically Trained Climber**

Duration →

Anaerobic threshold

Maximum contraction

0  10  20  30  40  50  60  70  80  90  100

Movement intensity as percent of maximum

Two graphs illustrating the result of improving the aerobic energy system. Graph 1 represents an aerobically untrained climber; his anaerobic threshold is at 40% of his maximum movement intensity. Graph 2 shows that after training, his anaerobic threshold has increased to 60% of maximum. Whereas he would have incurred an oxygen debt in graph 1 at an exertion level of 50% of maximum, he would still be climbing aerobically in graph 2.

These provide for more efficient processing of nutrients into ATP, thereby using less muscle glycogen and producing less lactate waste. Third, the relatively low intensity level, extended climbing time, and low stress required by aerobic training provide the ideal environment for movement practice. Engaging in lots of good-quality, repetitive movement exercise will help develop and ingrain solid wall contact and movement skills. Finally, the tendons of the lower arms are strengthened. Although there currently is not much evidence, some data support the view that engaging in low-intensity exercise over an extended time frame may be best for increasing tendon strength, according to Jozsa and Kannus's *Human Tendons*. Tendinous tissue regenerates at a much slower rate than muscle and therefore adapts more slowly to training. Additionally, if training is too intense, tendons can actually lose strength and become

more susceptible to injury. Many new climbers jump wholeheartedly into bouldering, become much stronger in a short period of time, and then injure an elbow or finger tendon because their muscles adapted quickly and overpowered tendons that did not.

## Aerobic Endurance Workouts

Performance is dependent on the intensity and duration of the exercise. In aerobic exercise, intensity is much lower than your maximum and the duration much longer than your typical performance. To expand the capillary network, you must raise the blood pressure in the targeted

**Cross Section Muscle Comparison of Sparse and Dense Capillary Networks**

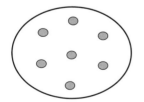 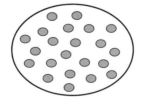

A denser capillary network provides better flow of material into and out of muscle cells.

**Aerobic Conditioning as It Relates to Performance**

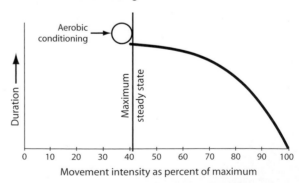

Aerobic conditioning

Duration →

Maximum steady state

0  10  20  30  40  50  60  70  80  90  100

Movement intensity as percent of maximum

Aerobic training is best performed by maintaining an intensity just under your anaerobic threshold for 20 to 40 minutes.

muscle tissue and keep it there for an extended period of time. If the intensity of the exercise is too low, no change to the capillaries occurs. If it's too high, the muscles pinch off the blood flow, and without blood flow, there can be no growth. Most experts today agree that the exercise intensity needed to improve aerobic conditioning must be just below your anaerobic threshold.

There are four components to any workout routine: duration, level of intensity, timing, and location. At least twenty minutes of sustained activity is necessary to achieve any aerobic improvement. Lydiard recommends that middle-distance runners train for up to two hours, at a pace between 70 and 100 percent of their anaerobic threshold. Climbers typically don't require two-hour endurance workouts, but they can certainly benefit from sessions lasting up to forty-five minutes.

The question of intensity is very important to aerobic training. Too little or too much exertion is wasted effort, so how can you determine if you're training in the effective intensity zone? Runners use heart monitors to gauge their exertion level as they try to maintain a heart rate of around 70 to 80 percent of maximum. But heart rate is not affected to the same degree in climbing. Here the best method is to gauge what you feel happening in the forearms. Look for a very slight burning in your forearms, which signals that you are near the anaerobic threshold. You should know you are using your arms, but they should not be tight or pumped. At first it may be difficult to tell if you are working at the right level of intensity. You may spend some time working too hard or not hard enough, but with experience you'll learn how to stay in the right range. If you begin to feel a stronger pump coming on and must stop and shake out, this is an obvious sign that you are working too hard. If at the end of thirty minutes you don't feel much of anything, then you need to increase the intensity.

ARCing a long traverse is one of the best ways to improve your local aerobic conditioning.

Try to schedule aerobic workouts for off days and hours. Depending on your daily training schedule, aerobic conditioning can be completed either as you warm up or at the end of your training session. With extended sessions approaching an hour, and depending on your seasonal training plan, this exercise can also be your only activity on certain training days. Because aerobic training sessions require access to a climbing wall for an extended amount of time, as well as a controlled level of intensity, it's best to use a climbing gym. Gyms, however, can be crowded at times, making this particular exercise difficult, as it requires the use of a wall for up to forty-five minutes. These activities can be performed outdoors if suitable access to numerous routes at the right grade is available.

## Exercises

Aerobic restoration and capillarity, or ARCing, is well known as the foundation of local endurance training for climbers. It refers to continuous climbing for thirty to forty-five minutes at a level that keeps your forearms warmed up and working, but not tight or pumped. ARC training can be done by lead or top-rope climbing or by traversing.

Aerobic training can be somewhat tedious; there is little challenge in climbing endlessly over the same easy terrain. To make the best use of this time, practice movement skills, especially those techniques new to you. The safe, easy climbing performed in aerobic training is the ideal environment for learning new skills. You can take your time, learn new skills, and gain the benefits of aerobic conditioning all at the same time.

### Activity 32: Lead or Top-Rope Climbing

You can do this form of ARC training by climbing up and down routes either indoors or out. Find a crag or a part of your gym that has several routes of the correct difficulty near each other. Climb up and down one route, either leading or using a top rope, then move to the next, and so on for thirty to forty-five minutes. You may climb each route multiple times.

Roped routes have the advantage of being assigned a standard grade, thereby providing you information on the climbing intensity involved. A gym provides the additional benefit of several routes on one rope line, allowing you to use any holds, create alternative sequences to marked routes, or start on one route and end on another. Don't limit yourself to what the course setters have marked; be creative and have fun.

Belaying for thirty to forty-five minutes may sound like a long time, but if you trad climb or belay friends on projects, chances are you regularly perform longer belay sessions. Finding other climbers with similar goals will provide you with motivated partners who are willing to trade off belay duty. Some gyms have auto-belays. These relieve the belayer and are available at any time, making them ideal for this exercise.

### Activity 33: Local Endurance Traversing

Traversing allows you to train at your own pace without need of a belayer. This exercise works best in a gym where you can choose among the holds already on the wall to allow the ideal level of intensity. Many gyms place a variety of handholds six to eight feet off the padding all the way around the gym, making for a single-length traverse of up to two hundred feet. This exercise session should last for thirty to forty-five minutes.

## Making Your Workouts More Effective

Climbers sometimes have difficulties with aspects of these exercises. Here are some ways to overcome problems, as well as several tips to make your workouts more effective:

• Many climbers just can't do thirty-minute ARCs without getting a pump, no matter how easy the climbing. If this is the case, your only option is to shorten the duration of the workout. Try starting with fifteen-minute ARCs and working up from there. Do several fifteen-minute workouts, then several at twenty minutes, and so on until you can last for thirty minutes or more.

• Make sure the intensity of your workouts is not too high or too low. If you are working too hard, you will feel yourself develop a pump. Drop the grade of your climb, use bigger holds, or try a less steep wall. If you never need to rest and don't feel much in the forearms, the intensity is too low. Try using a more difficult route, smaller holds, a steeper wall, or more difficult sequences.

• Climbers sometimes find local endurance training dull or boring. If so, one solution is to train with a friend who also has climbing goals. It's easy to maintain a conversation during local endurance training, so getting together with a training partner can help pass the time more pleasurably and help you get psyched. Another solution is to listen to music while climbing. Use a small device that won't interfere with your climbing.

• Set endurance training goals and reward yourself for meeting them. It can take a large number of workouts to get your local endurance to a level that will affect your performance, so set benchmarks and treat yourself to something small when you reach them.

• Your local endurance will improve much more quickly if you do five or more ARCs per week. By concentrating on your local endurance training, you can make noticeable gains in a shorter time, and since the intensity is relatively low, you won't have to worry about overtraining. Once you can ARC for forty-five minutes, you can reduce the number of sessions per week.

• Measure the intensity of your workouts in performance terms by asking yourself what the highest grade is that you can climb continuously for thirty minutes without getting a pump. The answer may be 5.10 for some and 5.4 for others, but the important thing is to have a concrete answer. Make it your goal to increase this grade, and you'll see a direct effect on your climbing.

• Keep track of your improvements. First get your duration up to forty-five minutes, and then begin raising the intensity. If you can ARC for forty-five minutes at 5.8, move up to 5.8+. Record your progress, and keep working on your local endurance until you have reached a level that is consistent with your performance goals.

• If your gym does not have interconnected walls, or if the difficulty of different sections is either too easy or too hard, step off the wall and move to a better section.

• Make use of a variety of hold types and positions. At first you may need to stay on larger holds, but as you gain fitness, push yourself to use all different types. Endurance training is a great place to practice using the holds you don't like, since the intensity is low enough to allow their use.

## QUICK TICKS

✓ Climbing is a local endurance sport that stresses the specific muscles engaged but doesn't put much pressure on the cardiopulmonary system.

✓ Your local anaerobic threshold determines the difficulty of moves you can climb continuously before a pump starts to set in. Raising your anaerobic threshold is the goal of aerobic endurance training for climbing.

✓ Aerobic restoration and capillarity workouts (ARCs) are the best endurance workouts for climbers and can be performed while traversing, top-roping, or leading.

✓ ARCs should make your forearms feel warm and active with a very slight burn but not stiff or pumped. The exercise intensity should be just below the anaerobic threshold, and the duration long.

✓ ARCing exercises work best at a consistent level of difficulty for more than twenty minutes at a time.

**When the anaerobic clock starts ticking, you need a large reservoir.** PHOTO: MIKE NANNEY

Within the climbing community, the term power endurance is a more common but less precise term for anaerobic endurance. Both terms refer to climbing at a high enough intensity that you cross your anaerobic threshold and your muscles rely more heavily on energy produced by the anaerobic energy system.

Raising your local aerobic capacity will help you delay crossing the anaerobic threshold. But climbing is an anaerobic sport, and it is inevitable that you will eventually derive a significant portion of your muscle energy from your anaerobic system, accumulate lactic acid, and feel pumped. Anaerobic endurance training will raise the maximum amount of lactic acid you can tolerate and, in so doing, extend the time you'll be able to stay on any climb that taxes your anaerobic system. The limit of your ability to sustain anaerobic work is referred to as your anaerobic reservoir.

A number of factors determine how quickly your anaerobic reservoir fills with lactic acid. One is the intensity of the moves. The more difficult the moves, the faster lactic acid accumulates. As the intensity of the exercise increases above the anaerobic threshold, lactic acid accumulates at a geometric rate. A doubling of exercise intensity will more than double the lactic acid produced. Another factor is the duration of intense moves. The longer you grasp holds requiring intense effort, the sooner your reservoir fills with lactic acid.

The quality of your movement also can have a significant impact on how quickly your reservoir fills. If you move inefficiently, you increase the effort and the time necessary to move through a particular sequence and complete a route. Climbing efficiently ensures that you get all you can from your physical conditioning. Inefficient effort wastes your capabilities.

The size of your anaerobic reservoir is also a factor. If your tolerance for lactic acid concentration is low, your reservoir fills quickly. But if you have a high tolerance for lactic acid, you can accumulate much more waste before the affected muscles shut down. Just as you can raise your anaerobic threshold, you can also increase the size of your anaerobic reservoir through training.

In climbing terms, it is useful to distinguish between different intensities and their corresponding uses of the aerobic and anaerobic systems. Low-intensity anaerobic endurance consists of longer efforts with less intense moves that provide a deep pump over the course of roughly five minutes or more. This means that even though you have crossed your anaerobic threshold, your muscles are relying on both the aerobic and anaerobic systems. On-sighting a long, continuous route is an example of low-intensity anaerobic endurance.

On the opposite end of the scale is high-intensity anaerobic endurance, in which the aerobic system provides very little energy. An example would be redpointing a short, desperate route on which every move is hard. High-intensity anaerobic endurance will give you a good pump, but it won't be as deep and crippling as that delivered by low-intensity anaerobic exercise.

Between these two extremes lie many different combinations of intensity and duration, and you should have some awareness of this in your training. Remember that performance equals movement intensity times duration, and that matching the demands of your training to your performance goals will produce the best results.

## Benefits

Mercy Seat (13a/b) in the Coliseum at Summersville Lake, West Virginia, overhangs some fifty feet in its eighty feet of height. A successful ascent involves pulling fifty feet of continuous V2 to V4 moves on a 45-degree face before reaching a large, positive jug, known as the Seat. On redpoint, most climbers find it advantageous to recover on the Seat, if possible, before attempting the crux, even though much of their body weight is supported by their arms. Climbers need to be able to sustain high levels of exertion, recover under stress, and continue to be successful on this route. To do so, you need both well-conditioned local aerobic and anaerobic systems.

If you can increase your anaerobic capacity, you'll be able to climb longer after you cross your anaerobic threshold. That is the primary goal of anaerobic endurance training.

Anaerobic training causes several physiological adaptations. The first is an increased concentration of glycolytic enzymes. These enzymes are key to the production of anaerobic energy, and they enhance the ability of the muscle to produce ATP from glucose. The studies proving this adaptation, such as Costill et al.'s "Adaptations in Skeletal Muscle Following Strength Training" in the *Journal of Applied Physiology*, were based on observations of individuals undergoing anaerobic training. Data collected from strength-training

Mike Helt rests below the crux on Mercy Seat. After 60 feet of sustained 45° V2–V4 climbing, recovery at the Seat is critical to sending the crux directly over his head.

activities reported by Sale et al., in "Comparison of Two Regimes of Concurrent Strength and Endurance Training" *Medicine and Science in Sports and Exercise*, showed that no enzymatic adaptation occurred, leading to the conclusion that athletes who engage in sports with large strength and anaerobic components need to train both in order to maximize their performance. For climbers, this means that you need to engage in specific training exercises designed to tax your anaerobic system. Strength training alone is insufficient to increase the size of your anaerobic reservoir.

Anaerobic training also increases mitochondrial, or oxidative, enzyme activity, which enhances the aerobic

High intensity anaerobic endurance, such as that required by a long, steep boulder problem, is best improved by using the 4x4. DREW CAIN ON THE BAD V5, TRIASSIC, UTAH. PHOTO: NATHAN SMITH

system. If you engage in anaerobic training, your aerobic system will also improve, although not to the extent as with aerobic training. Again, the message is that you need to train both aerobic and anaerobic endurance with targeted exercises to be most effective.

High-intensity exercise produces increased concentrations of lactic acid in the muscles employed, resulting in muscle fatigue and a lowered blood pH. With anaerobic training, the muscles adapt and are better able to tolerate higher levels of lactic acid. Sharp et al.'s 1986 "Effects of Eight Weeks of Bicycle Ergometer Spring Training on Human Muscle Buffer Capacity" in the *International Journal of Sports Medicine* found that this buffering is a result of an increased ability to produce base compounds such as bicarbonate, which counteract the acidity of the lactate. Studies show that athletes who train anaerobically can improve their tolerated lactate concentrations by 9.6 to 50 percent.

Strangely enough, aerobic endurance training can enhance the anaerobic system. Although the mechanism is unclear, individuals who have trained aerobically have lower concentrations of blood and muscle lactic acid at subanaerobic threshold levels, according to Holloszy and Booth's 1976 "Biomechanical Adaptations to Endurance Exercise in Muscle" in the *Annual Review of Physiology*. Simply put, aerobic training both extends the time it takes for you to reach the anaerobic threshold and effectively increases the size of your anaerobic reservoir by lowering the starting level of lactic acid in the blood.

## Anaerobic Interval Workouts

Performed correctly, interval workouts designed to boost your anaerobic capacity are debilitating. The intensity and duration of the exercises are such that you

## Interval Training as It Relates to Performance

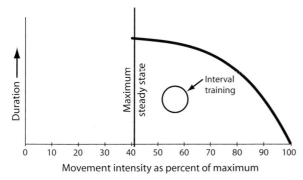

A single set in an interval session like a 4x4 consists of moderately high movement intensity over moderate time periods.

will feel exhausted, even beat up, afterward. Because anaerobic training involves repeatedly building and relieving your muscles of lactic acid, postworkout fatigue and soreness can last several days. You need a good cooldown and adequate rest between sessions to prevent overtraining.

High-intensity anaerobic interval workouts involve repeated exercises at a moderately high level of intensity (70 to 80 percent of maximum) for the duration of an average sport climb (three to five minutes). The interval is the timed rest period between the three- to five-minute physical efforts. The rest must be long enough to allow some, but not full, recovery. You should vary the exertion and interval periods based on fatigue, but a good place to start is with three minutes for both the exercise and rest interval. The number of repetitions you should do depends on your conditioning, current abilities, and the intensity level of the workout.

## Interval Training Exercises: Bouldering Circuits

In anaerobic training, you'll need one to three days to recover from each interval session. Increasing your anaerobic reservoir to its maximum requires only a few weeks of training, and you should not continue anaerobic training beyond six to ten consecutive weeks. Do not repeat these exercises more than twice a week, or you risk overtraining and possible injury.

## Activity 34: The 4x4

Perhaps the best-known anaerobic endurance workout is the 4x4. In the early 1990s, climbers experimented with how best to train for the short and very sustained sport routes found in climbing areas such as American Fork, Utah. At crags like the El Diablo wall, the very difficult routes consist of twenty to forty feet of nearly continuous technical and very powerful bouldering without rests. It was in answer to the question of how to train for these routes that the 4x4 was born. The logic was that climbing these routes shares a similarity with middle-distance running, both of which require a very high intensity of effort over a period of two to five minutes. If middle-distance runners could reap great benefits from repeating powerful efforts at shorter distances without full recovery, couldn't climbers realize similar results?

The 4x4 consists of four sets of four boulder problems done back to back, for a total of sixteen problems. The four problems in each set are completed in sequence, with no rest in between, followed by a two-and-a-half- to four-minute rest after each completed set, depending on the set duration and the climber's fatigue. Longer set durations or higher fatigue should result in longer rests. The same problems are used for each set.

The effectiveness of this exercise was immediately apparent, as climbers began turning in impressive results in a short period of time. Now, more than a decade later, 4x4s are known across the country. Performed correctly and combined with adequate rest, the 4x4 can have a dramatic effect on your anaerobic endurance and, as a result, your climbing performance. Doing 4x4s forces you to learn to stay cool and focus on movement even when pumped senseless. The exercise teaches you to keep climbing even when you don't think you have another move left in you. In fact, the cumulative effect of a hard 4x4 will be more emotionally or physically difficult than a redpoint at an equivalent level.

Because the problems need to be in close proximity to each other, safe, and have specific technical characteristics, climbing gyms are the ideal venue for 4x4s.

The really difficult part of the 4x4 is choosing appropriate boulder problems. If they are too easy, you won't tax your anaerobic system enough and the workout won't be effective. If they're too hard, you'll pump out and won't complete the workout. The correct mix of problems depends on your current conditioning and short-term goals.

There are two different ways to choose effective 4x4 problems. The first is to pick a range of problems that present different types of holds, moves, and technical demands to create a generalist 4x4. This will provide a broad range of challenges to help you prepare for a variety of routes. The second method is to choose problems that closely simulate the challenges of a hard redpoint project in your targeted pyramid. In creating a targeted 4x4, you select a mix of four problems that mimic the intensity and technical demands of the climbs for which you are training. Here's an example: Quinsana Plus (13a) in West Virginia's New River Gorge is seventy feet in height and slightly overhung. It has two distinct crux sections: one at thirty feet (V4) and the other near the finish (V6). Between the cruxes, the climbing is stiff and the rests are difficult to use. If you were creating a 4x4 to prepare for Quinsana, you would want the first problem to be moderately difficult, followed by a harder problem, then another of moderate difficulty, and finally the hardest of the four—perhaps V2, V3, V2, V4. You would want all four problems to be located on a slightly overhanging wall matching that of the climb.

Choosing the right boulder problems is critical for achieving the proper workout. Ideally, you want to be able to complete all four sets—that is, all sixteen boulder problems—but just barely. You should almost fail on the sixteenth problem. The ideal set is hard to create and may require some fine-tuning as you train in subsequent sessions. If you are aspiring to reach a certain level but are not there yet, start with easier problems and work your way up.

Begin by determining your consistent bouldering redpoint grade—that is, the grade you can almost always complete after some work and up to ten attempts. Drop two to four grades from this level to find a good starting point. If you're a V5 boulderer, choose V1s, V2s, and maybe V3s.

The best way to choose your problems, especially when you are new to 4x4s, is to create a set based on the suggestions above, test it, and then adjust the problems or their order to make the workout easier or harder. When you are creating a 4x4 not targeted to a specific route, arrange the problems in descending order of difficulty at first, and depending on how it feels, mix them

up on subsequent sets. Make sure you are familiar with each problem you choose, that you know the location of the holds and efficient sequences. Because you'll accumulate lactic acid and tire quickly, you will lose some of your ability to judge and apply movement. Knowing the holds and sequences will help you complete the exercise and maintain reasonably good form.

All anaerobic endurance training should be done with a partner; these workouts are too intense to do alone. A partner can spot for you and take weight off when necessary to help you complete a problem, as well as record your times and give you a countdown for your rest interval. A partner also provides important encouragement and gets you back on track if you get confused. You'll need a stopwatch plus a pen and paper for your partner to time and record your problems and set and rest durations.

Since you'll be using a gym, it's a good idea to perform this exercise during nonpeak hours, when there are few people using the bouldering area. Waiting for someone to vacate a wall so you can do your next problem is frustrating.

To begin, climb the first problem, then move as quickly as possible to the second. Spend as little time down-climbing and on the floor as possible; hustle to the next problem and get climbing. It's especially important in such a taxing workout to focus on your movement. You'll know these problems well, so climb them exactly the way you know they need to be climbed. In addition, climb with a rhythm and keep your breathing under control. Continue until you have completed all four problems and then immediately start your rest interval.

Have your partner record your set duration time. Rest for three minutes. Drink water, sit, pop your shoes off, and relax. If your heart rate is going through the roof, lying down on the floor helps it calm down faster. Have your partner keep track of your rest period and let you know when you have thirty seconds left, then twenty seconds, and so on, so that you get back on the first problem at exactly the right time. Repeat the progression three more times.

Although you should minimize the rest time you spend on the floor between the problems, you should not try to race through the climbing. A 4x4 is not a speed-climbing contest. Be deliberate, stay in control, use good form, and follow the efficient sequences you worked out beforehand. Try to climb at the same pace you would use on a redpoint.

If someone gets in your way, it's more important to continue climbing than to wait for the next problem in your set, even if you have to do the problems out of the intended sequence or repeat a problem you have already completed in the same set. Whatever you do, keep climbing.

If you are about to fall during a problem, have your partner take a bit of weight off by supporting you lightly at the waist or shoulders. It's more beneficial to keep climbing even if you need someone to support you than to interrupt a set with falls. If you fall on the first half of a problem, get right back on the same problem. If you fall on the second half, move to the next problem.

Climbers sometimes choose problems that are too difficult and fail to complete the exercise. If you were not able to complete all sixteen, back the grades down for your next 4x4. Did you feel that the problems were too easy? If you were able to complete the exercise without feeling beat up and abused, you can increase the grade of one or more problems next time. Keep pushing the grades up until you get a solid burning pump but are still able to complete all sixteen problems.

*Activity 35: Roped Laps*
Roped laps are a popular climbing fitness tool. You can find climbers lapping down at any gym or crag. In most cases, they do not take the requisite rest interval, opting instead to repeat one lap immediately after the other. Although there is nothing wrong with this procedure, it is not the best way to increase your anaerobic endurance. Like the 4x4, roped laps must include a rest interval to be effective as an anaerobic training exercise.

Roped laps can be used to warm up or cool down, to practice movement, or for anaerobic endurance training. To lap down for anaerobic endurance, you want to do four to six laps with a timed rest that does not allow full recovery.

When deciding what route to choose for this workout, you have a few options in terms of route characteristics and difficulty level. One option is to choose a lap route that mimics your targeted project. Choose a matching wall angle, and then look for a route where the cruxes and rests fall at about the same heights as your targeted project. To simulate Quinsana Plus for

roped laps, a good route would overhang slightly, with cruxes at 30 and 90 percent of full height. A difficult rest on a sloper at 80 percent of full height would be included as well.

It's not always easy to find routes that simulate your projects, so another option is to choose a route that is continuous in nature, with limited resting opportunities and no easily discernible crux section. This will provide fairly continuous movement intensity and will foster a very deep pump.

You can also choose either a longer or shorter route. Doing laps on a short, steep climb will have more difficult moves and is roughly equivalent to doing a 4x4. A long route will have less difficult moves and will lead to a deeper, more painful pump because the durations are so much longer. As a guideline, laps on a short route should take about two to two and a half minutes per lap. Laps on longer routes should take between three and five minutes per lap. This time difference is important. As you use this activity, it's a good idea to choose routes of different lengths for different workouts so that you do not adapt to the same lap time. You can lead or top-rope. Keep it simple—what matters is the creation and relief of local oxygen debts as well as the mental aspects of staying focused and climbing well when pumped.

Because laps on routes can be done so many different ways, you need to be smart about your choices and know exactly what intensity of anaerobic endurance you want to target in the workout. If you are in good anaerobic shape and know the route well, you may be able to perform this exercise anywhere from two letter grades below to a letter grade or two above your onsight level. If it's been a while since you've trained anaerobically or you're new to this type of training, drop a full number grade below your on-sight level. The goal is to complete all four to six laps without falls, just finishing the last lap.

The procedure is similar to the 4x4. You'll need a stopwatch or clock with a second hand. Be sure you know the route well; this is not an exercise in on-sighting. If your local gym does not have an autobelay device mounted on your lap route, you'll need a belayer.

Climb the route at your redpoint pace and lower off. Your rest interval begins as soon as you weight the rope at the top of the route. Sit at the base of the route, drink water, take off your shoes, but stay tied in. After the rest interval, repeat the climb. Continue in this manner until you have finished four to six laps. You should feel a strong burning in your forearms. If you fell off before completing all four laps, choose an easier route next time or extend your rest by up to one minute.

This is not a speed contest. Climb at a comfortable pace, and follow the efficient sequences you worked out previously. Maintain good form; you will learn whatever you practice, good or bad, so be precise and smooth.

Attempting multiple redpoints on the same day requires stamina.

### Activity 36: Interval Traversing

Another variation on anaerobic intervals is to do them on long traverses in the gym. While very similar to intervals on routes, traversing has a few advantages. First, traversing makes it easy to create your own sequences to target specific movement intensities, types of holds, and types of moves. Second, it's easy to get back on if you make a mistake and fall off. Third, it's easy for your partner to give you a power spot if necessary. Finally, in many gyms it's possible to create traverses that are longer than the routes, so if you want to do long intervals of over fifty feet, traversing is often your best bet.

Some gyms have traverses set for this purpose; others don't. If yours does not, you will have to create and memorize the traverse a day or two before coming in to do your workout. This is a creative process, so have fun and don't be surprised if you need to do some editing here and there during your workout.

### Activity 37: The 6x8

Once you can recover from a properly executed 4x4 or roped lap workout in thirty minutes, consider moving up to a 6x8. You need to feel worked and fatigued at the end of an anaerobic session to realize its benefits.

A 6x8 is an extended 4x4. Six sets of eight boulder problems are climbed in sequence, for a total of forty-eight problems, with rest intervals between sets. The rest intervals should be three to six minutes in length, approximately the same time it takes to climb all eight problems in the set. The problems will need to be much easier than those used in the 4x4, roughly four to five grades below your redpoint boulder grade. Again, the ideal is for you to just barely complete the last set and to finish all forty-eight problems without falling. Whereas 4x4s effectively target the fitness level required for short, hard routes, 6x8s are of lower intensity and longer duration and target the fitness level required for on-sighting.

## Stamina

Stamina is the ability to sustain high, on-off workloads over the course of a day. It also means having the capacity to repeatedly recover from sustained high-intensity work. The goal in building stamina is some-

**Enhanced stamina improves recovery between runs.** DREW "THE ICON" BEDFORD ON COITUS FRUSTRATUS 5.13A, AMERICAN FORK, UTAH.

what different than that for anaerobic endurance: It is to make repeated high-quality, high-intensity attempts on a project route in the course of a single day. It is the recovery between attempts that is important, rather than increasing the capacity to sustain continued high-intensity activity.

The typical climber can make two, possibly three, solid redpoint efforts on a project in a single day before becoming fatigued. This will often leave the climber short of a redpoint, as it can take two or three tries to learn the most efficient sequences, discover the rests, and develop an overall understanding of what is expected. Thus, having the ability to make four or even five solid attempts in a single day significantly improves your chances for success.

The stamina exercise described here also can serve as a good plateau buster. Stagnation occurs when training no longer produces an increase in performance.

When this happens, the following exercises can help propel you to the next level.

In stamina training, there is more complete recovery during rest intervals. The exercises are of moderate intensity and duration, and the rest intervals are not timed.

*Activity 38: Bouldering Pyramids*

A bouldering pyramid consists of fifteen boulder problems: one problem at your current best, two problems at one grade less than redpoint, four problems at two grades less than redpoint, and eight problems at three grades below redpoint. If you can redpoint V6, for instance, your pyramid would consist of one V6, two V5s, four V4s, and eight V3s.

You can select a variety of problems or choose to focus on problems that reflect the nature of the routes on your targeted pyramid. You should be familiar with

**Stamina Training as It Relates to Performance**

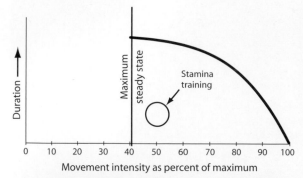

Stamina training consists of many short efforts at moderate intensity.

Stamina workouts are physically exhausting, but the goal of making four to five redpoint attempts in a single day is well worth the effort.

and able to send all the chosen problems in three tries or less; this is not an on-sight exercise.

Begin with the easiest grade. Climb the first four, resting after each ascent. The length of the rest period does not matter in this exercise, as long as you get enough rest. It may be necessary to force yourself to take a two- to three-minute rest between problems to prevent you from developing a pump. Attempt the next problem when you feel able. After four problems of the easiest grade, climb two of the next harder grade, again resting as much as you like after each. After the two, climb one of the next-to-hardest grade problems. Rest and then climb the most difficult problem.

Now that you've come up one side of the pyramid, descend the other side in reverse order. Do one at the next-to-hardest grade, two at the next-easiest, followed by four at the easiest grade.

**Sample Bouldering Pyramid**

| Order | Grade | Number to complete |
|-------|-------|--------------------|
| 1 | V3 | 4 |
| 2 | V4 | 2 |
| 3 | V5 | 1 |
| 4 | V6 | 1 |
| 5 | V5 | 1 |
| 6 | V4 | 2 |
| 7 | V3 | 4 |

*Activity 39: Continuous-Intensity Repetitions (CIRs)*

Another form of local endurance training, which is at an intensity level higher than ARCing, is known as continuous-intensity repetitions, or CIRs. This does not refer to continuous climbing, but to a continuous level of difficulty.

This workout consists of doing ten to fifteen laps at the most difficult grade you can climb without getting a pump. This is not interval training; you need to rest sufficiently between each lap so that the cumulative effect does not give you a pump. The route will feel too easy at the beginning of the workout, but around lap number eight, you will feel fatigue setting in. By repetition number fifteen, you will be exhausted and it will take a lot of concentration to finish the route, and all without ever getting a pump.

It will take some experimenting to discover the correct grade and how many repetitions you can handle.

Climbers with less experience in training endurance may need to start with eight to ten repetitions and work up from there. This workout is powerful and can deliver fast gains in local endurance, especially when combined with ARC training.

✓ The goal of anaerobic training is to increase the size of your anaerobic reservoir, allowing you to climb longer at movement intensities above the anaerobic threshold.

✓ Factors that affect anaerobic endurance are movement intensity, exercise duration, anaerobic reservoir size, and movement efficiency.

✓ Anaerobic training helps teach you that you can climb competently even if pumped.

✓ The best exercise for improving anaerobic endurance is interval training, represented in climbing by the 4x4.

✓ The most effective 4x4 mimics your targeted route and consists of problems you can just barely complete on the fourth set.

✓ Stamina is the ability to sustain high, on-off workloads over the course of a day. Stamina is the capacity to repeatedly recover from sustained high-intensity work in order to make four or five solid redpoint runs per day.

**Enhanced stamina improves recovery between runs.** DREW "THE ICON" BEDFORD ON COITUS FRUSTRATUS 5.13A, AMERICAN FORK, UTAH.

what different than that for anaerobic endurance: It is to make repeated high-quality, high-intensity attempts on a project route in the course of a single day. It is the recovery between attempts that is important, rather than increasing the capacity to sustain continued high-intensity activity.

The typical climber can make two, possibly three, solid redpoint efforts on a project in a single day before becoming fatigued. This will often leave the climber short of a redpoint, as it can take two or three tries to learn the most efficient sequences, discover the rests, and develop an overall understanding of what is expected. Thus, having the ability to make four or even five solid attempts in a single day significantly improves your chances for success.

The stamina exercise described here also can serve as a good plateau buster. Stagnation occurs when training no longer produces an increase in performance.

When this happens, the following exercises can help propel you to the next level.

In stamina training, there is more complete recovery during rest intervals. The exercises are of moderate intensity and duration, and the rest intervals are not timed.

### Activity 38: Bouldering Pyramids

A bouldering pyramid consists of fifteen boulder problems: one problem at your current best, two problems at one grade less than redpoint, four problems at two grades less than redpoint, and eight problems at three grades below redpoint. If you can redpoint V6, for instance, your pyramid would consist of one V6, two V5s, four V4s, and eight V3s.

You can select a variety of problems or choose to focus on problems that reflect the nature of the routes on your targeted pyramid. You should be familiar with

**Stamina Training as It Relates to Performance**

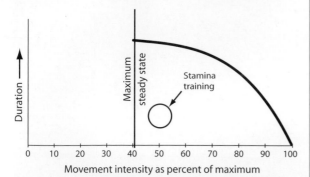

Stamina training consists of many short efforts at moderate intensity.

Stamina workouts are physically exhausting, but the goal of making four to five redpoint attempts in a single day is well worth the effort.

and able to send all the chosen problems in three tries or less; this is not an on-sight exercise.

Begin with the easiest grade. Climb the first four, resting after each ascent. The length of the rest period does not matter in this exercise, as long as you get enough rest. It may be necessary to force yourself to take a two- to three-minute rest between problems to prevent you from developing a pump. Attempt the next problem when you feel able. After four problems of the easiest grade, climb two of the next harder grade, again resting as much as you like after each. After the two, climb one of the next-to-hardest grade problems. Rest and then climb the most difficult problem.

Now that you've come up one side of the pyramid, descend the other side in reverse order. Do one at the next-to-hardest grade, two at the next-easiest, followed by four at the easiest grade.

**Sample Bouldering Pyramid**

| Order | Grade | Number to complete |
|-------|-------|--------------------|
| 1 | V3 | 4 |
| 2 | V4 | 2 |
| 3 | V5 | 1 |
| 4 | V6 | 1 |
| 5 | V5 | 1 |
| 6 | V4 | 2 |
| 7 | V3 | 4 |

*Activity 39: Continuous-Intensity Repetitions (CIRs)*

Another form of local endurance training, which is at an intensity level higher than ARCing, is known as continuous-intensity repetitions, or CIRs. This does not refer to continuous climbing, but to a continuous level of difficulty.

This workout consists of doing ten to fifteen laps at the most difficult grade you can climb without getting a pump. This is not interval training; you need to rest sufficiently between each lap so that the cumulative effect does not give you a pump. The route will feel too easy at the beginning of the workout, but around lap number eight, you will feel fatigue setting in. By repe-

It is very seductive to believe that most problems you face in climbing can be overcome simply with additional strength. It's quite true that getting pumped, feeling weak on a particular handhold, and coming up short on a move all feel like sure signs that you lack strength or power. The common lament around gym and crag is "If I were just a little stronger I could. . . ." Although strength and power are important, it is skill that matters most. Learn and practice proper movement, and your strength and power will carry you much farther.

Strength and power, as expressed in efficient movement and defined by its relation to performance level, are essential elements of climbing. But many climbers don't realize that the physical aspects of climbing, including strength, need to be understood through the master categories of balance and movement. Strength and power are essential; there can be no debating this fact, but you must understand and contextualize them correctly in order to develop them properly.

Within the climbing community, strength and power are used interchangeably to mean the force that can be exerted on a hold, usually a handhold. Outside of climbing, however, the terms have distinct definitions. Strength, or maximum strength, is the force that can be exerted without regard for the time necessary to reach maximum exertion. A pull-up is an example of applying strength. Power, on the other hand, is force times velocity. It is the ability to apply force quickly, as in throwing a ball or sprinting. With power, time matters.

In most sports, power is a highly desired attribute. Sprinting, throwing, jumping, and hitting a ball all require power. Climbing has both strength and power components. Strength is important in static climbing, whereas power is the key in dynamic movement. Dynamic moves require power to explode toward and quickly exert force on the next hold. Being able to latch a hold is a desirable skill that results not simply from strength applied with speed, but also from well-timed movement. Power can be developed only by improving speed, strength, and efficient, effective movement.

Because strength and the speed at which you can apply it are important performance components in climbing, you need to improve both. But strength gains alone will never outperform improvement in strength combined with efficient application.

A route can be viewed as nothing more than a set of stacked boulder problems, and your ability to successfully ascend the hardest problem embedded within that route is an indicator of whether you can send the whole thing. For example, if your maximum bouldering grade is V3, it is unlikely that you will be able to send any routes 12b or higher, because you would likely encounter sequences that are V4 or harder. Your maximum boul-

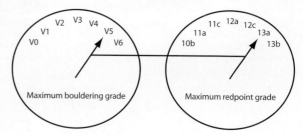

The setting on the left dial determines the setting on the right.

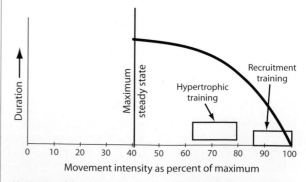

**Hypertrophic training is best performed at high intensity levels and low duration, while recruitment requires very high intensity combined with very short durations.**

dering grade is the grade you can consistently send after many attempts.

Additionally, strength and power are hold and position specific. Climbing relies on isometric contractions in the forearms, so there is no shortening or lengthening of the muscle as force is applied. The fingers don't move once set in position, and the amount of force applied by the forearm is exactly equal to the force working to pull your fingers off the hold. Isometric strength is dependent on joint angle, in this case at the knuckles and wrist. This means that becoming stronger at crimping will not translate well to slopers, sidepulls, underclings, and so on; you must therefore train using all types of holds and positions.

## Strength and Power Determinants in Climbing

The amount of force you can exert on a hold and the speed with which you can attain that force are determined by several factors. The first is your genetic potential. Musculoskeletal makeup can account for significant differences among individuals. Humans have two types of muscle fibers: slow twitch (Type I) and fast twitch (Types IIa and IIb). Slow-twitch fibers are great for endurance, fast-twitch fibers for producing force and speed. The fast- and slow-twitch makeup of your muscles is, for the most part, determined by genetics. Some studies suggest that a small percentage of muscle fiber can, through training, be switched from one type to the other, but you are mostly stuck with a predetermined ratio. If you were born with a high percentage of slow-twitch fibers, you will never be able to jump like Michael Jordan or throw like John Elway. Nevertheless, it's unlikely that you will ever be able to see the effects of genetics in your climbing, unless you are either extraordinarily limited or gifted. And even then, this would likely be most evident when you are a rank beginner. Muscles respond incredibly well to training, and it would take far more time and dedication than most climbers can allocate to reach their genetic ceilings.

The second factor in determining the amount of force you can exert is intermuscular coordination. Climbing puts strength to a real use. Here you are not moving an inanimate object through a controlled range of motion, as in lifting weights. Climbing movements are remarkably complex, involve the entire body, and require intricate timing between different body segments in an infinite number of combinations, positions, and movements. Isolated strength in a few large muscles is not helpful; you must train your muscles, from large to very small, in a wide range of motions to see overall improvement.

The size of your muscles is the third factor. The bigger the muscle, the larger its potential for exerting force.

The fourth factor is recruitment, or the percentage of your muscle fibers that can be brought to bear in a single contraction. Your neuromuscular system cannot stimulate all the muscle fibers to respond at once, but the higher the percentage that can be recruited in a single contraction, the greater the force that can be applied. As a load is placed on a muscle, the individual fibers are recruited in sequence, with the most efficient slow-twitch fibers called up first. If the slow-twitch fibers are unable to sustain the required load, Type IIa fast-twitch fibers are brought to bear, followed by Type IIb if necessary. The sooner and more fully you can recruit fast-twitch fibers, the more force you can apply.

The amount of force you can exert on a hold can be improved by increasing either the size of the muscle, called hypertrophy, or the number of muscle fibers recruited in a given contraction. Hypertrophic training is fiber type specific. Since muscle growth results from physiological adaptation to stress, the force of the contraction determines which muscle fiber types are targeted. In general, doing many repetitions with low amounts of force recruits only the slow-twitch fibers, whereas doing fewer reps with higher force requirements recruits the fast-twitch fibers. Fast-twitch fibers are your source of strength and power, so it is on this part of the muscle tissue that you want to concentrate your efforts at promoting hypertrophy and recruitment.

## Hypertrophic Training

Improving strength in climbing is a two-step process. Hypertrophic training increases fast-twitch muscle fiber size, and recruitment exercises ensure access to as many of those fibers as possible in a single contraction. To increase the size of the targeted fast-twitch fibers, you must put your muscles under a sufficient load to recruit and fatigue the Type IIa and IIb fibers. Too little a load and you will recruit only the slow-twitch fibers; too great a load will fatigue a smaller percentage of the fast-twitch fibers.

Recruitment increases as you increase the speed of contraction, the force you are applying, or the length of time you sustain the load. This is why weight training involves multiple repetitions of the same weight. As you increase the time you sustain the load over the course of a repetition set, more and more muscle fiber is recruited, until it has all been fatigued to the point of failure. Thus if you use too much load, you will fatigue only a portion of the fast-twitch fibers.

Hypertrophy in Type IIa and IIb muscle fibers is best achieved at loads that require six to twelve repetitions to reach failure. If you have ever lifted weights, you'll recognize this commonly recommended range. It is the best for producing hypertrophy in fast-twitch muscle.

Unlike lifting weights, climbing typically does not load the same muscles repetitively for six to twelve moves. This lack of consistency in strength-training movement makes hypertrophic development difficult. The science is clear, though: You need six to twelve reps at equal loads on the same muscles to see effective Type II muscle growth.

Over the past twenty years, climbers have developed several methods of hypertrophic training, including hard bouldering, hang boards, system walls, and campusing. The question is how effectively each of these workouts increases your strength and improves your climbing performance. It's one thing to say that a system wall, because it addresses all the accepted principles of strength training, will undoubtedly produce the greatest strength gains, but another to say it's the best strength-training method to improve your climbing performance. To date, that question has not been answered. Because of the amazing complexity of climbing movement, the completion of individual moves is dependent upon many factors working together. This makes it nearly impossible to determine what the contributions of strength and power are to any given climbing move.

This last point is the best argument for using bouldering for hypertrophic training. Bouldering directly trains all the movement skills of climbing, can be done in a way that emphasizes specific types of holds and moves, and works all the muscles involved in difficult movement, including the legs and trunk, rather than just the arms. Thus your bouldering level can be measured and compared objectively to the demands of individual climbs. Proficiency at bouldering has a direct and measurable relationship to overall climbing performance.

Bouldering, however, is less effective at accurately targeting and training the muscles. Hang boards and system walls present very precise and systematic methods of achieving this end. The only problem is that there's no way of measuring the trade-offs between how well these workouts target the forearms and upper body and the effect of losing all the climbing-specific elements present in bouldering, such as balance, timing, and intermuscular coordination. How to use and combine these various activities depends on the amount of time you have to train, the resources available, and your ability level, motivation, and specific goals.

If you lack access to quality bouldering or have limited time to train, you might be best served by using nonbouldering methods. Certainly hang boards, campus boards, and system walls fit into a basement or garage more readily than a home climbing gym. Another consideration is how well your local bouldering matches the needs of your performance goals. If you are training for routes with pockets and pinches, yet your local bouldering area or gym lacks these holds, adding nonbouldering methods of training may be the only way you can build the forearm strength you need for these holds.

If you have good access to bouldering and ample time to climb, you can combine various hypertrophic activities as you see fit, as long as you do not completely drop hard bouldering from your training. Apply any strength you gain through nonbouldering activities to the complexities of challenging moves. In addition, all the other muscles not trained by system walls, hang boards, or campusing need to be worked at high intensity levels, and this can best be achieved through bouldering.

The impressive musculature of many boulderers attests to the effectiveness of building muscle mass through this activity. The simple act of spending several hours each week attempting difficult boulder problems will improve your upper-body strength. Bouldering is a great way to practice technique and build strength throughout the body in a fun, supportive atmosphere. The group support commonly found among boulderers at gym and crag has encouraged many climbers to put forth the effort necessary to adapt and strengthen their muscles.

**Bouldering has become a popular branch of climbing due in part to its very social nature.**

Bouldering to increase muscle mass is an effective type of training to a point. Boulder problems generally do not require the same motion at the same intensity move after move. Instead, an interesting problem will require the use of several different types of holds in various positions. A given problem consisting of various elements has limited effectiveness for recruiting and fatiguing all the fibers in a particular muscle. This is why the addition of the nonbouldering strength-training activities described below may be helpful in giving the forearm muscles the best stimulus. Record all your workouts in a journal, including grades and numbers of repetitions, so you can track your progress.

*Activity 40: Bouldering with Continuous-Intensity Repetitions (CIRs)*

This exercise consists of ten to fifteen boulder problems all at the same level of difficulty, with at least two to five minutes of rest between each problem. You need to be familiar with most of the problems in the workout, but it's okay to include some new ones as well. The difficulty of the problems should be such that you can do each problem in one to three tries. For the V5 boulderer, this might be V3. The intensity of this workout is roughly consistent with your current bouldering on-sight level.

CIR packs a high volume of climbing into a single workout and guarantees that you will be exposed to a wide variety of hold types and movement styles. This workout is highly effective at raising your base level, improving your stamina, and preparing you to increase your current best bouldering grade. The only drawback is that it is quite fatiguing, and for most will require two days or more of rest. At the beginning of the workout, the routes may feel too easy, but somewhere between problems eight and eleven, your fatigue should increase, making the workout a struggle to complete.

You can repeat some problems if necessary. Always climb with good movement, and force yourself to rest between problems, even if you don't think you need it; getting a pump defeats the purpose of this workout.

*Activity 41: Bouldering Pyramids with Variable-Intensity Repetitions (VIRs)*

VIR is similar to CIR, but instead of many problems at one grade, vary the difficulty. For example, let's say you are trying to increase your bouldering base from V3 to V4. After doing CIR on V3 problems, it would be too big of a jump to go straight to doing ten to fifteen V4s; you simply would not be able to handle it. So you work up to the new level in steps by doing a workout that mixes V3 and V4 problems.

This exercise consists of doing sixteen problems of different grades in one session. The hardest grade should be your current best; for example, if your best is V5, you would choose a set consisting of one V5, two V4s, four V3s, and eight V2s. A specific order of problems works best. Start by doing half of the problems at the lowest level first. In this example, you would first complete four V2s, then two V3s, one V4, and then the V5. Then you work back down the pyramid: one V4, two V3s, and finally four V2s. This puts the most difficult climb in the middle of the workout, making it fairly challenging to complete. Use problems you know well, especially at the higher grades. Avoid getting a pump during this workout; rest two to five minutes between problems.

*Activity 42: Campus Board Hypertrophic Training*

It's generally agreed that Wolfgang Gullich invented the campus board as he prepared for his redpoint of Germany's Action Direct (14d). Consisting of small edges,

Due to the isometric nature of a forearm contraction in climbing, crimp strength does not translate well to slopers, and vice versa. To be a well-rounded climber, you need to specifically build strength in many different hand positions.

pockets, and slopers on an overhung wall, the board helped Gullich improve his recruitment.

With large enough holds spaced at appropriate distances to allow six to eight repetitions, a campus board can be an effective hypertrophic tool. Once you can do eight reps per arm, increase the intensity by skipping rungs, using smaller rungs, or adding a weight vest.

The exercise is simple enough: Grab a rung with both hands, lift your feet off the ground, and reach for the next hold. Proceed hand over hand for twelve to sixteen moves (six to eight per arm). If this is too difficult at first, try matching each hand move: Move your right hand up one rung, then place your left hand on the same rung, move the left hand up another rung, match the right to it, and so on.

You should be able to do three sets of six to eight repetitions per arm and, ideally, reach failure at the last repetition of the last set. This sufficiently fatigues a large number of the muscle fibers, which prompts your body to adapt by adding a small amount of mass to your muscles.

There are several ways to adjust the difficulty of the sets to accomplish your objective of reaching failure on the last rep. Campus boards typically contain several different rung sizes; you can use a different set of rungs to make the sets more difficult. You can reach farther to make your workout harder. And you can add weight, using a weight vest, to increase the intensity of the individual repetitions.

Campusing solves the bouldering issue of nonrepetitive moves, but since all the rungs require a straight-down pull on similar type holds, you still will not hit all the hand and arm positions required of isometric conditioning. To get everything you're looking for in a hypertrophic program for climbers, you need to add the system wall to your bouldering program.

### Activity 43: System Wall Hypertrophic Training

To get the desired hypertrophy in targeted muscles, you need to perform six to eight identical repetitions per arm. System wall training was developed for just this purpose; it is essentially repetitive bouldering. A systematic grid of identical handholds is spaced at twelve- to fifteen-inch increments in a ladderlike pattern up an overhanging wall. Footholds are spaced uniformly as well. The idea is to repeat the exact same bouldering move twelve to sixteen times (six to eight per arm).

Strengthening a static hand position requires training in that specific position. Applied to a system wall, this isometric principle means that you need to perform training sets with all the different hold types and positions. A good system wall has crimpers, slopers, pinches, and a variety of pockets in sidepull, undercling, gaston, and straight-down positions. That's sixteen possible combinations, without counting any of the myriad body position variations. Multiply that by two to three sets per combination, and this makes thirty-two to forty-eight sets in a workout—far too many for any given training session. Target your combinations on weaknesses and do no more than a dozen sets—any more than that and you risk injury.

There are many possible exercises for the system wall, but the basic tenet of stressing a specific muscle to failure over six to eight reps per arm always holds true. Once you are able to do eight reps per arm, raise the intensity by either decreasing the size of the holds or, on a well-built hinged system, increasing the steepness of the wall. You can also make the exercise more intense by adding a weight vest.

The exercise itself is fairly straightforward. Choose a hold type, size, position, and wall angle that force you to failure at the end of the third set of sixteen moves (eight per arm). Once you can do three sets of sixteen, raise the intensity. Do three sets of each hold type and position you've targeted for improvement. Climb at your redpoint pace, and use the same body position by keeping the foothold location constant relative to the handhold in use.

A training session on the system wall might look like this: three sets of straight-down slopers, three sets of sidepull crimpers, and three sets of angled pinches.

System wall training can also be used to build lock-off strength, or the ability to hold a position with one hand. During each reach, hold the lock-off position for three to six seconds before grabbing the next hold. Lock-off strength can be an important tool when you need to gain careful control of the next handhold or, in the case of an on-sight, you are unsure of its size and characteristics.

## Recruitment Training

The second step in climbing-strength improvement is to recruit as many muscle fibers in a single contraction as possible. A single contraction, even under a heavy load, uses only a portion of the muscle fiber available. Since climbing often requires a small number of powerful moves in a crux sequence, it is important for you to have quick access to as many of your fast-twitch fibers as possible. Recruitment training helps your muscles apply greater force by improving your neuromuscular coordination; your nervous system can be trained to stimulate more muscle fibers at one time. Recruitment exercises require the use of loads large enough that you can perform only one or two repetitions. Once you can do three reps, raise the intensity.

Climber Brendan Perkins uses threshold bouldering to improve the recruitment of muscle fiber in a single contraction. PHOTO: NATHAN SMITH

Recruitment exercises are at the upper limit of intensity and have the lowest duration of all the activities in this book. You're likely to feel that you haven't worked very hard at the end of your session. But the point is not to fatigue the muscles; rather, it's to shock them into recruiting more muscle fibers in each contraction. Once you can no longer generate powerful moves at your limit, you've accomplished your objective, and your body will react by adapting slightly to the new load being placed on it.

Because these activities are so intense, a word of caution: The loads placed on your fingers will be quite large. Warm up well, stretch, and be aware of the warning signs of overload, such as nagging finger soreness. If your body tells you to take it easy, then back off. The first rule of improving your performance is that you have to be physically able to climb. If you're injured, you can't improve.

### Activity 44: Threshold Bouldering

Threshold bouldering is climbing at or very near your limit. Your goal is maximum exertion over a very short time span to promote a recruitment adaptation. Choose boulder problems two to three grades harder than your maximum and work the individual moves. Your best efforts should last only two or three moves and make you feel as though you are at your absolute limit. This exercise can be frustrating, because you're going to fall repeatedly after one or two moves. Progress is measured in millimeters over many tries, as you edge closer to snagging that next hold.

To make the most of this workout, choose three different problems that are very different in hold type, wall angle, and technical demands of the movements. Spend a limited amount of time on each problem. Individual efforts may last ten to thirty seconds and will not lead to a pump. Rest a minute or more between efforts. Despite the high intensity levels, the short efforts and long rests mean that you won't feel tired at the end of the workout, and you may be tempted to continue. Don't. You'll be working at the limits of your one- or two-move strength, and once you begin to tire even a little, the exercise diminishes markedly in effectiveness. When the time is up, take your rest and move on to the next activity.

**Campusing can be used for hypertrophic or recruitment training.**

and additional attempts, eliminate those footholds or gradually reduce their size and effectiveness until you can do the move with the prescribed holds.

### Activity 45: Campus Board Recruitment Training

Recruitment training using a campus board follows the same procedure as that for building mass, but with increased intensity. Either decrease the rung size or add weight with a vest or belt so that only one or two repetitions per arm are possible. When you can do three reps at this load, increase the intensity.

Thirty minutes spent campusing for recruitment in any one workout is sufficient. Again, because of the lack of fatigue associated with recruitment training, you may feel as though you haven't accomplished much at the end of thirty minutes of work. But if the duration of your sets begins to decrease, and you can't do as many reps per set, you'll know you've had enough. Remember, the point is not to fatigue the muscles; rather, it's to shock them into recruiting more muscle fibers in a single all-out burst of exertion. Once you can no longer generate powerful moves at your limit, it's time to move to other activities.

### Activity 46: System Wall Recruitment Training

System wall recruitment training is simply the same exercises as those for hypertrophy, with an increased load. If you can do three reps, increase the load by decreasing hold size, adding weight to your vest, or increasing the wall angle. A good system wall has the advantages of different types of holds in varying positions and a changeable angle.

## Power Training

Power equals velocity times force. It is speed and strength combined. For many sports, power rather than simple strength is a key component of success. Baseball players seek sprinting speed, arm power for throwing, and bat swing speed to hit. Swimmers competing in sprints want churning arm speed. Boxers wish to throw fast and forceful punches. But the force that can be applied decreases as speed increases, so the faster you want to contract a muscle, the less strength you will be able to use. Theoretically, the maximum force

If you are in a recruitment training phase, threshold bouldering should be performed near the beginning of your training session and should last no longer than forty to fifty minutes. Warm up adequately first, but get this very powerful training done early, before some of your strength is drained off by other activities.

If you are having trouble with a particular move, there are a couple of training tricks to help. The first is to have a partner or spotter take some weight off by lifting you at the ribs just enough to allow you to do the move. The amount of help is then gradually decreased over subsequent tries, as you become stronger and more familiar with the moves. The second method requires the use of a climbing gym. Simply add some more footholds to the problem you are working. Over time

you can apply is available isometrically, when velocity is zero.

Climbing demands both strength and power. The strength to grasp and use the tiniest holds is the isometric expression of your maximum finger strength. Power is needed to explode dynamically and apply force quickly to a distant hold.

Developing forceful and speedy contractions means utilizing plyometric or ballistic training of the arms, legs, and trunk. Plyometrics involves a fast, loaded eccentric, or negative, contraction just prior to a concentric, or positive, contraction. Often called stretch-shortening exercises, plyometrics attempts to invoke an involuntary protective reaction to a muscle being quickly stretched. Among others, Bobbert et al., in their 1996 study "Why Is Countermovement Jump Height Greater than Squat Jump Height? published in *Medicine and Science in Sports and Exercise* 28: 1402–12, showed that the stretch reaction results in a more powerful contraction and has been shown to improve power performance above that derived from strength training alone. Bosco et al.'s 1982 "Combined Effect of Elastic Energy and Myoelectric Potential During Stretch-Shortening Cycle Exercise," published in *Acta Physiologica Scandinavica* 114:557–65, showed that improvements of 18 to 20 percent are possible in jumping.

Whereas plyometrics uses your body weight and a bounce reaction to build power, ballistic training uses added weight combined with fast contraction speed. Ballistics falls somewhere between recruitment training and plyometrics; it is strength training at speed.

### Activity 47: Campus Board Two-Handed Drop and Throws (Plyometric Approach)

For the plyometric approach, begin by hanging with both hands on a rung midway up the campus board. Drop to a lower rung simultaneously with both hands, and then immediately pull up and bounce back to the starting position. Do not try to stabilize on the lower rung; rather, attempt to immediately spring back to your beginning position. Repeat to failure at somewhere between three and five repetitions. When you can do six reps, increase the intensity by using rungs spaced farther apart.

### Activity 48: Campus Board Two-Handed Throws and Weighted Deadpoints (Ballistic Approach)

Ballistic training with a campus board is simply weighted throws. Using a weight vest, perform two-handed campus throws by dead hanging from one rung, pulling up forcefully, and then simultaneously jumping both hands to a higher rung. Put enough weight in the vest that you can do only three to five repetitions. When you can do six reps, increase the weight in the vest instead of the rung spacing. To get the most out of this exercise, you must explode as powerfully as possible during each throw.

A single-handed, weighted deadpoint is another effective ballistic training method. Again using the weight vest, dead hang from one rung, pull up as fast as possible, and move a single hand to the highest rung you can reach. Drop the higher hand back to the starting rung and repeat the throw, this time reaching with the other hand. When you can do six reps with each arm, increase the weight in the vest.

The ability to apply force to holds is important, but it's not the only aspect of climbing performance. The many complexities of climbing movement complicate the application of that force, and as a result, they obscure the efficacy of the various strength-training regimens developed for climbers. A combination of bouldering, which allows you to refine movement skills and build some strength, along with other training methods designed to target muscle development, seems to be the best strength-training methodology for improving climbing performance.

Your forearms contract isometrically in climbing, and since increasing isometric strength requires training at the specific joint angles to be used, you need to exercise in those positions. Becoming strong with crimpers will not translate well to slopers or pockets.

Strength is dependent on several factors. The larger your muscles, the greater the force you can typically apply. In addition, the larger the percentage of muscle fibers you can use in a single contraction, the greater the force you can exert. In an applied sport such as climbing, the coordination of many muscles is required to create movement, and it is those muscles working in concert that allow the effective use of force.

You can build strength by increasing the size of your muscles, known as hypertrophy, recruiting more fibers in a single contraction, or both. The best exercises for hypertrophy are a combination of bouldering and system wall training. For recruitment, threshold bouldering is best.

Climbers need power, or the ability to apply force and speed simultaneously, principally to latch the hold at the end of a deadpoint or dyno. The best way to improve power is by applying principles of plyometrics to climbing exercises.

### QUICK TICKS

✓ Strength and power are essential elements in climbing performance, but we must understand and contextualize them in terms of efficient movement to develop them properly.

✓ Strength, or maximum strength, is the force that can be exerted without regard to the time necessary to reach maximum exertion.

✓ Power is force times velocity. It is the ability to apply force quickly.

✓ Strength and power are hold and position specific because climbing relies on isometric contractions in the forearms.

✓ The amount of force you can exert on a hold and the speed with which you can attain that force are determined by your genetic potential, proportion of fast- and slow-twitch muscle fibers, intermuscular coordination, muscle size, and recruitment.

✓ Strength can be improved by either increasing the size of the muscle, called hypertrophy, or increasing the number of muscle fibers recruited in a given contraction.

✓ Bouldering is the best hypertrophic training for climbers. Bouldering directly trains all the movement skills of climbing, can be done in a way that emphasizes specific types of holds and moves, and works all the muscles involved in difficult movement, including the legs and trunk.

✓ Hang boards, campus boards, and system walls present very precise and systematic methods of targeting and fatiguing specific muscles, particularly the forearms.

✓ The goal of recruitment training is to use as many muscle fibers in a single contraction as possible.

✓ The best exercise for recruitment training is threshold bouldering—climbing at or very near your limit in order to maximize exertion over a very short time span to promote a recruitment adaptation.

The physical training activities in this book provide direct emotional benefits to the climber. ARCing raises your basic comfort level in the climbing environment. Confidence and comfort on rock come only through many hours of climbing; ARCing will help you quickly stack up these hours. Continuous-intensity repetitions will teach you to keep performing at a consistent level during a long day of climbing and will increase confidence in your capabilities, even when you are very tired. Anaerobic endurance training will teach you to stay relaxed and focused when pumped and that you always have more climbing in you, even when you think you can't do another move. The point at which you *think* you have reached failure occurs before you actually fail. In fact, you should have between two and five moves left in you, and those few moves can mean completing the next clip or getting to an easier section or rest.

In addition, creating a route pyramid is as much an emotional tool as it is a performance tool. Posting your pyramid where you can see it every day not only keeps you focused but helps you realize that you will be climbing at a higher level in the near future. Over the course of a few weeks your attitude toward your goals can change. At first they may be exciting and somewhat intimidating, but in time the intimidation will wear off, and the idea that you can climb at the new higher level will become your assumption. This is an important change, as intimidation fades, confidence increases, and you accept that you really are becoming a significantly better climber. For a detailed description of creating your own targeted route pyramid, see chapter 12.

Sending the routes on your pyramid level by level and rewarding yourself for each climb will feed you a steady diet of success, build confidence, and create momentum in your climbing. Climbers thrive on success; training and climbing need to be structured to foster as much success in the shortest time possible.

The mental toughness and focus you gain from these activities can be applied every time you get on a route or boulder problem. The best mental training closely matches the emotional challenges of the performances you are training for.

## Creating a Positive Self-Image

Your self-image can have a marked impact on your climbing. The great movement teacher Moshe Feldenkrais emphasized that self-image helps determine every action. By self-image he meant cultural heritage, genetic composition, the manner and type of formal education, and amount of self-education. The process of becoming a better climber, of committing to a training program and to a set of goals, is a form of self-education that will force your self-image to change for the better.

Making the decision to become a better climber is exciting and motivating but also involves taking a risk. You are launching into the unknown, and change can be frightening. Learning to see yourself as the climber you are becoming rather than the climber you are is not always easy to do.

### Activity 49: Positive Self-Talk

Listen to the way climbers talk about their climbing. You'll notice a great deal of negativity, judgments, and put-downs. If you do this yourself, first write out a list of all the negative sayings you use to refer to yourself, others, or climbs. Next come up with a positive replacement for every negative statement. If you find yourself saying, "I can't," replace it with, "I will do it," "I can do it," or "I can learn how to do it." The idea is to release the burden of the negative judgment, thereby giving yourself the opportunity and authority to be successful. Find appropriate positive replacements and then banish the negative terms from your vocabulary. Use the positive replacements whenever you find yourself starting to say something negative. Because negativity can be deeply ingrained, it helps to keep your list of positives in close proximity to your route pyramid as a daily reminder of the habit you are trying to form. Additionally, let a friend in on your mission—a trusted climbing partner can be very helpful at pointing out when you are using your old negative statements.

### Activity 50: Positive Activators

We all have moments of doubt in climbing, such as when we are pumped, when we are unsure of a sequence, or when we are afraid of a possible bad fall, a run out, a hard clip, or tricky gear placement. The onset of doubt is accompanied by hesitation as we decide whether or not to keep climbing. This hesitation leads to lower levels of performance. It can be dangerous and is often accompanied by negative self-talk. In these situations, you need a focal point to keep you positive and moving forward. If you say the right thing to yourself in challenging situations, you are more likely to be successful.

Good activators are personal and short. Common general positive activators are "go!" or "keep moving!" but you should strive to find something more personal. One young climber found inspiration in a rap lyric and said, "C'mon sucka!" to himself as he launched into difficult crux moves.

The key to using activators is awareness. You need to know when your confidence begins to wane or when you begin to doubt and immediately counter those negative thoughts with something short, pithy, and motivating. In crux moves, when you're pumped, on a long run out, pull out your activator and repeat it to yourself.

# Fear

Fear is a part of climbing for many. Its performance-robbing nature demands that every climber conquer it. At its root, fear in climbing is most often based on the possible consequences of a fall, and this fear of falling can be exacerbated by characteristics of the route. For example, if you believe yourself to be unskilled with slopers, you will be more likely to fear routes requiring their use.

The practical method for coming to grips with the fear of falling is called desensitization. In this process, you adapt to the stimulus that frightens you by gradually increasing its severity. As you become familiar and comfortable with a given level of stimulus, you'll increase that stimulus slightly. For example, people afraid of flying are often led through a series of incremental small steps to completely overcome their fear. They may begin by simply sitting in the airport, becoming comfortable with the bustle, the arrival and departure monitors, ticket desks, and so on, and then returning home. On a subsequent visit, they might go through the security line and walk to the gate before going home. On the next visit, they might enter a plane

and sit in a seat. A subject does not advance to the next stage until he is comfortable at the current level. All these steps are designed to gradually turn uncertainty into familiarity, with the eventual goal of becoming comfortable with flying.

*Activity 51: Desensitizing Your Fear of Falling*

First you'll need to find the level at which you are not afraid. For example, if you are afraid of slopers, you may find that you are comfortable using these holds during easy traversing, top-roping, when the footholds are large, or where the wall angle is not so steep. Once you find your comfort zone, begin the process by practicing at that level. Spend an hour a day for six to ten climbing days before increasing the severity. Getting over the initial fear of specific hold types can take a number of practice sessions, but it's fairly easy if done in a playful manner. Experiment with all the different ways to use each hold, the subtleties of how you hold your fingers, how you can use your thumb, how the angle of your wrist and the positioning of your body affect how the hold feels to you.

For the next few sessions, slightly increase the severity by using somewhat smaller footholds or steepening the wall angle. Once you are comfortable at this level, incrementally increase the severity once again. Continue in this manner until you are comfortable leading overhanging routes that require the use of slopers.

A fear of falling is typically related to leading. You should approach a fear of falling in much the same manner as a fear of flying. Begin by getting completely comfortable on top rope at all wall angles and hold types. Make sure you are also comfortable with all types of top-rope falls, including swinging out from the wall on an overhanging face and pitching sideways when the route wanders.

Once you can truly approach any top-rope situation with complete comfort, you're ready to address your fear of leading. Begin by mock leading on a belayed top rope by trailing a lead rope. Get comfortable making all the clips and managing the lead line. Next begin leading very easy climbs, say four or even five number grades below your maximum. As you gain confidence in your leading, gradually increase the grade.

When you get within two or three number grades of your maximum, begin taking practice lead falls. Make

Fear of falling can rob you of your potential. You can apply desensitization to overcome this fear by gradually adapting to the stresses of possible falls. HEATH CHRISTENSEN ON TEARDROP 5.13A, AMERICAN FORK, UTAH. PHOTO: NATHAN SMITH

sure the route you choose for this exercise is slightly overhung and free from ledges or other projections. Climb to the third or higher bolt and have your belayer hold you so you're as close to the draw as possible. Now get back on the wall, have your belayer slack you as if you were about to climb. Then let yourself fall. The impact of the resulting fall should be similar to that experienced on a top rope. Repeat as many times as necessary so you're comfortable with this short fall. Next climb a foot above the draw before dropping off, and repeat as necessary to gain comfort. Increase to two feet, then three, then four, and so on until you can drop off from ten feet or so above your last bolt. It could take weeks or even months to gain this level of comfort. Go slowly, gaining confidence at every step; if you over-reach, you'll only end up reinforcing your fears.

## Fear of Success and Failure

Even ambitious climbers who already climb at a fairly high level can struggle with fears of success and failure. This type of challenge is best worked out in a support-ive environment with a mental health professional and a good coach who can keep you on track by helping to limit self-sabotaging behavior. Our goal here is to pro-vide assistance in recognizing some of the symptoms and consequences of these problems.

Fear of success sounds like a contradiction—who could be afraid of success? But some people are, and this fear is an expression of their deep-seated negative feelings about themselves. Such feelings have any number of potential origins rooted in emotional trauma. Individuals who fear success are typically frightened of rising performance standards that they'll need to live up to and maintain. They can be very critical of themselves and are in the habit of prejudging their ability. They may also feel they are undeserving of success. Such individuals may outwardly be confident or arrogant, attitudes that serve as a defense against their internal sense of unworthiness. People who suffer from fear of success may actually be somewhat successful, but they rarely exceed their comfort zones. Climbers suffering from a fear of success are likely to downgrade routes they send. This kind of chronic downgrading is one way of protecting themselves from success, since they never

have to admit they have ever done a more difficult route. Downgrading is also a way of reducing the accomplishments of others and claiming superiority without having to perform at a higher level.

Fear of failure involves a fear of disapproval; the fear of losing affection or social status is the usual underlying cause. Climbers who fear failure may have felt a great deal of pressure to succeed at an earlier time in their lives. As with fear of success, fear of failure also prevents climbers from moving out of their comfort zones, thereby slowing progress. Fear of failure mani-fests itself in placing blame on the belayer, other climbers, the climb, and just about anything else they can think of. People who are afraid of failure may have a tendency to be grade inflators. Inflating grades is a way of claiming greater success without risking the potential failure associated with getting on a route that is beyond their comfort zone.

Fears of success and failure also express themselves in the way climbers speak. A consistent flow of nega-tive language such as "I can't" or "this is too hard" can only hinder progress and risk becoming a self-fulfill-ing prophecy. Using this kind of language can be an honest expression of frustration, but it is more often a way of judging or placing blame for a poor perform-ance, neither of which has a legitimate place in your climbing. Your goal as a success-oriented climber is to analyze the elements at work in each performance from how you execute movement to your fitness level to your emotional state and more. By letting go of the urge to judge, you give yourself permission to remain analytical and are more likely to discover what is work-ing for and against you. In short, analysis is necessary and productive, but judging or placing blame serves no useful purpose.

Learn to send consistent positive messages to your-self as you train and climb. By setting goals and making this kind of commitment, you are making a full effort to be the best climber you can be. You should celebrate yourself and your ambitions and not put unnecessary obstacles in your way. An important step in doing this is committing to the idea that you will be objective about success and failure. Success and failure are not acci-dents; they are constructed and are a result of what you are or aren't doing in your training and climbing.

Visualizing a successful performance prior to the attempt is a powerful method for improving your climbing.

## Visualization

In chapter 5 we described several ways to use visualization during a climb to make movement more precise, control force, and increase enjoyment. Another type of visualization provides a powerful tool to help prepare for an entire performance. To visualize a route or boulder problem means creating a complete mental picture of the entire performance before you attempt to send it and being able to see yourself climbing the correct sequence for the entire route from bottom to top. This mental picture will contain many details, including the entire movement sequence, how each move feels, the pace and the rhythm of your movement in different sections, and changes in your mental approach, such as when you need to focus on precision or where you want to be more aggressive. Proper visualization includes all the ways you plan to initiate and control individual moves.

But why use visualization? Years ago, a psychology experiment divided a bunch of equally talented basketball players into two groups. The first group spent all their time trying to improve their free throws by practicing the shot over and over. The second group did nothing but learn to relax into a meditative state and visualize themselves making perfect free throws. After weeks apart, both groups were tested on their actual free throw abilities. It turned out that the visualizers improved their free throw percentage to a greater degree than those who spent their time actually practicing the shot!

Visualization aids the learning process. Attempting to visualize a route while you are learning it will quickly reveal which sequences and details you know and which you don't. It gives you an immediate way of assessing your pragmatic knowledge of a route, making goals for the next learning burn easier to set, and it reinforces the learning that you have already done. In addition, visualization prepares you for the redpoint. Even after you know the sequences, hold and movement details, and rests and clips, it can be difficult to visualize the route from bottom to top with no mistakes, falls, or lapses in concentration, but the effort will aid in the learning process.

You may visualize your climbing from a number of different perspectives. You can use a third-person viewpoint and remain outside of your body, as in watching a movie. Or you may opt for a first-person perspective, experiencing everything as if you were actually climbing. A complete visualization will also include specific keys for each move, such as a foothold that is difficult to see or a handhold that you need to use in a very specific way. You may also want to include how your muscles will feel and imagine yourself climbing well and with precision even while experiencing considerable fatigue.

*Activity 52: Visualization*

Begin visualization by putting yourself into a meditative state through relaxation. The mind must be prepared to accept and internalize the images you will visualize. A simple relaxation technique is to lie on a comfortable piece of furniture in a quiet room. Close your eyes and breathe in deeply through the nose, hold your breath for a moment, and then release it through your mouth by sighing. With the first breaths, allow your fingers and toes to relax. On subsequent breaths, let your hands and feet and then arms and legs relax completely. Lastly, let go of the muscles in your torso. Release all the tension in your muscles, and feel your body sinking into the furniture. Try to think of nothing, or simply concentrate on the number of breaths you have taken thus far; the object is to open the mind to the suggestions that will follow.

The subconscious does not know the difference between reality and imagination. Your goal is to show your subconscious the perfect movie of your upcoming redpoint, and the more real you can make it, the more believable it will be. If the subconscious internalizes the images of your success, you will enhance your chances of sending the route. What will you hear while you're climbing? What will you smell? How does the sun feel on your skin? Be confident and experience the world around you. Visualize preparing for the redpoint, and then apply all the subtlety and nuance of movement you discovered to your desired sequences. Visualize every hold and sequence in detail and in order. What does each hold feel like? What is its texture? See yourself confidently ascend the route in perfect style, noting the look and feel of all the holds and movements and in complete harmony with your surroundings. After seeing yourself confidently ascend the route, visualize your calm celebration of the achievement. Then bring yourself slowly out of the meditative state by repeating the breathing exercise for a few breaths and gradually coming back to consciousness.

To create a positive self-image, use self-talk and activators. Talk to yourself in a positive manner, reinforcing the good in everything you do. Create an activator that motivates and inspires you and that contributes to the positive self-image you desire.

Fear is the great paralyzer in climbing, whether derived from the possibility of injury, success, or failure. Learn the warning signs and take steps to reduce fear to a manageable level.

Visualization is mentally practicing, in perfect detail, a successful performance before it is attempted. Learn to put yourself in a relaxed state and feel yourself moving flawlessly up your targeted route. This mental practice will help you learn the route more quickly and create a positive picture for your subconscious.

✔ Physical training activities provide direct emotional benefits by raising your basic comfort level in the climbing environment.

✔ Sending the routes on your pyramid and rewarding yourself for each climb will build confidence, develop a positive self-image, and create momentum in your climbing.

✔ Your self-image can have a marked impact on your climbing. Use positive self-talk and activators to improve your self-image.

✔ Fear robs performance. Use desensitization to overcome a fear of falling.

✔ To visualize a route or boulder problem means creating a complete mental picture of the entire performance before you attempt to send it. Visualization can help make movement more precise, control force, and increase enjoyment.

With such a variety of activities, methods, and workouts, how can you organize your training program so that it's fun, reasonable, and propels you to the next level? This chapter walks you through the process that we use as coaches to assess abilities and identify goals. In the next chapter, we'll help you produce a workable and motivating plan that includes exciting and achievable performance goals.

Many climbers place too much emphasis on physical strength; although maximum strength is an important component of overall performance, it is not the only or even the most advantageous aspect of your climbing worthy of improving. Additionally, climbers tend to work on improving areas in which they already excel. Climbers, like all humans, tend to gravitate toward that which provides greater gratification. This means that if you are good at something, you'll tend to do more of it, especially if you receive internal or external rewards, such as acknowledgment from your peers. Not surprisingly, then, climbers are attracted to routes with characteristics that tend to favor their abilities.

A climber who is expert at crimper use would naturally find it more satisfying to send a V5 crimper problem than to repeatedly work a V3 slopefest. Mapping your course to improvement begins with an assessment of your current abilities, especially determining and then addressing any weakness. Keep an open mind; it is human nature to overlook one's weaknesses, but if you can critically and objectively evaluate your abilities and skills, you'll be rewarded by learning where to begin your improvement program. You can gain valuable insights into your current abilities, both physical and mental, by evaluating your climbing history, considering your partners' observations, examining your emotions, and performing some simple yet effective physical-conditioning assessments.

## Evaluating Your Climbing History

Begin your self-assessment by evaluating your climbing history, using climbing pyramids to spotlight your strengths and weaknesses.

## Climbing Pyramids

A climbing pyramid is simply a list of the routes or boulder problems you've sent in the last twelve months, in descending order from hardest to easiest. It is called a pyramid because of the shape that such a list often takes, as in this example:

12c

12b  12b

12a  12a  12a  12a

11d  11d  11d  11d  11d  11d  11d  11d

Your experience may not take on a pyramid shape, but the patterns that are revealed can be very helpful in determining your climbing strengths and weaknesses.

You will complete four pyramids: one each for indoor and outdoor routes and indoor and outdoor bouldering.

Start with a pyramid of your redpoints. Use the upper section of the Self-Assessment Worksheet, which you'll find on the DVD and at the end of this chapter, to record, one climb to a line, in order from hardest to easiest, the most difficult outdoor and indoor routes and boulder problems you have sent in the last year. Start at the top grade level, and record all the climbs you have completed at that level. Then work your way down the worksheet one letter grade at a time. Do not include any climbs you have not sent. Note the number of redpoint attempts you made to eventually send the route.

Next, describe the following route characteristics for each climb on your pyramid:

- *Wall angle:* Is the route less than vertical, vertical, steep, or a mix?

- *Hold type:* What is the predominant hold type on the route? If the hold types vary significantly, what are the holds like in the crux section?

- *Length:* What is the length of the route, measured in feet?

- *Crux location:* Is the crux located at the start, middle, or end of the route?

- *Continuity:* Is the route sustained without crux moves substantially harder than the rest of the climbing, or does the route have distinct crux sections with rests or easier ground in between?

Once you have completed all four pyramids, take a look at the shape of each. Ideally, your pyramids will all have a similar look, with one route or problem at the top grade, two at the next hardest level, four below that, and eight at the lowest level (represented as 1-2-4-8). This standard shape shows good, solid progress through the grades. As you gain experience, acquire skill, and improve your physical conditioning, you should see a steady progression as represented by the 1-2-4-8 profile.

A steep pyramid, such as 1-1-2-3, or one with gaps, such as 1-0-2-8, reveals a climber who needs to develop a solid base of experience. As you reach your current potential, your experience should be reflected as the standard 1-2-4-8 pyramid.

A flat pyramid, such as 2-7-15-many, is indicative of a climber who has plateaued or has developed an impressive base and is ready to achieve the next level. A good rule of thumb to distinguish between the two is the number of redpoint tries you took on each route. A great many burns, more than eight to ten per route, indicates a plateau. Fewer than ten tries on the harder routes suggests a readiness to move to the next level. This form of self-assessment is quite beneficial to a climber who has plateaued. Uncovering strengths, weaknesses, and preferences, and then applying effort toward the broadening of skills and the improvement of weak areas, is the most effective means of breaking out of stagnation.

Now compare your indoor versus outdoor pyramids. Are there any major differences? Are you better or worse at climbing on plastic? If you're much worse at outdoor routes or problems, you may simply need more outdoor experience, or perhaps the character of the rock is markedly different from the gym routes you are used to. Gym problems have progressed toward more sloping, finger-friendly holds and fewer crimps, but many difficult outdoor routes require significant crimping strength. Training on slopers transfers poorly to crimpers. If your pyramids show a difference in achievement between indoors and out, consider the holds you are using, as well as the wall angles and size of footholds available on your indoor problems. If you're not practicing indoors what you wish to perform outdoors, you are training suboptimally.

Next, note any patterns in the types of routes and problems you've listed on your pyramids. Look for consistencies in the named route characteristics. Do you favor climbs with crimpers? Slopers? Long routes? Short ones? Routes with the crux at the beginning? At the end? If you look closely, you'll likely see several patterns emerge, and those patterns, which highlight route characteristics that attract you, are usually strengths in your climbing.

Conversely, if you discern a pattern denoting a strength, you may also discover a weakness. Many times a climber strong in one area can be weak in another, especially if he shies away from those climbs that are not satisfying to him. For example, if you were to find that many of your hard routes involve crimper strength at the crux, you may be weak with slopers. Or if your top routes are all discontinuous in nature, meaning the routes are broken into easy and hard sections, you may not have developed the aerobic or anaerobic capacity that would allow you to climb continuously difficult routes.

Take your time preparing and evaluating your route pyramids. This tool is very powerful in bringing preferences and patterns to light and should not be taken casually.

## Your Partners' Observations

Your climbing partners have watched you climb, and they know where you shine and where you don't. This knowledge can also be valuable in helping you form a picture of your skills. Ask your climbing partners the following questions, and record their answers on the Self-Assessment Worksheet. If your friends are honest and at least somewhat perceptive, they'll give you invaluable feedback about your abilities.

1. Which moves or movement skills do I perform repeatedly or am I good at? What types of moves do I usually try first when stuck? (For example, if you're good at heel hooks you'll tend to try them first and use them frequently.)

2. Which moves or movement skills do I avoid or am I weak in? (If your friends rarely see you use a particular movement skill, it's an indication that this skill may need improvement.)

3. What kinds of routes or boulder problems do I love? On what kinds of climbs can I smoke my friends?

What kinds of climbs do I hate? Specify wall angle, length, continuity, and crux position.

4. What hold types do I complain about or avoid? Which do I like? Do I have more confidence in some kinds of holds?

5. Do I make a lot of foot adjustments?

6. Am I able to turn back and forth easily?

7. Do I apply the appropriate movement skill when it's called for?

8. Are there certain skills at which I am particularly good or poor?

Now ask yourself the same questions you asked your climbing partners. Be truthful, and record your answers on the worksheet.

Compare your own answers with those of your friends. Look for consistent messages from among your partners. Does everyone agree on your preferences? On the areas where you seem to have difficulty? Look closely at any patterns that emerge from your thoughts and discussions. If you repeat a movement over and over, it's likely you have located a movement strength. Likewise, those types of climbs you prefer usually indicate an ability bias. On the other hand, those types of climbs, holds, or angles you avoid or complain about indicate areas needing improvement, and those movement skills you never use point out abilities you may lack.

## Emotions

Success and failure are never accidents. Whether you realize it at the time, success and failure are created in climbing by the collision of your abilities and level of preparedness with the demands of specific climbs. On top of this, your readiness to perform on any given day is largely a result of your state of mind—in short, your emotions. It's important to isolate those aspects of your emotional life that either enhance or hinder your performance.

Begin by looking back over your climbing experience. Decide what your all-time five very best and five very worst climbs have been. For this evaluation, pick specific climbs that represented real landmarks for you and your all-time worst climbs. They could be routes or boulder problems, on-sights, beta flashes or redpoints, trad or sport. In the next section on the Self-Assessment

Worksheet, record your answers to the following questions for each of these ten climbs:

1. What kind of climb was it? Describe the climb, along with its location and the date you sent it.

2. On a scale from one to ten, with one representing emotionally flat and ten denoting an excited and upbeat state, how did you feel as you were putting on your shoes and tying in just before you started the attempt? What was your level of fear, with one representing not frightened and ten very frightened?

3. What sorts of things were you saying to yourself the day before the climb? On the drive to the crag? During the approach?

4. What did your warmup consist of that day? How many climbs did you do? What grade were they? What were you thinking and focused on during your warmup?

5. What was your emotional energy focused on during the actual climb? What were you aware of, thinking, and trying to do while climbing?

6. What was your attitude toward your physical safety on the climb? On a scale from one to ten, with one being very worried and ten not worried at all, rate how you felt about your safety.

After you've answered the questions about each route performance, compare your answers for your best and worst climbs. Your answers form an emotional framework for how you climb each day. What were the differences in terms of your thoughts and feelings during the day leading up to the best and worst climbs? What were the differences in your focus during the climbs? In your concern for safety?

After evaluating the differences between your best and worst performances, you'll want to craft your thinking and alter your climbing in a way that fosters the best performances possible. Use the comparisons you just made to determine how you would like to be thinking and feeling before a challenging climb. What is the best way to focus your attention before and during the climb? Once you know the difference between successful and unsuccessful emotional performances, it makes no sense to leave your state of mind up to chance. Your goal each day should be to create an emotional state that will help you succeed.

Recommended reading for psychological training includes *Thinking Body, Dancing Mind*, by Chungliang Al Huang, and *The Mental Edge: Maximize Your Sports Potential with the Mind/Body Connection*, by Ken Baum and Richard Trubo.

## Physical-Conditioning Assessments

Physical abilities are only strengths or weaknesses relative to one another. For instance, a V5 boulderer with a route pyramid topping out at 5.11b may be lacking endurance, because his V5 bouldering strength should enable him to do any individual sequences up to mid-5.12. This section will help you determine your level of conditioning in four key physical attributes: strength and power, aerobic endurance, anaerobic endurance, and stamina.

### Strength and Power

Benchmarking your strength and power is as simple as reviewing the bouldering pyramid you constructed on your Self-Assessment Worksheet. For now, note the highest bouldering grade you can consistently send in a dozen or so attempts. Also note any significant differences between your indoor and outdoor pyramids. A large difference might simply indicate a lack of experience in one or the other, but it could highlight route or hold type preference. Maximum strength and power are strengths or weaknesses only if they are at markedly different levels than your other physical abilities.

To determine your maximum strength, refer to the following table, which displays a rough guide for determining the hardest moves you're likely to encounter on a roped route of a given grade. They are presented in the form of a range in which the lower V grades tend to be found on longer routes of a continuous nature, whereas the higher, more difficult grades are located on shorter or discontinuous routes.

The hardest problems in your bouldering pyramids determine the most difficult routes you'll be able to send. If your peak bouldering grade is V5, it is unlikely you'll be able to send a 5.13c, as you do not have the move-by-move strength and movement skill necessary to climb one or more of the route's sequences.

If your bouldering and route pyramids do not top out at the same level as shown in the table, you have an

| | |
|---|---|
| 5.10 | V0– to V1 |
| 5.11a and b | V1 to V2 |
| 5.11c and d | V2– to V2+ |
| 5.12a and b | V2 to V3 |
| 5.12c and d | V3 to V5– |
| 5.13a | V5 to V6 |
| 5.13b | V6 to V7– |
| 5.13c | V6 to V8 |
| 5.13d | V6 to V9 |
| 5.14a | V7 to V10 |
| 5.14b | V8 to V11 |
| 5.14c | V8 to V12 |

indication of a strength or a weakness. It is unlikely that your route pyramid will peak at a grade equivalent above your maximum bouldering grade. The situation whereby peak bouldering grade exceeds that for routes, however, is quite common and indicates well-developed maximum strength relative to endurance. This is the case for many boulderers who train by exerting maximal bursts of effort for very short durations but spend little time improving their endurance.

### Aerobic Endurance

Your aerobic conditioning determines your anaerobic threshold, making it an important component of your overall physical state. Testing your current local aerobic-conditioning level is a simple matter of determining the highest grade at which you can climb continuously for twenty minutes without crossing your anaerobic threshold. You'll need an autobelay or a patient belayer and a clock. Pick a climb with a vertical or slightly overhung angle that will allow you to climb up and then back down again. Once you start climbing, you may not touch back down on the ground until the twenty minutes are up. Ideally, you're looking for a very slight burning sensation in your forearms—any less and the climb is not hard enough; any more and the climb is too hard. Experiment with several grades until you arrive at the ideal, and record that grade on your Self-Assessment Worksheet.

The typical difference between your maximum continuous climbing grade and the top of your route pyramid is 2.5 number grades. For example, if your route pyramid tops out at 5.13a, your maximum continuous climbing grade should be around 5.10c (13a minus 10 letter or 2.5 number grades). If the difference is less, aerobic conditioning is a strength; if more, a weakness.

## Anaerobic Endurance

To determine your anaerobic endurance, perform the 4x4 exercise (activity 34). Instead of varying the grades of the boulder problems selected, however, use four different problems of the same grade. Find the highest grade whereby you can complete all sixteen problems in the workout without becoming too pumped to continue; you want to be able to complete all sixteen problems, but just barely. Record the grade of the four problems on the worksheet.

Your maximum 4x4 grade should be three to four grades below your peak consistent bouldering level. If you can send V6 boulder problems in a dozen or so attempts, you should be able to do a 4x4 at V2 or V3. Much less, and anaerobic conditioning is probably a weakness; more, and it's a strong point relative to your maximum strength.

## Setting Long- and Short-Term Goals

Goals serve the dual functions of specifying a destination and providing the motivation for getting there. Setting goals is a necessary and enjoyable part of effective training. Without goals, it's impossible to track your progress and measure your improvement. It's also impossible to know how to train properly if you have no basis on which to decide what activities to use or what level of skill or fitness you need to realize. Additionally, having goals that excite you is one of the most powerful motivational tools available. Your long-term and interim climbing goals will not only mark your destination, but also evoke a positive visceral reaction whenever you think about them. When climbers create goals that excite them, that get them thinking about and anticipating a positive future, they are more likely to be successful.

Climbing often plays a large role in climbers' lives. When they aren't climbing, they're thinking and talking about climbing, and their most powerful relationships are often with other climbers. Climbing success and failure play a very real role in shaping their self-perceptions, which carry into other areas of their lives. Achievement in climbing can therefore be a step toward improving the overall quality of your life.

You should set both long- and short-term goals. Climber turned business guru Jim Collins, in a *Harvard Business Review* article entitled "Building Your Company's Vision" (September–October 1996, with Jerry Porras) proposed a methodology for creating a long-term vision. The process is based on his research into why some companies produce consistently superior results (see *Built to Last: Successful Habits of Visionary Companies*, by Collins and Porras, 1994). Vision begins with what Jim called the Big Hairy Audacious Goal (BHAG). The BHAG is an outrageous but motivating aspiration that drives the strategy and tactics necessary to achieve it. It's a North Star, an unwavering long-term goal that sets a direction. In the early 1980s, Microsoft's BHAG was a computer on every desk, at the time a seemingly ludicrous goal. In fact, IBM, then the industry leader, did not think there was a need for every worker to have his own computer, believing that the future was in big mainframes. Microsoft's vision led the company to make some very crucial decisions leading to dominance in the PC software market.

The second step is setting interim, short-term goals, or what Jim, in a climbing metaphor, calls base camps. These are way stations along the path to the summit (BHAG) that inform you of your progress. Unlike the BHAG, the base camps must be measurable so that you can track your progress and reward yourself for the achievements.

### Setting Your Long-Term Goal

You can use the BHAG principle to create your own North Star. What would be the ultimate climb or climbing achievement for you? Be specific; simply saying 5.13b is not very motivating. Say instead something like "I will send Apollo Reed, The Pod, and Mercy Seat in the Coliseum at Summersville Lake, West Virginia." BHAGs do not come with time frames, nor will many of your friends believe them attainable. But they tap into your dreams and aspirations about what you, at your best, are capable of achieving.

To help you find your BHAG, ask yourself what your climbing dream goal is. If all your limits were pushed, if everything went right, if you had all the time you needed to climb, if you never had to worry about obstacles such as injury, illness, or bad weather, what would you be capable of achieving as a climber over the course of your career? Think about routes you have seen, or even a number grade that inspires you. The key to a valuable long-term goal lies in what you find inspiring or in what you dream about doing someday. What are the routes you have looked up at and said to yourself, "Someday. . . ."?

## Setting Short-Term Goals

Begin setting interim, short-term goals by considering what steps will be necessary to reach your long-term goal on both an annual and a seasonal basis. What is a realistic performance goal for this year? The answer to this question could be considered base camp number

one. Consider your present skill and fitness levels, level of motivation, potential to improve, and the amount of time you have to climb. What do you think you can reasonably achieve in climbing this year? The base camp needs to be achievable but challenging. If the goal is too low and the outcome certain, there is not much motivation to work hard, since your success is guaranteed. If the goal is too difficult and you perceive very little chance of success, your motivation is also diminished, because you'll feel you can't succeed no matter how hard you try. Your goals must stretch you, but only to the point where you believe you can succeed with effort.

What would your base camp look like next year? The year after that? In this manner, you'll lay out a step-by-step set of annual or seasonal goals that lead to your long-term goal.

Here's a little guidance on setting an appropriate short-term or seasonal goal. If you have ample time, are highly motivated, can climb three to four days each

**Choose routes for your pyramid that are similar to your long-term goal. If your goal consists of steep climbs, your targeted pyramid will require climbs at a similar angle.** ERIC HARRISON ON THE DIGGLER 5.13A, MAPLE CANYON, UTAH.

**If your goal consists of vertical or slab routes, your targeted pyramid will naturally include similar route angles.**

ment in a single season is likely to be less than four letter grades and depends on many of the same conditions.

Given the attainment of your first goal, what should your next base camp consist of? Think about what you need to achieve in your second year or season, and so forth, leading to your BHAG. If you look at your long-term goal as a set of achievable steps, each built on its predecessor, the vision becomes clearer and your perception of success improves.

Use the following questions to help you clarify your base camp goals. Give some thought to the answers before setting them.

1. For your area of interest, what is the most difficult climb you have successfully completed as a project? How many tries did this take?

2. What is the most difficult project you have sent this year? How many tries did it take?

3. What is your consistent on-sight level? This is the grade at which you have a 90+ percent chance of a successful on-sight attempt.

4. What is your level of commitment to yourself? Regardless of the outcome, can you learn from your experiences and be accepting of yourself? Will failure to achieve your desired goals cause you to lose self-respect, or can you use failure to make yourself stronger?

5. Can you try to do your absolute best every day? No matter how you feel or what conditions are like, can you be satisfied by achieving the goal of giving your best effort? How and why?

## Creating a Structural Framework: Progressive Performance Pyramids

Now that you have competed the self-assessment and considered your goals, you need to compare the two and measure the difference. This comparison is essential on two levels. First, it gives you a good idea of whether or not your initial and future base camp goals are realistic. The greater the difference between your current best performance and your goals, the more time and effort it will take to achieve them. Second, you must structure your climbing to provide you the type and quality of experience that will lead to

week, live in an area with good weather, have frequent access to outdoor routes, and have good climbing partners, you can conceivably gain four letter grades in a single climbing season. If you are not so fortunate to have the time, weather, partners, and so on, but you can maintain a climbing schedule of two or three sessions per week, step your goals back a bit to perhaps two letter grade increases. With less available time, your goal may simply be to maintain your current level. At higher starting performance levels (5.12 and higher), your improve-

achievement of your goal. This structural framework is created by constructing a targeted performance route pyramid. These pyramids work extremely well, providing a large amount of relevant experience in a short period of time, and can help climbers create real momentum for improvement.

You start by constructing a target pyramid to help you achieve your first base camp, choosing routes that you have not sent but will provide you the experience necessary to move you toward your BHAG. The Coliseum example is a good case in point. Each route is severely overhung and requires a broad range of technique and movement skills related to steep terrain. If your current pyramid tops out at 5.12c and consists mostly of thin face climbs, your first base camp might be completing a pyramid consisting of steeply overhung routes topping out at 5.12c, such as the following:

| | | |
|---|---|---|
| 5.12c | Scar Lover | The Hole at Kaymoor |
| 5.12b | Chunky Monkey | Beauty Mountain |
| | Ly'n and Steal'n | Summersville Lake |
| 5.12a | Narcissus | Summersville Lake |
| | Tobacco Road | Summersville Lake |
| | Yowsah | The Hole at Kaymmor |
| | Smoking Guns | Beauty Mountain |
| 5.11d | eight overhung routes | |

Your next base camp might consist of moving your top grade up one notch to steep 5.12d. In this case, you'd need to add one 5.12d (perhaps Lactic Acid Bath

in The Hole), one 5.12c, two 5.12bs, and four 5.12as to keep the geometric pyramid shape that denotes the experience progression desired. You thus could create a series of pyramids, each of which is an interim goal, or base camp, that move you from where you stand today to where you want to be tomorrow.

## Constructing Performance Pyramids

Creating your first pyramid is often the most difficult planning task associated with progressive pyramids. The first step is to determine your current, or base, level, defined as the grade at which you have completed eight or more routes or boulder problems in the past twelve months. In some cases the base level is easy to determine, for example, a climber whose experience is defined by a 1-2-4-8 pyramid with 5.12a at the top and 5.11b at the bottom. If the on-sight level is 5.10d/5.11a and he can redpoint 5.11b in less than five attempts, his new pyramid will begin at 5.11c and overlap the old pyramid as follows:

**5.12b**

5.12a **5.12a**

5.11d 5.11d **5.11d 5.11d**

5.11c 5.11c 5.11c 5.11c **5.11c 5.11c 5.11c 5.11c**

5.11b 5.11b 5.11b 5.11b 5.11b 5.11b 5.11b 5.11b

*regular type = past experience, bold = new pyramid*

The climber's goal is to redpoint eight new routes, upping his hardest redpoint by one letter grade and building a new base at 5.11c. Climbing three to four

### A Sample Pyramid Progression

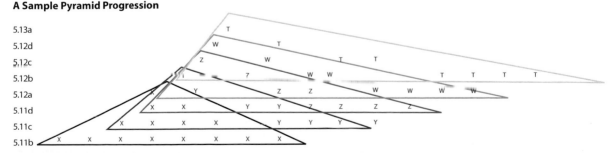

When one pyramid has been completed, set the next by moving all four levels up one grade. Then send all the new routes beginning with those at the lowest level. For example, after finishing pyramid X, the climber should target the Y climbs for completion. After Y is complete, the climber should target the Z climbs and so forth until sending the ultimate goal of the 13a T climb.

days per week can produce these results in seven to ten weeks. That still leaves a lot of climbing season, so he might add more routes and raise his base level to 5.11d. The new pyramid would look like this:

**5.12c**

5.12b **5.12b**

*5.12a* 5.12a **5.12a 5.12a**

*5.11d 5.11d* 5.11d 5.11d **5.11d 5.11d 5.11d 5.11d**

*5.11c 5.11c 5.11c 5.11c* 5.11c 5.11c 5.11c 5.11c

*5.11b 5.11b 5.11b 5.11b 5.11b 5.11b 5.11b 5.11b*

*italics = original pyramid, regular type = second pyramid, bold = third pyramid*

Now let's say this climber's season ended here. In fourteen to twenty weeks, he would have sent sixteen new routes, raised his new redpoint best from 5.12a to 5.12c, increased his base level from 5.11b to 5.11d, and redpointed six routes as hard as or harder than his previous best. It's also reasonable to expect that this climber's on-sight level would go from 5.10d/5.11a to 5.11b/c. All in all, this represents what would be a banner year for most climbers, and this is a fairly conservative program. In our coaching experience, we have seen many climbers move up two, three, and even four letter grades in a single season using this progressive system. One memorable climber took his redpoint level from 5.11d to 5.13a in six months.

Let's look at a few other examples. What if this climber started out with the same base-level pyramid, a 1-2-4-8 pyramid topping out at 5.12a, but had on-sighted three of the routes at the 5.11b level and sent the others in two to six tries. As long as the 5.11cs took between four and nine tries each, it's reasonable for this climber to set 5.11d as the new base level, bypassing 5.11c. His new pyramid then would look like this:

**12c**

**12b 12b**

12a **12a 12a 12a**

11d 11d **11d 11d 11d 11d 11d 11d**

11c 11c 11c 11c (11c 11c 11c 11c)

11b 11b 11b 11b 11b 11b 11b 11b

*regular type = old, bold = new*

In this example, the climber adds twelve routes to his existing pyramid and raises his best redpoint to 5.12c. This is a completely reasonable progression for someone climbing three to four days per week, but it might take nine weeks or more to complete the twelve routes. Even if it took twelve weeks to complete this pyramid, there still would be time left for the climber to add more routes and potentially raise his best redpoint to 5.12d.

What about climbers who don't fall into this easy pattern? It's common to see small or incomplete pyramids and to have forgotten some climbing experiences. A climber's pyramid might look like this:

5.11c

5.11b

5.11a 5.11a

5.10d 5.10d 5.10d

Say this climber has been climbing two to three days per week for three years, has flashed one of the 5.11as, and is sure there are other routes he can't remember that would fit on the pyramid. He does not remember enough of the 5.10s he's done to determine with any certainty what his base should be. In this case, he can simply use his consistent on-sight level to determine his initial base. If he doesn't know offhand, he'll need to spend one weekend making on-sight attempts. He's looking for the grade he can consistently on-sight. A safe place to start his pyramid is one letter grade above this level. So let's say that he found his on-sight level to be 5.10b. This means that his base pyramid will start at 5.10c and look like this:

11c

11b **11b**

11a **11a 11a**

10d 10d 10d **10d 10d**

**10c 10c 10c 10c 10c 10c 10c 10c**

*regular type = old, bold = new*

This case differs from the usual pyramid by adding thirteen new routes without raising the redpoint level. Climbers with incomplete pyramids often need to complete a large number of successful ascents in a short amount of time. They need to learn what they are capable of, refine their tactics, and develop their base so that it's solid and strong for the next step in the progression. In all likelihood, this pyramid will not be difficult for the climber. He'll flash a few of climbs at the 10c level and maybe even one at the 10d level. The other routes may take two to five tries each. If he stays on task, his pyramid will be completed quickly despite the large number of routes. In roughly six to eight weeks, he should be ready to start a new pyramid. The new pyramid will depend on his success with the first. If he flashes three of the 10cs, does the 10ds in two to four tries, and completes one or both of the 11as in one day, he can choose either 10d or 11a as the new base level. If he were to choose 11a as the new base, the pyramid would look like this:

**11d**

*11c* **11c**

*11b* 11b **11b 11b**

*11a 11a* 11a **11a 11a 11a 11a 11a**

*10d 10d 10d* 10d 10d (10d 10d 10d)

10c 10c 10c 10c 10c 10c 10c 10c

*italics = original, regular type = second pyramid,
bold = new pyramid routes to add*

This climber has added twenty-two routes to his pyramid in two iterations. This is a big, but not unheard of, jump in ability. He'll develop a great base, raise his on-sight level, build confidence, hone tactics, and be ready to break into 5.12s in his third progression.

Now let's look at a bouldering pyramid. Say a boulderer's pyramid looks like this:

V4 V4 V4

V3 V3 V3 V3

V2 V2 V2 V2 V2 V2

*(too many V1s to count)*

This is another incomplete pyramid, but closer inspection shows that it's not a simple case of a climber with a good base who is ready to move higher. Assume he climbs three days a week at an indoor gym and has been climbing a total of seven months. His flash level is V1, and the V3s and V4s all took twelve or more tries each.

This reflects a common situation, in which a new climber has specialized very early and is already approaching a plateau. He is practicing all his motor skills at a very high level of difficulty, making it impossible to foster solid learning. A climber in this situation is not really ready to advance to V5. He needs a great deal more experience at the V2 level or lower. He'd benefit from diversity in his climbing, mixing routes and focused movement training in with his bouldering.

As a general rule, your beginning base level should be at the grade that normally takes you two to three attempts to send. For example, if you're after those Coliseum routes and you can currently send overhung 5.11ds in two or three attempts, set the lowest grade of your first target pyramid at that level. If it takes half a dozen tries to send overhung 5.11ds, begin your pyramid at a lower grade. If you can on-sight steep 11ds, begin at a higher grade. It is better to set your initial pyramid too low than too high, so be conservative in its construction.

This method of using a highly targeted set of routes designed to build experience for a narrow objective, such as Coliseum routes, will get you to your goal faster, because you'll be gaining knowledge, physical conditioning, and experience all directly related to that goal. If, however, you want a more rounded education, you can construct your pyramid from classic routes of all types. Choose a variety of route lengths, crux locations, hold and rock types, and wall angles, possibly biased a bit toward the weaknesses you discovered in your self-assessment.

## Rules for Using the Progressive Pyramid Method

Following a few simple rules when using progressive pyramids will keep you motivated and progressing at a good pace.

- Start at the bottom of your new pyramid and complete the lowest level before moving to the next higher grade. This will give you enough time to refine your tactics, build fitness, and earn the next level.

- Print out your pyramid and post it somewhere prominent: on your refrigerator, on the side of your computer monitor, or on the dashboard of your car. Regularly reading your goals will remind you where you're headed and what you still need to achieve.

- Celebrate your climbing successes. Reward yourself for every climb on your pyramid you complete.

Each is an important goal, so celebrate by going out to dinner or treating yourself to something you want. You deserve it, and you should do everything you can to reinforce your climbing successes.

• Target and track both indoor and outdoor pyramids. Because of route turnover indoors, targeting specific climbs may not be productive, but you can set a target of sending a certain number of 5.12as, for instance, by a specific date. Keep track of your progress by recording your sends and keeping an up-to-date pyramid in your training log.

• As much as possible, construct your pyramid from classic routes. Your pyramid will provide more inspiration and be more fun if it consists of classic, well-liked routes at each grade.

Planning is a key to success. Invest the time and thought necessary to clearly lay out a set of personal, relevant goals, and your training schedule will fall into place. Once you have laid out a clear set of goals, from your long-term BHAG to your short-term base camps, you can begin to put your improvement plan together.

This approach to climbing improvement has a progressive order. Begin by assessing your strengths and weaknesses to gain a thorough understanding of your current situation. Then examine your personal aspirations related to climbing and set challenging but attainable goals. Only after completing these two steps should you create a training plan. You must know where you are, where you want to go, and how to measure your progress along the way to receive the utmost from your training.

## QUICK TICKS

✓ Mapping your course to improvement begins with an assessment of your current abilities. Look for patterns in your climbing to help paint a picture of your strengths and weaknesses.

✓ Your redpoint route pyramid can tell you if you have a preference for specific wall angles, hold types, route lengths, crux locations, or continuity.

✓ Survey your friends about your climbing, and look for patterns in their responses. Examine your own likes and dislikes.

✓ Evaluate your physical condition relative to the general standards for your level.

✓ Set a long-term goal that truly excites you. Let it become your North Star.

✓ Set the intermediate goals (base camps) necessary to reach your long-term goal. These goals should be challenging but achievable.

✓ Use performance pyramids to target specific routes leading to your goal. Your beginning base level should be at the grade that normally takes you two to three attempts to send.

✓ Start at the bottom of your new pyramid and complete the lowest level before moving to the next higher grade.

## Current route pyramids*

| | Route name | Grade | # RP tries | Wall angle | Hold type | Length | Crux location | Continuity |
|---|---|---|---|---|---|---|---|---|
| 1. | | | | | | | | |
| 2. | | | | | | | | |
| 3. | | | | | | | | |
| 4. | | | | | | | | |
| 5. | | | | | | | | |
| 6. | | | | | | | | |
| 7. | | | | | | | | |
| 8. | | | | | | | | |
| 9. | | | | | | | | |
| 10. | | | | | | | | |
| 11. | | | | | | | | |
| 12. | | | | | | | | |
| 13. | | | | | | | | |
| 14. | | | | | | | | |
| 15. | | | | | | | | |

*complete a total of four separate pyramids, one each for indoor and outdoor routes and indoor and outdoor boulder problems.

**Patterns discovered:**


## Climbing partner critiques

**Movement skills feedback:**


**Route type preferences:**


**Hold type preferences:**


## Your likes and dislikes

**Movement skills:**


**Route types:**


**Hold types:**

**Emotional reactions**

Best climbing experience

    1. Emotional excitement level prior to climbing (rate from 1 to 10):

    2. Fear level prior to climbing (rate from 1 to 10):

    3. Self-talk prior to climbing:

    4. What did your warmup consist of?

    5. What were your thoughts during the climb?

    6. Physical safety (rate from 1 to 10):

Worst climbing experience

    1. Emotional excitement level prior to climbing (rate from 1 to 10):

    2. Fear level prior to climbing (rate from 1 to 10):

    3. Self-talk prior to climbing:

    4. What did your warmup consist of?

    5. What were your thoughts during the climb?

    6. Physical safety (rate from 1 to 10):

Compare performances:

    1. Thoughts and feelings:

    2. Focus:

    3. Fear:

**Physical conditioning**

Highest consistent bouldering grade:

Highest continuous climbing grade:

Highest 4x4 grade:

**CHAPTER 13**

# Your Personalized Training Plan

PHOTO: LESLIE RIEHL

Once you have performed a self-assessment and set both long-term and short-term goals, you are ready to bring everything you've learned to its logical conclusion: a training plan to take you from your current level to where you want to be.

## Training Methods

There are several methods of training that climbers currently use, including cross-training, periodization, and progressive training.

### Cross-Training

Cross-training refers to performing exercises outside the usual mode of training, normally in a completely different sport, such as a runner that periodically trains on a bicycle. Cross-training can help prevent overtraining by transferring stresses to different parts of the body, and it can aid in situations where the athlete is injured.

The efficacy of cross-training, however, leaves something to be desired. Studies have shown that although cross-training can help maintain a certain level of conditioning, it cannot improve sport-specific fitness to the same degree as exercising within the confines of the sport. This is why, for instance, there is little correlation between improvement in the number of pull-ups a climber can do and his climbing ability. If you want to improve your climbing, you'll need to spend your training time performing climbing exercises. Forget about lifting weights, doing pull-ups, or running. All are excellent general-purpose exercises, but they won't do much for your climbing.

### Seasonality and Periodization

For most climbers, there is one time of the year that produces the best weather conditions conducive to difficult sends. Typically, this corresponds to cool, dry seasons, which vary from location to location. In the east and many parts of the west, fall is best. Winter can be optimal for crags in warmer regions, such as Red Rocks in Nevada. Whatever your climbing location, you'll likely want to be at your best during the favorable season.

Although trainers have known for centuries that an athlete cannot maintain peak performance conditioning indefinitely, it was not until 1965 that a study on periodized training was published. Soviet scientist Leonid Matveyev formulated a model in which the calendar year is broken into three training phases: preparatory, competitive, and transitional. The preparatory phase was further broken into general preparation and specific preparation phases. As the year progresses from the general preparatory to the competitive phase, the volume of training decreases while its intensity increases. The transitional phase is a period of active rest between cycles, allowing the body to recover before the next cycle begins. Subsequent studies have shown the efficacy of periodized training. Study subjects using a periodized schedule gained significantly more strength than those in a nonperiodized control group. See, for example, Baker et al., "Periodization: The Effect on Strength of Manipulating Volume and Intensity," published in the *Journal of Strength and Conditioning Research* 1994, 8:235–42.

Today, periodization schedules for sports that have important endurance and strength components, such as climbing, have been adapted from Matveyev's work. They gradually transition from a period of high volume and low intensity to one of low volume and high intensity. The initial period of local endurance training (aerobic training) transitions to hypertrophy strength training (maximum strength training), moves on to recruitment (strength and power training), and culminates in interval training (anaerobic training) just before the competitive or cool, dry weather season. During the peak period, volume again decreases and intensity increases. After the performance season comes a period of active rest to allow recovery prior to the next cycle.

The longer the cycle, the longer the peak will last. Use an annual cycle and your peak can last a month or more. With a shorter cycle, your peak will be correspondingly less. A periodized annual schedule aiming for a performance peak in October would begin in early January by building your local aerobic capacity, transition slowly into hypertrophy training in March, move into recruitment in early June, and culminate with anaerobic intervals from late July through September. The latter part of November and December would be spent in active rest.

Periodized training can be a useful tool for putting you in the best shape possible for a single time period or an important event, but it's not for everyone. Periodized training schedules are challenging for most recreational climbers to sustain. The phases are long and require many similar training sessions. This repetition can cause a fun activity to feel more like work, making you less likely to want to continue the training. Also, most climbers simply don't want to peak for just a single season or event. Instead, they prefer to enjoy gratifying climbing year-round, opting for sustained, longer-term performance that is somewhat less than that for a periodized peak. Climbing for most is not a professional pursuit where every ounce of performance potential must be squeezed out of the body to win a competition or please a sponsor.

Although periodized training will produce higher performance peaks, it also will result in deeper lows. If you're not approaching a peak, your performance is likely to be at a level that is less than satisfying. Persevering through these troughs in the expectation of better performance for a relatively short time frame is emotionally difficult for most recreational climbers.

## Progressive Training

Progressive training is defined as more or less continual improvement over an extended period of time, whether it's a season or many years. With progressive training, the climber experiences gradually improved performance to intermittent plateaus. Instead of the peaks and troughs produced by a periodized schedule, progressive training generates a sustainable, albeit subpeak, performance level allowing for many more performance opportunities throughout the year, and thus this method is more in line with the needs of most climbers.

Progressive training also results in measurable improvement. The recurrent regular feedback loop of training-performance-training can help you gauge your performance level more accurately at any given point in time, and it provides the small success incentives so necessary to continuing any training program. Don't underestimate this point: All athletes experience an ebb and flow of motivation, but if you can see improvement on a regular basis, you're more likely to continue working toward your goals. Progressive training will help you realize goals on a regular basis, making your climbing regularly satisfying, and you are more apt to stick with a plan that is fun and satisfying.

In progressive training, pyramids again are the best technique to direct your efforts, measure your progress, and provide motivation for continuing your training program. The same methodology is used as in the previous chapter, when you targeted routes in a series of grade pyramids leading to your goal climb or grade. Progressive pyramids prepare you well at every step to proceed to the next grade level, directing your efforts to those improvements most relevant to your goal. If, for example, your goal is The Big R at Smith Rock, Oregon, you'll need finely tuned balance skills and crimping power, as well as a healthy dose of both aerobic and anaerobic endurance. If you follow the guidelines in this chapter, by the time The Big R shows up on your current target pyramid, you'll be fully prepared to tackle its difficulties.

Progressive pyramids also provide you a convenient means to measure your progress. Set targeted climbs and send them, marking them off your list as you go. As you record the sends, you are keeping track of your progress in a simple, effective manner. To achieve any goal, you need motivation, and there's nothing like constant success to keep you working and trying. Because of the continual reinforcement, progressive pyramids will keep you going back for more, and the more you return to climb, the better your chances of ultimately succeeding at you BHAG.

# Assessing Your Strengths and Weaknesses

Creating your training plan begins by comparing your current state with your goals. Your plan needs to address two broad areas for strengths and weaknesses relative to your goals. It should enhance those movement skills important to attaining your targets and improve your physical conditioning as necessary.

## Movement Skills

Improving deficiencies in movement skills can greatly affect your performance, especially if those specific skills are directly related to your goals. For example, if

# Performance Guidelines

| Consistent Redpoint Goal | | Local Aerobic level | Local Anaerobic level | | Strength | Stamina | |
|---|---|---|---|---|---|---|---|
| | | Continuous Climbing Level | Highest Intensity: 4X4 | Mid-level Intensity: Laps on Routes | Max Bouldering Level | C.I.R. Bouldering | C.I.R. Routes |
| **5.10** | 5.10a | 5.7/5.8 | N/A | 5.9- | VB - V1 | VB | 5.8+ |
| | 5.10d | 5.8/5.9- | VB-V0 | 5.9/9+ | V0/1 | V0 | 5.9/9+ |
| **5.11** | 5.11a | 5.9-/5.9 | VB-V1 | 5.10a/b | V1/V2 | V0 | 5.9+ -5.10a |
| | 5.11d | 5.9+ | V0-V2 | 5.10b/c | V2/V3 | V0/V1 | 5.10c-5.11a |
| **5.12** | 5.12a | 5.10a-c | V0-V2 | 5.10d-5.11b | V3/V4 | V2 | 5.10d-5.11b |
| | 5.12d | 5.10d-5.11b | V1-V4 | 5.11c-5.12a | V4/V5 | V3 | 5.11c/5.12a |
| **5.13** | 5.13a | 5.11b/c | V2-V4 | 5.11d-5.12b | V5/V6 | V3/V4 | 5.12a/b |
| | 5.13d | 5.11c-5.12b | V4-V7 | 5.12b-5.13a | V8-V9 | V5/6 | 5.12c-5.13a |
| **5.14** | 5.14a/b | 5.12b-c | V5 - V8 | 5.12d-5.13a/b | V9 - V11 | V7-V9 | 5.13a/b |

These general guidelines are consistent with solid performances such as on-sights, or fast redpoints, as well as with continued improvement to the next level.
They do not represent the minimum requirements necessary to climb at a specific grade.

## Sample Comparison of Current Condition to Target for a 5.9/5.10 Level Climber

| | Level Standard | Current Condition | Condition to Achieve Goal | Activities |
|---|---|---|---|---|
| **MOVEMENT SKILLS** | | | | |
| 1. Identify hand- and footholds | Quickly, first time | I can do this | Same as level standard | None needed |
| 2. Precise use of holds | No adjustment necessary | Adjust foot about every 5 moves | Same as level standard | Continue using silent feet and glue hands |
| 3. Climbing at differing speeds | Some ability to vary speed at will | I can do this | Same as level standard | None needed |
| 4. Turning | Detect uses for and apply twists and turns | Can't always see where to apply a turn | Must be able to apply turning | Line and flag, apply turning to every move |
| 5. Movement initiation | Minimize initiation from the arms | Still initiate many moves from arms | Must initiate from hips | Practice initiation from hips, legs, and so on |
| 6. Body awareness | Begin to develop a sense | I have done this | Same as level standard | Continue use of body awareness exercises |
| 7. Style | Begin to develop a style | Not sure if I have one yet | Same as level standard | Continue studying style |
| **PHYSICAL CONDITIONING** | | | | |
| 1. Aerobic endurance | 20 minutes continuous climbing at 5.8 | 15 minutes max at 5.8 | Same as level standard | Push continuous climbing duration |
| 2. Strength | V0 to V1 | I can send V1 in 6 to 8 tries | Must be able to send V1 when somewhat pumped | CIR |
| 3. Anaerobic endurance | CIR at V0 | I can't complete a CIR at V0 | Same as level standard | CIR on a mix of V0– and V0 |
| **TACTICAL SKILLS** | | | | |
| 1. Organizing time | Climb 8 pitches each day | I have done up to 6 | Same as level standard | Continue improvement to reach goal |
| 2. Quickly orienting to crag | Can find most routes | I can do this | Same as level standard | Continue improvement |
| 3. Preplanning each route | Attempted on every climb | I sometimes rush to start | Same as level standard | Use preplanning skills on every climb |

your goal is to send the easiest 5.13s in the Coliseum at Summersville Lake (Apollo Reed 5.13a, The Pod 5.13a/b, and The Mercy Seat 5.13a/b), you had better have your drop-knee skills down cold. Otherwise, you'll have to compensate by applying a larger percentage of the force necessary with the small muscles of the arm, making the movement inefficient.

### General weaknesses

General weaknesses are deficiencies relative to your current level, as noted in your self-assessment. Maybe you can send V3 boulder problems so long as they're vertical in nature, but when the angle steepens, you're able to pull only V1. Or you're able to pull V4s so long as all the reaches are static in nature, but add in a throw and you're down to V2. To keep you on a well-rounded course to improvement, you need to bring these sub-par elements up to speed. Begin a list by making a note of each.

### Goal-specific weaknesses

Examine your self-assessment. What movement skills did you note as strengths and which as weaknesses? Now compare that list to your goals. Are there any places where the two lists don't match up? Are there skills you need in order to attain your goals that you currently don't possess? Add any goal-specific weaknesses to the list you started in the section above. If, for example, your goal is to kick butt in Maple Canyon, an area known for its smooth cobbles, but you have a weakness with slopers, you would add this to a list of goal-specific weaknesses.

### Activities on which to concentrate

This is the easy part. Simply take your list of skills that need improving and consult chapters 1 through 6 for the appropriate activities. For now, note them on your list. You will add them to your improvement plan later.

## Physical Conditioning

As with movement skills, a deficiency in physical conditioning relative to your goals can lead to failure, but even without a specific weakness, you need to gain fitness in order to achieve your goals. Using the example of the easiest 13s in the Coliseum, you'd need V5 bouldering power, sufficient anaerobic endurance to finish a 4x4 consisting of steep V3s, and enough aerobic endurance to complete twenty minutes of continuous climbing at 5.10c. Without these attributes, it would be very unlikely that you could send any of the three routes.

### General weaknesses

Check your Self-Assessment Worksheet for any relative deficiencies in physical conditioning you discovered. These would be strength versus anaerobic endurance versus aerobic endurance differences greater than the ranges specified. Say your bouldering pyramid tops out at V5, but the highest grade for which you can complete a 4x4 is V1, when it should be V2. Or your route pyramid tops out at 5.12a, but the highest grade at which

you can climb continuously for twenty minutes without getting pumped is 5.8, when it should be 5.9. Add these to your list.

### Goal-specific weaknesses

In comparing your goals with your current condition, note any improvements you need to make. Have you developed enough strength to pull the cruxes of targeted routes? Do you have the endurance necessary? Add any discrepancies between your current situation and your targets to your improvement list.

### Activities on which to concentrate

Again, the choice of training activities to improve your weaknesses should be evident. Refer to the activities in chapters 7 through 11 for those exercises designed to improve the specific weaknesses on your list. Note them on your list to be added to your improvement plan later.

## Making and Measuring Progress

For each general ability level below, we have specified goals for tactics, movement skills, and physical conditioning. Attaining these goals will make you a well-rounded climber, ready to tackle the challenges of the next level.

According to the progression principle, once you have adapted to an intensity and duration level for a given exercise, you must increase one or both in order to see further progress. Keeping the intensity and duration constant will only maintain your current level of conditioning. If you are attempting to increase your anaerobic threshold through ARCing by traversing back and forth at an indoor gym, you must gradually increase intensity or duration, and once a given level is attained, you must push for the next by slightly decreasing the size of the holds, steepening the wall angle, or increasing the continuous time spent ARCing. In a 4x4, you might increase the grade of one problem (V2, V3, V2, V3 to V3, V3, V2, V3). If you can complete the new set, increase the grade of another problem.

Although the progression principle holds true for movement skills as well, it's more difficult to measure that progress. In order to reach the movement goals specified in each level, you will need to begin by practicing on wall angles and hold sizes that are easy and comfortable for you. Note the grade of these climbs. As you gain confidence with a particular skill, raise the intensity by increasing the grade; this effectively steepens the wall angle or decreases the size of the holds. Before you raise the intensity, be sure you can use the skill comfortably, and then continue to increase the intensity until it approaches your maximum; this is your goal within each level.

For both physical and movement training, it's important to know if you are pushing too quickly or too slowly. The best indication of raising the intensity or duration too quickly is an inability to complete the exercise. Back down until you can just barely complete the activity, and then increase intensity or duration slightly. If you can complete the exercise easily, you're not pushing hard enough. Keep increasing the grade slightly until you can just barely complete it.

The only good way of keeping track of your activities is through written records. Keep a training log, and each day record which activities you engage in, their intensity and duration, and your results. The next time you train, you can simply refer back to the previous day's records to see which exercises to perform and how difficult to make them. With one eye on your daily record and the other on the goals for your level, continue to push for improvement.

## Creating a Training Schedule

The scheduling of your workouts during the week and the arrangement of activities within a single session both require some forethought and planning.

### Weekly Schedule

How much time each week can you devote to your climbing? How many climbing sessions of what length can you fit into your schedule? Even though you'll be using the most time-efficient method for improving your climbing, you still need to devote several sessions of two-plus hours each week to see significant progress. If your life commitments will not allow for this kind of investment in climbing, expect your progress to be a bit slower, and consequently, you may need to extend your goals or adjust them downward.

The choice of which days during the week to train depends as much on your lifestyle as on the demands of your improvement goals. For progress to occur, you must get adequate rest between workouts so that your body can recover and compensate from the load you placed on it. You should devote between three and five days per week to training, depending on your conditioning and abilities. Except in unusual circumstances, such as a three-day weekend, try not to string more than two days together in a row.

### Training Days versus Performance Days

Improving your performance requires an appropriate mix of training and performance sessions. It also means committed and disciplined training, the point of which is to send hard routes. Training for training's sake is not your goal, and you need to keep that firmly in mind. Likewise, if your training consists only of trying to send harder routes every time out, you won't improve as quickly. When you create your improvement plan, you'll need to specify each day as either a training day or a performance day.

A training day is one in which you actively work on improving a particular area of your abilities or your conditioning. These sessions incorporate exercises and activities designed to help you improve as rapidly as possible and do not usually involve attempts to send hard problems or routes. A performance day, on the other hand, is spent making redpoint runs or on-sight attempts in an effort to add routes to your pyramid. In a four-day workout week, try to schedule two training days and two performance days.

Regardless of what kind of session it is, you should begin each workout with an adequate warmup. Warmups perform several functions. They get your muscles working, which opens up the capillaries and allows for good blood flow. Your aerobic energy production system, which takes a few minutes of low-intensity activity to engage, becomes active. This can help prevent a sudden muscle load that would immediately push your muscles into the premature and debilitating anaerobic energy production mode commonly known as a flash pump. The warmup is a great time to practice movement at the general patterning level. Do a few laps on a route that is three or even four number grades below your project grade. For example, if your current project is 5.11b, do

**Sample Weekly Schedule for a 5.10 Level Climber**

| | | Week 1 | Week 2 | Week 3 | Week 4 |
|---|---|---|---|---|---|
| **MONDAY** | | REST DAY | | | |
| **TUESDAY** | | TRAINING DAY | | | |
| | Goal | Correct deficiencies in movement skills and bring fitness to standard | | | |
| | Warmup | 17 minutes ARC traverse at 5.8 with silent feet | | | |
| | Movement training | 30 minutes line and flag on 3 to 4 easy routes | | | |
| | Performance | 1½ hours to send a new route for pyramid | | | |
| | Fitness | 30 minutes bouldering at V1 and V2 | | | |
| | Cooldown | 15 minutes fun, easy climbing at 5.7 | | | |
| **WEDNESDAY** | | TRAINING DAY | | | |
| | Goal | Correct deficiencies in movement skills and bring fitness to standard | | | |
| | Warmup | 17 minutes ARC traverse at 5.8 with glue hands | | | |
| | Movement training | 30 minutes movement initiation | | | |
| | Performance | 1½ hours to send a new route for pyramid | | | |
| | Fitness | • CIR V0–/V0<br>• 20 minutes continuous climbing (ARC) at 5.8 | | | |
| | Cooldown | 15 minutes fun, easy climbing at 5.7 | | | |

| | | Week 1 | Week 2 | Week 3 | Week 4 |
|---|---|---|---|---|---|
| **THURSDAY** | | REST DAY | | | |
| **FRIDAY** | | REST DAY | | | |
| **SATURDAY** | | **PERFORMANCE DAY** | | | |
| | Goal | Add routes to redpoint pyramid | | | |
| | Organization | Be climbing by 9:30 A.M. | | | |
| | Volume | 7 pitches | | | |
| | Warmup | 3 easy routes at 5.8 using line and flag, movement initiation from lower leg, and silent feet | | | |
| | Performance | Add 1 to 3 routes to pyramid | | | |
| | Cooldown | 3 laps on a 5.8 | | | |
| **SUNDAY** | | **PERFORMANCE DAY** | | | |
| | Goal | Add routes to redpoint pyramid | | | |
| | Organization | Be climbing by 9:30 A.M. | | | |
| | Volume | 7 pitches | | | |
| | Warmup | 3 easy routes at 5.8 using line and flag, movement initiation from hips, and glue hands | | | |
| | Performance | Add 1 to 3 routes to pyramid | | | |
| | Cooldown | 3 laps on a 5.8 | | | |

laps on a 5.7 or 5.8. Alternatively, do some light traversing for ten to fifteen minutes.

### Daily schedule for training days

1. Warm up as above.

2. Movement training. Because you need to be both mentally and physically fresh for movement practice, schedule it directly following your warmup. The optimal environment for practicing new movement skills is a wall with comfortably large holds, and easy climbing.

3. Strength training. Schedule your system wall or other repetitive strength workouts next. To recruit and stress the largest percentage of muscle fibers during strength training, you need to be relatively fresh.

4. Anaerobic training. Next do any intervals or other anaerobic exercises.

5. Aerobic training. Do your aerobic workout last. You don't need to be rested for this one; just keep the intensity below your anaerobic threshold.

### Daily schedule for performance days

1. Warm up by doing a route at a grade one and a half to two numbers or several boulder problems three to four grades below your project. If your project is 5.13a, for example, use a route at 5.11a to 5.11c. Don't skimp on the warmup; throw in an easy 5.12 or several 5.11s. A well-prepared climber will have plenty of energy to send a project. Keep warming up until your mind, body, and movement are all fully prepared for the routes you want to learn and send.

2. Make an attempt to send the desired route.

3. If you fail, wait at least twenty to forty-five minutes, and then try again. If you are well prepared, twenty to thirty minutes' rest is plenty. Don't rest too long or you risk cooling down between attempts.

4. Repeat step 3 up to two more times if necessary and if you have the juice for it. A climber with excellent stamina can make four solid learning or redpoint attempts in a single day. If you succeed, celebrate and take your well-earned accolades. If you do not succeed, keep your head up; the route will still be there on your next performance day.

5. Move to another potential project and work the moves to finish out your day.

## Making a General Improvement Plan Framework

To put your improvement plan together, you'll start with a general framework and customize it to your needs and goals. Climbers with the same broad ability level can benefit from similar training programs emphasizing movement skills, fitness conditioning, and improving general weaknesses. This is not to say that all climbers at a given level should train the same way, but certain skills and abilities should be acquired at each stage. You'll add your specific weaknesses to this general framework.

Begin putting together your framework by planning one week at a time. Sit down on Sunday night and make a plan for the week to come. After a few weeks, you can try planning for two weeks at a time, and eventually a month at a time. Creating a training schedule is a skill that must be acquired through practice.

In your framework, each day of training and climbing will share the same general structure: a warmup, movement training, fitness or performance activities, and a cooldown. The specifics of your daily schedule are determined by your self-assessment, where you are on your pyramid, and your fitness in relation to benchmarks. With this information in hand, you can select movement and fitness training activities to help you achieve your goals.

Rather than create a personalized schedule immediately, you can get a feel for what training activities are most helpful for reaching your goals by rotating through the movement and fitness training activities prescribed for your level. Do one or two of them each day at an appropriate level of intensity. By rotating through the activities, you'll gain experience in each activity and an understanding of how it works. For a few weeks, you'll never do the same training activities two days in a row; the diversity will keep things interesting and be a valuable learning experience. After you know how to execute each activity, how it feels, the results you can expect, and the amount of rest you need after each, you can begin to make informed decisions about which training exercises to choose and when to schedule them.

Here is a very basic example of a general framework for a training day. Plugging activities into this basic structure is relatively easy. It may feel like guesswork at first, but with experience, you will quickly learn what constitutes a good day and a good week of training.

1. Warmup: thirty minutes. Choose one body awareness activity and two movement training activities. Spend ten minutes on each.

2. Movement training: thirty minutes to an hour. Choose one movement training activity to target a weakness discovered in your self-assessment, and apply the activity to a route two to three grades below your current performance level.

   Another way to get your movement training in when climbing outdoors is by being playful with your warmup routes. We have emphasized that movement learning should be an act of enjoyable exploration. One great way to do this is to look at your warmup routes and see what kinds of games or challenges they lend themselves to. For example, any section of a route that is less than vertical can be attempted using one or no hands. You can also challenge your partner by seeing who can climb a route the fastest while still maintaining perfect hand and foot placement. If a route has many hand- and footholds, try marking some of them off-limits and seeing how you need to change your movement in those areas. There is no limit to the different ways you can engage a route and create movement learning challenges for yourself, so take the time to do it and have fun exploring and playing with movement.

3. Fitness: Choose one or two activities for aerobic endurance, strength training, or anaerobic endurance. If you choose two activities, they should target different types of fitness, such as one aerobic endurance and one strength exercise. The intensity of each is determined by comparing your current conditioning with your fitness benchmarks. Rest fifteen to twenty minutes between activities.

4. Cooldown: Fun easy climbing that takes ten to fifteen minutes to complete. At least fifteen minutes of stretching.

On your performance days, you will attempt to send a route or problem in your targeted pyramid. Unlike training exercises, performance activities will always be determined by your route pyramid. Send the routes at your current base level before moving up to the next grade in the pyramid, and send all the routes at that level before bumping up to the top.

## Maintaining Workout Records

With everything that swirls around in your head during any given work week, it's difficult to keep track of your climbing improvement progress by simply trying to remember. Get a spiral notebook and keep it with your workout bag. Every day you climb, record the following:

1. Date, time, and location of the workout.

2. The weather conditions, if outdoors.

3. How you felt before, during, and after the workout. Include emotional and physical feelings. For example: "Felt mentally tired upon entering the gym. Felt good while training and left feeling better mentally and tired physically."

4. Exactly what did you do and for how long? Record the specifics of each exercise, such as "2 x 15 minute ARC at 5.7" or "30 minutes of threshold bouldering. Made six good attempts on Fandango. Got to third hold today for the first time." If you're using a system wall, record the angle of the wall, weight in the vest (if applicable), and number of repetitions for each hold type and position trained.

5. Anything else that may have had a bearing on your workout, such as who you climbed with, the music playing, the condition of your shoes, and so on.

You can use the diary to track your progress and note any emerging patterns. You might see a boost in performance each time you climb with a certain partner, or that you seem to climb better in the afternoon than in the evening.

A good guideline for filling out your weekly and monthly training schedule is to use a hard day/easy day pattern. By looking at the intensity and volume of climbing on a given day, it is easy to tell if it will be a hard, moderate, or easy day. Be on the lookout for too many hard days in a row. You might be able to handle a week of all hard days now and then, but two or three weeks in a row of all hard days will wear you out more than it will help your climbing. By alternating between hard, moderate, and easy training days, you will be sure to vary your activities and your intensity levels over the course of a week.

Earlier we mentioned that it is essential to keep a climbing diary or log. As you consider the sample training weeks below, we need to emphasize that it's not enough to just make a plan; you must also review it and your results afterward. Each day and week of climbing contains many activities and goals. The only way to know if you are getting the proper amount of climbing in each week, if you are progressing, and if you are ready to move up in intensity is to record and review your progress. Our sample weeks include a lot of climbing, often suggesting thirty or more pitches per week, which is over a hundred pitches per month. It's not possible to remember that many pitches or how close you're coming to the various benchmarks without a written record. It is critical that you sit down at least every other week to review your climbing for the past two weeks. This is the only way to know if you are getting enough of what you need in your training and performance schedule. It's this review process that allows you to learn about making a schedule and to plan for the coming weeks and months.

The sample weeks that follow for each grade level are well-constructed examples that you should try. Realize, though, that they are not crafted to meet your individual needs. After you have tried the sample weeks for your current level, evaluate how it went and write out what your climbing will look like for the next week. Include activities that you didn't do in the sample week. Choose activities based on your priorities, current fitness level, and weaknesses. Anything that is a top priority you should be doing two, three, or more times per week. Movement learning and local aerobic endurance training can be done every day, while stamina and anaerobic endurance can each be performed up to two times per week at the lower levels and up to four times per week (for short periods) at higher levels.

In addition, after you have completed the sample week, assess it in terms of its difficulty. For each activity, determine if the intensity needs to be higher, lower, or the same as the previous week. Always be sensitive to the intensity of your climbing, looking for opportunities to increase it but being willing to decrease it when necessary as well.

Finally, we need to mention that all the sample training weeks that follow assume you are working with a training partner. A motivated and supportive partner (or partners) with goals similar to your own will be one of your greatest assets and will make meeting the demands of a rigorous climbing schedule possible. Without good partners, your chances of success are greatly limited. Finding these kinds of partners can be challenging, but they are out there in every community. In some cases, you need to be willing to change who you climb with. Partners who are lazy, don't have goals, are negative, or tend to do the same thing every day they climb should be replaced. You must be willing to meet new climbers, to climb with people much older or younger than yourself, or who climb harder than you do. It is often necessary and desirable to have a pool of good partners to choose from. Don't stop searching until you have a list of three to six motivated, supportive, and focused climbers that you can rely on for training and climbing.

## General Training Schedules for Common Climbing Levels

As you read the following sample schedules, there are several issues to keep in mind. The first is how much rest is desirable between climbing days. This depends on a number of variables. If you are new to training, you will likely need one rest day after every climbing day, but as you become more accustomed to training, your rest needs will change. Listen to your body. Take cooling down and warming up seriously; they are essential to reducing soreness and getting the most out of every day. Muscle soreness is not necessarily a sign that you must have a rest day; it may simply be a sign that you did not cool down adequately. Pain in tendons or joints, a general feeling of continued weariness, or fading motivation can be real signs that more rest is necessary.

The second issue concerns the balance of indoor to outdoor climbing and the substitution of activities. In the sample schedules, we state that specific days should be indoors or outdoors, and we do this because we know that most people will be climbing after work in a gym. In reality, if you live in an area with ample outdoor climbing you can do most of your training outdoors. Do so intelligently, however, by retaining the structure and emphasis of the schedule intact. On the other hand, bad weather or a lack of local outdoor climbing may force you to substitute the gym for a day that was supposed to be outdoors. Again, retain the structure of the day and substitute similar activities when necessary.

The third issue is the volume of climbing specified for each day, which may be higher than you are used to. Don't be intimidated; it might take a few weeks to become accustomed to this much climbing. The important thing is to stay organized, keep trying, and make the necessary adjustments in the intensity of each activity. Within two to four weeks you should be acclimated.

The fourth issue concerns the prescribed intensity level of each activity. It is only natural that the intensity we prescribe will be too hard or too easy for you. Feel free to adjust the difficulty of activities to match your current fitness level. Before you make any adjustments, though, please try the activity at the intensity level we prescribe with an open mind and a can-do attitude. Don't assume beforehand that the intensity we prescribe is wrong. By working your hardest at the prescribed intensity level, you gain the knowledge necessary to make the appropriate changes for future workouts. Changes in intensity should be based on experience and not on assumptions.

The last issue concerns all the activities we have not included in the sample weeks. There are far more activities in this book than can be included in a one-week schedule, so it's up to you to include the other activities as you construct future schedules based on your self-assessment. This is somewhat a matter of trial and error. Plan your weeks with an eye to your fitness, movement, and performance priorities and you should do well even if you make mistakes along the way.

## General Training Plans for the 5.9 to 5.10 Levels

This section is aimed at climbers who have a best red-point in the mid-5.10 range and an on-sight grade of 5.9 and who want to move those respective grades to 5.11a and 5.10. Your goal at this level is to create a solid foundation to support the more advanced skills and performances to come later. You'll spend a significant amount of time climbing at a submaximal level to improve your local aerobic fitness and gain the comfortable, confident feel of advanced climbers. Training and performance are structured to develop a number of skills, provide you with a depth of experience, and prepare you for the demands of the 5.11 grade. At this level, you're looking for targeted growth in tactics, movement skills, and fitness.

### Tactics

At this level, you likely need to work on the fundamental tactical skills that allow you to be efficient and productive at the crag or in the gym. This includes organizing your time, orienting yourself quickly at the crag, and maximizing productivity each day. These can be real challenges. A day of climbing often has quite a bit of downtime as you decide what to do, search for routes, rest, socialize, and have one or two mini-epics. In an eight-hour day, it's all too common for climbers to do four or fewer pitches. One climber learned from a boyfriend early in her climbing career to expect to get in two or three pitches per day. She was quite shocked to discover that barely constitutes a warmup under our schedule! Four or fewer pitches in a day is a very small number; you need to learn to efficiently manage your time at the crag or gym.

Get in the habit of doing your planning before arriving at your destination. By the time you reach the crag or gym, you should know what climbs you'll be doing and in what order. You may also want a backup plan if a route is occupied. It's easy to lose thirty to forty-five minutes between routes as you decide what to do next, resulting in lost productivity. A good day of climbing can have a rhythm to it that maximizes your climbing time and your enjoyment. It's common for 5.9 climbers to move at a pace of one pitch per hour or perhaps a bit slower. More seasoned climbers, on the other hand, are able to get two, three, four, or more pitches in per hour. A fast-moving team of expert sport climbers can do twenty or more pitches each in a single day.

Take a watch to the crag and time how long it takes you to get from the car to the point where someone is actually climbing. Also time how long each pitch takes and how much downtime you have between routes. Do this in the spirit of fun and not as a challenge. Climbing should equal fun, so the goal is to get in as much climbing per day as possible. You want to be excited about getting on the next route. As an initial goal, try to do more than one route per hour each. Can you do eight to ten pitches in a day? Try to work up to this level and then surpass it.

The second tactical skill is finding your way around the crag, especially at an area new to you. Climbers of any ability can get lost and disoriented at a new crag, but some don't. To stay oriented, you need either a lot of experience or a lot of information. Try to go with a local, look up topos on the Internet, buy the local guide-book, and get opinions about the best and most easily accessible routes. Study the guidebook thoroughly for the details of trail and route descriptions and the features of the cliff, but be ready for serious discrepancies between the book and reality. Look up photos and send e-mail to local climbers on the many climbing-related websites. Start getting the lay of the land before you ever set foot at the crag, and arrive with a plan.

The third tactical skill is planning your process for each route. You should know in advance whether the attempt will be for an on-sight or eventual redpoint. Approach it using the best tactics you can. Reading a sequence from the ground with intelligence and insight takes a lot of practice, and staying ahead of the pump and learning and memorizing moves quickly are skills that come only with experience. To foster rapid development of these skills, choose redpoint routes you can do in less than four tries, and do lots of climbing at your comfortable on-sight grade.

By learning tactical skills, you will gain confidence as you gain experience and quickly develop an idea of what is possible for you in a day of climbing.

## Movement Skills

The movement habits you develop today will affect your climbing for years to come, so take this training seriously, learn it well, enjoy it, and complete climbs for the sake of their movement, not just to get to the top. It's easy for 5.9 climbers to convince themselves that strength is the key to improvement. If this is you, keep two things in mind: First, you will quickly develop added strength as you follow this program, and second, your lack of efficient movement skills results in wasted effort that makes the climbing feel harder than it really is. Work on developing the following movement skills:

- Quickly identify both hand- and footholds.
- Make foot placements with precision; your foot should not need readjustment after it is placed on a hold.
- Work on using smaller footholds on all angles.
- Place hands correctly on holds the first time.
- Climb well at different speeds. A route might require moving with fast efficiency through a steep section, and then slowing down and being very precise on a technical, slabby section.
- Initiate movement in the legs.
- Create and control body tension where necessary.
- Apply turning and its variations where applicable.
- Resist or unlearn initiating movement from the arms.
- Develop body awareness.
- Develop some ideas about style of movement, figuring out how you want to move and how you want moves to feel.

## Fitness

At the 5.9/5.10 level, targeted training to develop fitness takes a backseat to gaining experience and developing the many tactical and movement skills described above. Fitness will come as you gain experience, but at this point, focus on the following goals.

### Endurance goals

Develop the ability to rest on climbs, recover in under thirty minutes between climbs, and handle longer routes. Work up to being able to complete eight to twelve routes in a day. Work your continuous climbing up to twenty minutes at 5.7+ to 5.8+.

### Strength goals

Bouldering is quickly becoming king in American climbing. This phenomenon poses a problem for less experienced climbers, in that it encourages spending excessive time working at or near your limit before your movement skills have developed enough to be effective at this level. Further, hard bouldering at this stage does not foster high-quality learning. Your goal here should be to complete many easier problems rather than fewer more difficult problems.

### Anaerobic endurance goals

You should develop a good base of low-intensity anaerobic endurance. Using high-intensity anaerobic endurance exercises such as 4x4s or 6x8s before you have developed an endurance base is not very helpful. In addition, not many routes at 5.9 or 5.10 require continuous climbing at a high level of intensity.

## Training Schedule

Creating your own training schedule can be a difficult task. Here is a sample schedule for guidance. With some creativity and a focus on the right priorities, you will be able to create a program that works for you. The following are the priorities for 5.9 to 5.10 climbers:

1. Adding routes to your pyramid.

2. Movement training.

• Body awareness activities: the press exercise with variations and blindfolded climbing.

• Movement activities: silent feet, glue hands, same-side-in traverse, same-side-in top rope, same-side-in with straight arms, one-foot-off traverse, one-foot-off with same-side-in, line and flag, and any additional activities from your self-assessment.

3. Fitness training: ARCing, laps on easy routes, CIR bouldering and routes, and developing a bouldering base.

The following weekly training plan for the 5.9 to 5.10 levels has climbing four days per week, two weekday training days indoors, and Saturday and Sunday as performance days outdoors. Your emphasis should be on having fun and creating success by focusing on your route pyramid and your movement training. After those come endurance, low-intensity power endurance, and bouldering.

### Training day 1 (indoors or outdoors)

WARMUP: 20 MINUTES

1. 5 minutes no-handed climbing with press exercise variations.

2. 15 minutes ARC. Choose three movement activities and spend 5 minutes doing each.

MOVEMENT TRAINING: 30 MINUTES
AT SUBMAXIMAL LEVEL

1. Two to three boulder problems that are of moderate difficulty. Do the problems using silent feet and glue hands. Repeat each problem until you can do it flawlessly as judged by your partner and then move to the next problem.

5- to 10-minute rest.

FITNESS: 2.5 TO 5 HOURS
Choose one activity:

1. Aerobic CIR 10 x 5.8+/5.9 (or whatever grade is appropriate for you). Focus on your movement. Can you do specific movement activities on some of these routes? Remember that you never want to get pumped during CIR, so force yourself to rest no less than 5 minutes between each route.

2. Stamina on-sight/flash day. Attempt no less than six on-sights or flashes, at whatever grades are appropriate for you.

COOLDOWN: 15 MINUTES STRETCHING

### Training day 2 (indoors)

WARMUP AND MOVEMENT TRAINING: 40 MINUTES

1. 20 minutes ARC traversing. Choose four movement activities from above or from your self-assessment and spend 5 minutes doing each.

2. Three easy routes, 5.7 to 5.9 range, on top rope or leading. Perform the simplest activities such as glue hands or silent feet on these routes. This is a chance to engage in movement learning at the submaximal level.

PERFORMANCE: 1 HOUR, 30 MINUTES

1. Choose one route to add to your pyramid. If you complete it early, move on to your fitness training.

FITNESS: 30 MINUTES

1. Low/moderate-intensity power endurance: four laps on 5.8 or 5.9 with a 2- to 4-minute rest between laps.

COOLDOWN: 30 MINUTES

1. 10- to 15-minute ARC on very easy routes (any holds).

2. 10 to 15 minutes stretching.

### Performance day 1 (outdoors)

WARMUP AND MOVEMENT: 45 MINUTES

1. Three easy routes, choosing one appropriate movement activity for each route. For example, no-handed climbing on a slab or same-side-in on a vertical climb with many hand- and footholds. When in doubt about which activity is best for a specific route, do the simplest activities, such as silent feet, glue hands, straight arms, or the press exercise. Have fun; climb with the goal of completing the activity, but also climb for enjoyment. These activities are not meant to be dreary; they provide you with ways of exploring your movement.

PERFORMANCE: 4 TO 6 HOURS

1. Add routes to your pyramid. The goal is to work on or add one to three routes to your pyramid. If you are working at the bottom level of your route pyramid, try to on-sight or flash each route, and redpoint only if you are not successful on your first try. If you are higher on your pyramid, make each burn count; try to learn everything in one or two tries, and then send.

COOLDOWN: 20 MINUTES

1. Three to four laps on an easy route (5.7 to 5.8) that you really like. Up- and down-climb the route for a 15- to 20-minute ARC. Make all your movements smooth and graceful. Enjoy it!

### Performance day 2 (outdoors)

WARMUP

1. Use a warmup similar to what you did on the first day outdoors. If you are sore or tired, extend the warmup by including two or more routes that are easy for you.

PERFORMANCE: 4 TO 6 HOURS

1. Add routes to your pyramid. The goal is to work on or add one to three routes to your pyramid. If you are working at the bottom level of your route pyramid, try to on-sight or flash each route, and redpoint only if you are not successful on your first try. If you are higher on your pyramid, make each burn count; try to learn everything in one or two tries, and then send.

COOLDOWN: 30–45 MINUTES

1. 15- to 20-minute ARC by doing a few laps on a very easy route that you really enjoy. Climb it well and have fun with it.

2. 20 minutes of stretching.

If you follow this schedule, at the end of the week you will have:

- Completed approximately 34 pitches.

- Done several boulder problems.

- Added 1 to 4 routes to your pyramid.

- Performed an endurance workout and a stamina workout.

- Completed close to 2 hours of targeted movement learning.

- Spent up to 2 hours stretching.

Keeping track of these totals is important. You need good structure and a high volume of climbing to increase your fitness, add routes to your pyramid, and acquire solid movement skills. Consider how this experience adds up. If you were to do this for a month, you would finish 136 pitches, add no fewer than 4 routes to your pyramid, complete a number of endurance workouts, and so on. With this volume of targeted climbing, you will make significant gains in only a few months.

## General Training Plans for the 5.10 to 5.11 Levels

The 5.11 level is a significant milestone for many climbers. Although not difficult by today's standards, it is nonetheless the grade at which the quality of the skills and fitness acquired at lower grades begin to be evident. At 5.10, many climbers can get away with poorly developed movement by relying heavily on physical conditioning. At 5.11, these climbers struggle. The holds are smaller, requiring increased precision, and the routes are more continuous, making recovery between more difficult sections less likely. Misspend your energy adjusting, readjusting, and applying improper movement skills and you're likely to hit a roadblock to progress at 5.11.

Many 5.10 climbers want to hurry to get to 5.11. This level has some social capital in the climbing world, and one who can climb at this level can claim solid standing in sport climbing. But the poorly prepared 5.11 climber will be stymied by more difficult grades. Learn the movement skills well, and prepare yourself physically for what is truly the grade that many envy.

## Tactics

At 5.11, you are still acquiring and learning solid tactics. Although you may not reach proficiency at this level, begin to develop the habit of learning everything you possibly can from the ground, including the ability to see rests, cruxes, and specific sequences. Continue to master the redpoint process of working a route from the top, discovering efficient sequences, and then linking them together into longer sections. By the time you move to 5.12, you should be able to follow this procedure flawlessly.

## Movement Skills

The 5.11 climber should already have developed a number of solid movement skills:

- Recognizing and applying the proper use to all hand- and footholds.
- Near perfection in placing the foot precisely where it needs to be.
- Initiating movement from the legs.
- Basic proficiency with turning and flagging.
- Proficiency with body awareness.
- Developing body tension.

In addition, you'll continue to learn new skills at this level to enhance your ability to meet the challenges that 5.11 routes contain. The 5.11 climber should continue to work on improving these skills:

- Refining performance in situations of offset balance.
- Fully applying turning, flagging, and drop knees.
- Developing an understanding of initiating movement and creating movement centers in the knees, hips, spine, and shoulders.
- Developing dynamic movement and more precise movement timing.

## Fitness

### Aerobic endurance goals

Raise your continuous climbing level to a minimum of 5.9, your CIR level to between 5.10a and 5.10c, and your bouldering CIR level to V1 or V2.

### Strength goals

Add the necessary problems to your pyramid to get your bouldering grade up to V3. If you can already send V3 in a few tries or less, work on bringing your bouldering on-sight level up and increasing the volume of V2 and V3 you can handle in one bouldering session, such as by doing CIR bouldering on V2 and V3. You don't need to boulder at a higher level for your current performance goals, so don't spend a lot of time working harder problems that will not contribute effectively to your performance goals.

### Anaerobic endurance goals

If you are at the lower end of this level, your 4x4 goal is to include problems from V0 to V2. A typical set pattern looks like this:

> 5.11a/b: V2, V1, V1, V0 or V0, V1, V1, V2
>
> 5.11c/d: V2, V1, V2, V1 or V3, V0, V2, V1

Your 6x8 goal is to include problems from Vb to V1. Here are some sample sets:

> 5.11a/b: Vb, Vb, V0–, V0, Vb, V0–, V1, V0
>
> 5.11c/d: Vb, V1, V1, V0, Vb, V0–, V1, V0–
>
> or: V1, V0, Vb, V1, V0–, V1, V0, V1

When doing laps on routes for anaerobic endurance, you may start out only being able to do laps on 5.9, but the goal range should be from 5.10a to 5.10c.

## Training Schedule

This sample schedule for levels 5.10 to 5.11 is a weekly training plan with four climbing days per week, two training days indoors and two performance days outdoors.

### Training day 1 (indoors)

WARMUP AND MOVEMENT TRAINING:
30 MINUTES

1. 10 minutes two-handed dynos on a vertical wall with many holds. Place emphasis on feeling light, creating tension, and using the best path for each dyno.

2. 20 minutes on routes. Pick one or two specific movement activities that are well-suited to the angle and style of each route. Pay special attention to weaknesses you listed on your self-assessment.

MOVEMENT TRAINING AT SUBMAXIMAL LEVEL: 45 MINUTES

1. Apply the concepts from the discussion of body awareness in chapter 3 to a route at the 5.9 level. Feel the muscles working and try to anticipate how moves will feel before doing them. In addition, identify what muscles are at work in the move; what muscles are you relying on most and why?

FITNESS: 1 HOUR, 45 MINUTES, TO 2 HOURS

1. 15 minutes bouldering warmup on easy problems. Emphasize moving well and preparing emotionally for the workout to come.

2. 45 minutes threshold bouldering.

3. 15-minute rest.

4. 4x4 on V2, V1, V0, V1.

5. 15-minute rest (or until the worst part of your pump wears off).

COOLDOWN: 25 MINUTES

1. 25 minutes easy ARC traversing.

### Training day 2 (indoors)

WARMUP: 40 MINUTES

1. 25 minutes ARC traversing with emphasis on two or three movement weaknesses from your self-assessment.

2. 15 minutes top-roping. Do your choice of two to four movement activities, spending about equal time on each.

MOVEMENT INITIATION AT SUBMAXIMAL LEVEL: 45 MINUTES

1. Choose one or two V2s that you have not done, and give them each a flash attempt.

2. Go back and examine each individual move in terms of the lower body. Work on each move in terms of the following areas: Did you use the best possible foot sequence? Did you press as much as you could have from the legs? Did you keep the lower body engaged as your hands reached each new hold? Did you use the best movement initiation and centers possible in the legs? Repeat each move as many

times as necessary to answer these questions. Link each problem using all the movement advantages you learned while working the problem.

FITNESS: 1 TO 2 HOURS

1. CIR on routes: 8 to 12 repetitions at 5.9+ to 5.10c (whichever is right for your current level), with full recovery between repetitions.

COOLDOWN: 20 MINUTES

1. 20 minutes stretching.

### Performance day 1 (outdoors)

WARMUP: 45 MINUTES TO 1 HOUR

1. Do two to four routes, starting three number grades below your target performance level for the day. Make each subsequent route two to three letter grades more difficult than the one before it, and do each route more than one time if necessary. You want to feel that you climbed each route well, moving at a good pace, with rhythm and a light and strong feel on each route.

PERFORMANCE: 4 TO 6 HOURS

1. Try to on-sight two routes at your current on-sight level.

2. Three burns on a redpoint project. If you are building your base, you should send the route in three burns; if you are working at the higher levels of your pyramid, your goal should be to end the day having memorized most or all of the moves so you can begin true redpoint attempts on the next day.

COOLDOWN: 20 MINUTES

1. Four laps on a classic 5.9. Make your movement look smooth and feel great. The route should be easy enough that you don't get pumped. It should be enjoyable and provide an opportunity to practice movement.

### Performance day 2 (outdoors)

WARMUP: 30 TO 45 MINUTES

1. Do three routes, starting two and a half number grades below your performance level for the day, and working up from there. Keep warming up until you feel confident, light, and mentally ready.

PERFORMANCE: 3 TO 5 HOURS

1. Either try to redpoint the route you were on the previous day or learn the moves on a different route at the same level on your pyramid.

COOLDOWN: 20 MINUTES

1. 20-minute ARC on routes. Be playful, climbing the routes in different styles and at different speeds. Have fun.

At the end of this week, you should have:

- Completed between 21 and 23 pitches of route climbing.

- Completed 22 to 27 boulder problems.

- Engaged in about 3 hours of movement learning.

- Added at least one route to your pyramid.

- Completed 4 total workouts covering aerobic endurance, anaerobic endurance, strength, and stamina.

# General Training Plans for the 5.11 to 5.12 Levels

Continued movement refinement and significant physical conditioning improvement are usually required to move up to 5.12. Although 5.12 is not a magical grade or any more difficult to achieve than other grades, it's a very exciting level for many climbers. At this level many classic routes in renowned areas are opened to you in places such as Rifle, Colorado, and American Fork, Utah. As you gain competence, it is essential that you continue to mature as a climber, because there is still a great deal to learn in all areas.

At 5.12, you should be able to handle a higher volume of climbing each day, so your training days will include several challenging activities and your performance days will consist of many on-sight or redpoint attempts. Your training can be crafted to meet the needs of your pyramid, adjusted for weaknesses you discover as you explore different routes, and geared to meet the fitness needs of your current projects.

Climbers moving up to 5.12 can become very focused on performance. Some have come to believe that a warmup may take too much energy and nega-tively affect performance burns. If you think this is happening, it's a sure sign that you lack endurance and the ability to handle a reasonable volume of climbing in a day. You should be able to do three to six warmup routes and up to four working burns or redpoint attempts, as well as two or three cooldown laps or routes. If you are really fit, it's also possible to both redpoint and on-sight in the same day. If you are warming up thoroughly and correctly, it will never detract from your performance.

## Tactics

At the 5.12 level, you want to really refine your tactics. In on-sight situations, work on becoming proficient at learning everything you possibly can from the ground, including being able to see rests, cruxes, and specific sequences. When redpointing, you must be disciplined about your process and take enough rests while working the route so that you do not get pumped. You should be getting good at reviewing each section immediately after you climb it and develop the habit of reviewing the entire route as soon as you lower to the ground. You want to develop a precise understanding of when you know enough to be finished learning a route to begin making redpoint attempts. One good way to gauge your readiness is by reviewing the route from the ground. Go through every move, handhold, foothold, clip, and rest in your mind. If you are really good at this you will also know how each move should be initiated and what you should be thinking and feeling at each point of the climb. If you can do this with no gaps or errors, then you are ready to switch from learning burns to redpoint burns. You also need to develop a sense for seeing the necessary interim goals for every burn leading up to a redpoint.

## Movement Skills

Many climbers at this level can scrape and flail their way up 5.12 routes, but there are also plenty who have developed their movement skills well enough to move with authority. As you work into this level, strive to become an excellent model for all the basic movement skills, as well as continuing to develop more complex skills. The 5.12 climber should excel at the following:

- Hand and foot placement on all sizes and types of holds.

- Initiating movement from the legs.

- Body awareness.
- Climbing at different speeds depending on the demands of the climb.
- Good use of turning and flagging.
- Using body tension in many situations.

The 5.12 climber should continue to improve these movement skills:

- Refining the ability to deal with moves that require offset balance.
- Full use of turning, flagging, and drop knees.
- Ability to initiate movement and create movement centers in knees, hips, spine, and shoulders, with special emphasis on movement initiation from the hips and lumbar spine.
- Using the full range of dynamic movement and movement timing.

## Fitness

### Endurance goals

Raise your continuous climbing level to a minimum 5.10a; it's better if you work it up to the 5.10d level as you approach redpointing 5.12d and on-sighting 5.11d. Raise your CIR level to between 5.11a and 5.11c and your bouldering CIR level to V3.

### Strength goals

Add the necessary problems to your pyramid to get your bouldering grade up to V5. If you can already send V5 in a few tries or boulder harder than V5, work on bringing your bouldering on-sight level up and increasing the volume of V4 and V5 you can handle in one bouldering session, such as by doing CIR bouldering on V4 and V5. You don't need to boulder any harder than this for your current performance goals, so don't spend a lot of time working harder problems. If V6 seems close, however, add the necessary experience to your pyramid and go for it. Your threshold bouldering level should be between V7 and V8. At 5.12, begin to use the system wall to improve your strength.

### Anaerobic endurance goals

If you are at the lower end of the 5.12 level, your 4x4 goal is to include problems up to V3. Typical set patterns look like this:

5.12a/b: V2, V0, V2, V1 or V1, V1, V2, V1

5.12c/d: V3, V2, V2, V2 or V3, V2, V1, V2

If you are at the upper end of the 5.12 level, your 4x4 goal should include problems in the V2 and V3 grades, but it's fine to include a V1 or even a V4 if there is one you can handle, such as in the following examples:

5.12d: V3, V2, V1, V3 or V4, V2, V1, V3

Your 6x8 workouts will consist of problems from Vb to V2, with many problems at the V1 level. Here are some sample sets:

5.12b: V2, Vb, V0, V1, Vb, V0, V1, V0

5.12c/d: V2, Vb, V1, V0, V0, Vb, V1, V0

or: V3, V1, Vb, V2, V0, V0, V1, Vb

When doing laps on routes for anaerobic endurance, your goal can range from 5.11a/b at the lower end to 5.11c to 5.12a at the upper end.

## Training Schedule

The following sample schedule for the 5.11 to 5.12 levels is a weekly training plan with four climbing days per week, two training days indoors and two performance day outdoors.

### Training day 1 (indoors)

WARMUP AND MOVEMENT TRAINING: 30 MINUTES

1. 10 minutes easy and moderate two-handed dynos on vertical or very slight overhang. The goal is to make the moves feel like gliding. Do each move by initiating from the hips or lumbar spine and finishing by driving hard from the legs. Create a line of tension from your toes all the way up your back as you approach the target holds.

2. 20 minutes on routes: Pick specific movement activities that are appropriate for each route. Treat several skills, such as flagging, the press exercise, and pacing, with extra attention.

MOVEMENT TRAINING AT SUBMAXIMAL LEVEL: 45 MINUTES

1. Apply the concepts from the discussion of movement initiation in chapter 5 to a route at the 5.10+ or 5.11– level that you have never done or don't know

very well. The goal is to examine every move on a fairly easy climb and find the best method of movement initiation for each one, and then climb the entire route using the proper initiation for every move. It will probably take a few tries before you can do this without making any mistakes.

WARMUP: 15 MINUTES

1. Bouldering on easy problems.

FITNESS

Choose either A or B below.

A

1. 45 minutes threshold bouldering.

2. 15-minute rest.

B

1. 4x4 on V3, V2, V1, V2.

2. CIR 15 repetitions at V3. Include some flash attempts and some problems you already know. You may need to repeat some problems if your gym doesn't have enough at this particular grade.

3. 15-minute rest (or until the worst part of your pump wears off).

COOLDOWN: 25 MINUTES

1. 25 minutes easy ARC traversing. Include five movement activities of your choice and do each for 5 minutes.

### Training day 2 (indoors)

WARMUP: 50 MINUTES

1. 10 minutes no-handed climbing.

2. 10 minutes blind climbing on top rope.

3. 30 minutes ARC traversing, with emphasis on four movement activities: changing pace, one-foot-off same-side-in, pressing, and passing your farthest point.

MOVEMENT INITIATION AT SUBMAXIMAL LEVEL: 45 MINUTES

1. Choose one or two V3s that you have not done, and give them each a flash attempt.

2. Go back and examine each individual move in terms of the lower body. Work on each move in terms of the following issues: Did you use the best possible foot sequence? Did you press as much as you could have from the legs? Did you keep the lower body engaged when your hands reached each new hold? Did you use the best movement initiation and centers possible in the legs? Repeat each move as many times as necessary to answer these questions, and then complete each move perfectly. Link each problem using all the movement advantages you learned while working it.

FITNESS: 1 TO 2 HOURS

1. CIR on routes: 10 to 15 repetitions on 5.11b level, with at least 5 minutes of rest between repetitions.

COOLDOWN

1. 30 minutes stretching.

Two days rest recommended.

### Performance day 1 (outdoors)

WARMUP: 45 MINUTES TO 1 HOUR

1. Two to four routes, starting three number grades below your target performance level for the day. Make each route two to three letter grades more difficult than the one before it, and do each route more than one time if necessary. You want to feel that you climbed each route well, moving at a good pace, with rhythm and a light and strong feel on each route.

PERFORMANCE: 4 TO 6 HOURS

1. On-sight climbing (1.5 hours): Try to on-sight two routes at your current on-sight level. Take your time and do your best to read, plan, and visualize the climbs before you make your on-sight attempts. Rest 20 to 30 minutes between attempts.

2. Redpoint (up to 4 hours): Three to five burns on a redpoint project. If you are working at the lowest level of your pyramid, you should send the route in a few burns; if you are working at the higher end, your goal should be to memorize most or all of the moves and to link sections.

COOLDOWN

1. Four laps on a classic 5.10. Make your movement feel great. The route should be easy enough that you don't get pumped.

### Performance day 2 (outdoors)

WARMUP: 30 TO 45 MINUTES

1. Do three routes, starting two and a half number grades below your performance level for the day, and working up from there. Keep warming up until you feel confident, light, and mentally ready.

PERFORMANCE: 3 TO 5 HOURS

1. Either try to redpoint the route you were on the previous day or learn the moves on a different route at the same level on your pyramid.

COOLDOWN: 20 MINUTES

1. 20-minute ARC on routes.

# General Training Plans for 5.12 to 5.13 and Above

Although 5.13 and 5.14 are considered the elite realm of professionals, there are still plenty of average climbers out there getting up these routes with a combination of amazing determination and sticking to routes that match their strengths. Routes rated 5.13, 5.14, and higher are within the range of many climbers. This may be difficult to believe, since in the contemporary environment 5.14d is considered very difficult by just about everyone. Keep in mind, though, that in the 1970s, 5.12 was considered very difficult. Three decades later, many thousands of climbers around the world easily climb at the 5.12 level. The standards of the climbing community are always evolving and rising. Talented, committed, and motivated climbers cannot rely on contemporary standards to determine what their performance level should be. As your redpoint pyramid fills up with 5.14s, don't assume you are approaching the limits of your ability just because you are approaching the limits of the community's expectations of what you can do. You may need to travel more, or spend time seeking out first ascents, but this is to be expected, since at a certain point it will be your job to surpass and redefine the standards of your day.

When working at the 5.13 level and above, it's important not to develop the all too common bad habit of flogging overly difficult routes into submission over the course of fifteen, twenty, or more working burns rather than concentrating on on-sights and faster redpoints. This greatly lowers productivity and slows down the climber's development. Such climbers often are great on routes they know well but do poorly on anything new, even climbs that should be easy for them. Some climbers working on 5.13b and harder don't have a chance of on-sighting 5.11d. This is a sign that lengthy projects have had a negative effect on their fitness, tactics, and movement skills.

## Tactics

At 5.13, you should be an expert at all the on-sight skills described for the lower levels and be able to imagine the look and feel of the expected sequences before actually attempting them. In addition, you should have an idea of how to initiate crux moves and have a resting and pacing plan for the route. You should also be more relaxed as well as skilled at finding good alternatives to sequences that don't work. In redpointing, the solid skills you refined at the 5.12 level will carry over nicely to 5.13 and above.

## Movement Skills

Even at this level, no one knows all there is to know about movement. Continue to refine the more advanced aspects of movement, with special emphasis on mastering the nuances of balance and timing. Practice working with the three different types of balance as detailed in chapter 1, until you can identify each in practice and confidently apply the appropriate methods for resolving the difficulties encountered with each. Expand your practice to include balance on many different wall angles and hold types, and apply what you learn to many kinds of rock.

At this level, some climbers have obvious flaws in their movement that are easy to spot. You may or may not see obvious problems in your hand and foot placement. You may have discrepancies such as being great on slopers but terrible on crimpers. On the other hand, it's a good guess that you have favorite moves that you use instead of others, for example, substituting a back step for an inside flag even when a flag is the better solution. Or you may have deeply ingrained habits such as using the same pace of movement on everything regardless of the nature of the balance and demands of the moves.

A good way to discover your weaknesses is to videotape a session when you are failing, then examine the tape frame by frame. You can see examples of this kind of analysis on the DVD and apply it to your own climbing. When reviewing the videotape of 5.14 climbers it is easy to see them having difficulty with movement initiation and the timing of their moves. Or we see movement skills deteriorate as the climber fatigues. An important issue to consider is how many of your movement skills have reached the autonomous stage. Naturally, the quality of your movement will always deteriorate as fatigue sets in, but if most of your movement skills are in the autonomous stage, it will take a very high level of fatigue to diminish your movement. This is something that can be assessed on videotape.

## Fitness

### Aerobic endurance goals

Raise your continuous climbing level to 5.11b or higher if you are a 5.13a climber or 5.12b to 5.12d if you are working from 5.14a to 5.14c. At the 5.13a level, try to bring your CIR level on routes above 5.12a. For the 5.13d climber trying to move up, raise your CIR on routes to ten repetitions of 5.13a.

### Strength goals

To redpoint at the 5.13a level, the hardest move you are likely to ever encounter is V6. At the 5.14a/b level, it's rare to find sequences harder than V10, and for the 5.14c level, V11/12. For the 5.13a climber, get your CIR bouldering level up to V4 to V5. For those moving up to 5.14c, get your CIR bouldering level up to V8 or V9.

### Anaerobic endurance

For 5.13a climbers, 4x4 sets should include a mix of problems up to V5, such as V5, V3, V2, V3. At the 5.13d/5.14a level, they should include a range of prob-

lems from V4 to V7, with emphasis on V5, such as V7, V5, V4, V5. When doing laps on routes for anaerobic endurance, your goal can range from 5.12c to 5.13b, depending on your current fitness.

## Training Schedule

Return to your self-assessment and review your strengths and weaknesses. In order to grow once you have reached this advanced level, you need to address those fitness areas and movement skills where you are weak. Whittle away at them one by one, until you can turn each of those weaknesses into a strength. Your schedule should be highly specific to your needs, focusing on both your weaknesses and your goals. The proportion of time you spend on each training area should be similar to that in the sample training schedule for the 5.12 level.

The following sample training schedule is for the climber progressing from 5.13a toward the 5.13d redpoint level, with four days climbing per week.

### Training day 1 (indoors)

WARMUP AND MOVEMENT TRAINING: 40 MINUTES

1. 10 minutes easy traversing with straight arms. Work on using multiple movement centers for each move, such as starting moves in the knees and ending them with the spine.

2. 5 to 10 minutes two-handed dynos.

3. Perform a series of six to eight easy and moderate boulder problems V1 to V5.

MOVEMENT TRAINING FOR PERFORMANCE
APPLICATION LEVEL: 1 HOUR

1. Choose a boulder problem in the V6 to V7 range that you do not know very well and that you find awkward. Videotape both you and your training partner on the problem. For each move, identify the type and quality of balance. Are you using the best balance available for each move? Examine each move frame by frame on the videotape and determine how you are initiating each one. For every move you initiate from your arms or that just feels awkward, experiment with initiation from the spine, knees, or hips until you find

a better way of doing the moves in question. Also examine the speed and timing of each move. Make changes based on what the video reveals.

FITNESS: 2 TO 3 HOURS

1. 1 hour of threshold bouldering working at the V9 to V11 level. Remember that the goal is not to complete each problem but to link disparate sections one to three moves in length. Use frequent power spots. Training partners need to provide a lot of support for each other. Efforts should be very short and rests long. You should never feel pumped or even very tired in this workout.

2. 10 minutes rest. This should be an easy and short ARC session as a way of flushing lactate from your forearms.

3. 6x8 bouldering circuit. Choose a variety of problems in the V1 to V3 range, for example, V2, V1, V1, V3, V0, V1, V2, V1. Vary the angle and include problems that have many different types of holds.

4. 15 minutes rest.

COOLDOWN: 30 TO 40 MINUTES

1. Low-intensity ARC. Move as well as you can and keep the intensity very low. You should feel much better at the end of the ARC than you did when you started it.

2. 15 to 20 minutes stretching. Pay special attention to your forearms. Even after the easy traversing, they still may cramp up without a long gentle stretch.

### Training day 2 (indoors)

WARMUP

1. Progression of four to six routes from 5.10a to 5.12b.

MOVEMENT TRAINING: 45 MINUTES
AT SUBMAXIMAL LEVEL

1. Choose one or two routes in the 5.11c to 5.12b range that you are familiar with and that target a specific weakness. Examine the route move for move; find the best balance, timing, and initiation for each move and then lead the route, executing each move perfectly. Really engage each move and hold yourself to a high movement standard. Don't be surprised if it

takes considerable time and several attempts to do the entire route perfectly with no mistakes in any aspect of your movement.

FITNESS: 1.5 HOURS

1. Two 30-minute ARCs at 5.10+ to 5.11c level. Rest for 30 minutes between each ARC. Be sure to use the ARCs to work on movement, and do what you need to do to keep them fun; listen to music, do the workouts on routes, traverse with friends and make a game of it.

COOLDOWN: 20 MINUTES

1. 20 minutes of stretching.

### Training day 3 (indoors)

WARMUP: 1 HOUR

1. Four easy routes. Start on 5.10+ and work up to 5.12–. Rest enough between efforts so that you don't get a pump. While climbing, focus on the most basic elements of your movement and prepare mentally for a hard day of training. This is the time to use self-talk, to commit to what will be a grueling workout. Your warmup can end when you feel warm and are emotionally ready.

2. 30 minutes of moderate bouldering.

FITNESS: 2 HOURS

1. Anaerobic endurance: 4x4 bouldering circuit. This should be a challenging circuit for you, for example, V4+, V5, V5, V3.

2. 30 minutes rest. While you put your partner through his 4x4, put some extra clothes on (even in warm weather) to make sure you don't cool off.

3. Anaerobic endurance on a route. Four to six laps on a route you know well in the range of 5.11c to 5.12b, whichever is right for the day, considering you just did a hard 4x4. Choose a route that is continuous in nature and that you are comfortable on. Make your rest between burns as short as it can be while still allowing enough recovery so that you can finish your next lap. You can do the laps on lead or on top rope. It can be good to lead the first few laps and then switch over to top rope as you become more

exhausted. When top-roping, don't let yourself start sprinting; keep your top-roping laps the same duration as your leading laps. Having to stop to unclip some directionals can help keep you moving at the right speed.

4. Rest 15 minutes or more as you belay your partner. Stay warm.

COOLDOWN: 30 MINUTES

1. 15 minutes up- and down-climbing a high-quality but very easy route, 5.9+ or 5.10a. The goal is to help flush out your muscles. This cooldown will be tempting to skip because you will be very tired and your skin very sore. Do it anyway; your muscles need it. It may feel terrible at first, but at the end you should be feeling pretty good.

2. At least 15 minutes stretching.

You will need two days rest before your next climbing day.

### Performance day 1 (outdoors)

WARMUP: UP TO 1.5 HOURS

1. Four to six routes starting at 5.10+ and working up to 5.12. Remember to attend to all aspects of the warmup. You want your movement, your mind, and your body to feel good and ready by the time your warmup is complete.

PERFORMANCE: 4 TO 6 HOURS

1. Adding routes to your pyramid. How productive you are depends, as always, upon where you are in your pyramid. If you are on the first or second level, you may be able to add a route or two in a day if you have stamina and enough skin on your tips. If you are higher in your pyramid, your performance goal may be to put four good learning burns in your project. The important thing is to set reasonable goals for the day and to keep track of your progress.

COOLDOWN: 40 MINUTES

1. 20 minutes of easy ARCing by up- and down-climbing an easy route 5.9 to 5.10.

2. 20 minutes of stretching.

### Performance day 2 (outdoors)

Repeat the pattern from performance day 1. Let how you feel determine what route you attempt. You may want to try a different route from the same level of your pyramid.

After you have put in three to five good efforts on your project, rest for 30 minutes and spend the rest of the day doing whatever you like, such as trying a number of easy on-sights or repeating a few easy but classic routes.

COOLDOWN: 20 MINUTES

1. 20-minute ARC on an enjoyable easy route.

The following is a sample training schedule for a climber moving from 5.13d to the mid-5.14 redpoint level.

### Training day 1 (indoors or outdoors)

WARMUP/MOVEMENT TRAINING

1. Three to six route progressions starting at 5.10+/ 5.11a and working up to 5.13a. Include some routes that tap your weaknesses and climb them as well as you possibly can, repeating them if necessary.

FITNESS: 2 TO 3 HOURS

1. Anaerobic endurance: Four to six laps on a sustained 5.13a or 5.13b 50 to 60 feet in length. Make rest time equal to performance time. As always, keep your times consistent. Do not start to sprint as you get tired.

2. 30 minutes rest.

3. Anaerobic endurance: Four to six laps on a short, powerful 5.12d/5.13a with 2 to 3 minutes rest between laps.

4. 20 to 30 minutes rest.

COOLDOWN: 50 MINUTES

1. 25 minutes moderate-intensity ARC. Using a long and sustained route between 5.11a and 5.11d, up- and down-climb the route for 25 minutes. If you don't recover or start to get a pump, move to an easier route.

2. 25 minutes stretching. After a day of high-intensity climbing, good stretching is important for reducing soreness and preventing your arms from cramping up and taking a few days to loosen again.

### Training day 2 (indoors or outdoors)

WARMUP

Same as day 1, unless you are feeling sore and sluggish from the previous day, in which case do a number of easier routes 5.10 to 5.11. Have fun with them and don't increase the difficulty until you are ready.

FITNESS: 1.5 HOURS

1. 30 minutes ARC on 5.11d or harder.

2. 30 minutes rest.

3. 30 minutes ARC on 5.11d or harder.

COOLDOWN: 30 MINUTES OF STRETCHING

### Training day 3 (indoors)

WARMUP: UP TO 30 MINUTES OF EASY
BOULDERING V1 TO V5

Use this time for movement training as well. Pick specific skills to work on that are appropriate for each boulder problem. Repeat each problem as many times as you need in order to feel that you climbed it perfectly.

FITNESS: 2 HOURS

1. CIR bouldering: 15 repetitions of V7 or V8.

COOLDOWN: 45 MINUTES

1. 15 to 20 minutes easy ARC traversing.

2. 25 minutes stretching.

No less than two days rest.

### Performance day 1 (outdoors)

WARMUP: 1 TO 2 HOURS

Do a progression of four to six easy and moderate routes starting at 5.10+ and working up to 5.13a. Take your time and rest as much as you need between routes. You should already know and enjoy the harder routes. As always, use your warmup to work on your movement and prepare yourself mentally.

PERFORMANCE: 4 TO 6 HOURS

Choose either 1 or 2.

1. Work on your route pyramid. As with all climbers, what you can achieve depends upon where you are in your pyramid. What we expect to see at this level is an increase in the number of productive attempts you can make on a route. It is reasonable to expect that five to seven good-quality attempts can be made on one or two routes. The biggest limiting factors are probably skin and time rather than fitness.

2. Stamina redpoint day. If choosing this activity, we assume that your two- to three-try redpoint level is between 5.13a and 5.13d. Ideally you will put in no fewer than six to eight attempts. The goal is to redpoint two to four routes in a day at this level.

COOLDOWN

1. One to three easy routes 5.11 to 5.12 on which you can enjoy moving well without getting a pump.

2. 30 minutes of stretching. This is critical to prevent your forearms from locking up and to reduce soreness during the next few days.

All the principles, practices, activities, thought processes, plans, and goals discussed in this book are brought together in the form of your personalized training regimen. If you've carefully examined your current climbing, set goals, and prepared a plan, you're ready to begin training.

Now it's up to you to get busy. Climbing requires diligence and effort. Stick to your plan and you'll see improvement. Good luck in your training and many successful sends, but remember that climbing is a journey and not a destination. Enjoy your time in the vertical world. As our friend Boone Speed says, "The day I started climbing was the day I was born."

## QUICK TICKS

✓ Progressive training is the preferred method of training for recreational climbers. It's a more or less continual improvement over an extended period of time, whether for a season or many years.

✓ A training day is one in which you actively work on improving a particular area of your abilities or your conditioning. A performance day is spent making redpoint runs or on-sight attempts in an effort to add routes to your pyramid.

✓ Before setting a training plan, examine the differences between your goals or performance standards for your level and your current condition. Choose activities based on this assessment.

✓ Set up your schedule so that time is allocated to the specified activities. Be sure to include an appropriate mix of performance and training days in your schedule. Record your progress by keeping a daily diary.

# Sample Improvement Plan for a 5.9 Climber

### Route pyramid

| Grade | Target | Actual |
|-------|--------|--------|
| 10c | 1 | |
| 10b | 2 | |
| 10a | 4 | |
| 9+ | 8 | |

### Bouldering pyramid

| Grade | Target | Actual |
|-------|--------|--------|
| V0+ | 1 | |
| V0 | 2 | |
| V0− | 4 | |
| V0−− | 8 | |

| Movement skills to master | Movement skills mastered |
|---------------------------|--------------------------|
| Proper use of holds | |
| Silent feet | |
| Glue hands | |
| Line and flag | |

| Current physical condition | Targeted condition | Current condition |
|----------------------------|--------------------|-------------------|
| Bouldering | V1 | |
| 4x4 | V0− | |
| Continuous climbing | 30 minutes @ 5.7 | |

### Daily workout plan

| Date: January 21, 2005 | Target | Actual | Exercises performed | Accomplishments |
|------------------------|--------|--------|---------------------|-----------------|
| Warm-up | 15 min | | | |
| Movement training | 30 min | | | |
| Routes | 30 min | | | |
| Threshold bouldering | 30 min | | | |
| ARC | 30 min | | | |

### Sample entry in training journal for a single day

| Date: | Target | Actual | Exercises performed | Accomplishments |
|-------|--------|--------|---------------------|-----------------|
| Warm-up | 15 min | 15 min | Light traverse | |
| Movement training | 30 min | 35 min | Silent feet | Bumped 4 times |
| Routes | 30 min | 20 min | 2 x 5.9 | |
| Threshold bouldering | 30 min | 40 min | Worked V3 "Smurf" | Linked 2nd & 3rd moves |
| ARC | 30 min | 2 x 15 min | 5.7 autobelay | Had to break into 2 segments |
| Feelings | | Tired when arrived at gym but felt good at end of session | | |

# Glossary

**anaerobic reservoir:** An individual's capacity for tolerating lactic acid concentrations.

**anaerobic threshold:** The limit of the body to acquire, transport, and use oxygen for energy production. Climbers are concerned with the local anaerobic threshold of the forearm muscles. This is the highest grade you can continuously climb without getting a forearm pump.

**ATP:** Adenosine triphosphate, the energy-storing compound in muscle tissue.

**automatic response selection:** Decision making that requires little or no conscious thought. For example, the manner in which experienced climbers automatically position their bodies in relation to specific holds such as slopers or sidepulls.

**back step:** Standing on the outside edge, or little toe, of the foot.

**balance:** The relationship of the center of gravity to its base of support.

**base of support:** Points of contact with the rock that allow you to resist the constant force of gravity.

**body tension:** The intermuscular coordination of muscles in the trunk, hips, and legs necessary to prevent the body from falling away from the rock. Often required in moves on steeper climbs.

**campus board:** A slightly overhung, suspended board with evenly spaced horizontal rungs.

**center of gravity:** The point at which the body is balanced in space. Also called the center of mass, it is the focal point of gravity's pull on the body.

**chossy:** Unstable rock of a crumbly nature.

**closed-loop control system:** Applies to any movement you can change based on feedback.

**concentric contraction:** Muscles shorten to move a body segment.

**continuous-intensity repetition (CIR):** A stamina or anaerobic training exercise consisting of ten to fifteen boulder problems of the same difficulty with complete recovery between each problem. CIR can also be applied to routes, but rest durations will be longer and the intensity lower.

**controlled response selection:** Decision making that requires conscious thought. For example, the manner in which new climbers look at and touch each handhold before choosing how to use it.

**crimper:** A flat (horizontal) or in-cut (sloping down from the outer lip to the back) hold one inch deep or less.

**crimping:** A handhold position whereby the second knuckle is held at a 90-degree angle while pressing down and in on the hold with all of the fingertips.

**drop knee:** A turned body position used primarily on overhung terrain where the foot of the inside hip is placed high and the knee is turned downward for leverage.

**duration:** The amount of time a climb, or each of its sections, will take.

**dynamic balance:** Any position or movement in which the center of gravity passes outside the base of support.

**eccentric contraction:** Muscles lengthen to resist movement of a body segment.

**edge:** A foothold where the surface is either horizontal or slopes from the front of the hold to the back (in-cut).

**flag:** A move where, instead of placing his foot on a hold, the climber positions his leg so that its weight moves his center of gravity closer to the center of his base of support, thus improving his balance.

**flash:** Sending a route on the first attempt. Any information can be gathered before the attempt.

**gaston:** Any handhold requiring that force be applied horizontally away from or across the body.

**glycolysis:** The primary means by which cells produce energy if there is not sufficient oxygen available to produce energy through respiration.

**hypertrophy:** Increasing the size of a muscle.

**interval training:** Moderate- to high-intensity efforts separated by intervals of timed rests.

**isometric contraction:** Muscle remains the same length while contracting and therefore produces no movement in a body segment.

**isotonic contraction:** Muscle shortens or lengthens during contraction, resulting in the movement of a body segment.

**kinesphere:** A conceptual model proposed by Laban that consists of an invisible sphere or shell surrounding the body where every point on the sphere is connected by a line to the body's physical center.

**kinesthesis:** The senses through which we detect bodily position, weight, or movement of the muscles, tendons, and joints.

**lock off:** Holding a body position while the elbow of one arm is partially or completely flexed. This move requires contributions from the entire body, but climbers often incorrectly regard it as little more than an arm move.

**motor learning:** The process we undergo to acquire new physical skills.

**movement center:** The ability to place physical, emotional, and cognitive focus at key points in the body in order to aid in the execution of movement.

**movement initiation:** The origin of a movement in the body; the specific muscles and joints that begin to work first and set everything else in motion.

**movement intensity:** The difficulty of each section of the climb as measured on the V or YDS scale.

**offset balance:** Any position or movement in which the center of gravity approaches the edge of the base of support.

**on-sight:** Sending a route on the first attempt without any prior information other than what you can learn with your own eyes by viewing the route. You may not speak with anyone about the route, watch anyone climb it, or have touched any of the holds prior to the attempt.

**open hand:** A handhold position whereby the second knuckle is held at an angle greater than 90 degrees.

**open-loop control system:** Any movement we cannot change based on feedback.

**oxygen debt:** The quantity of waste product accumulated in muscles operating over the anaerobic threshold.

**performance:** Successfully completing a route, boulder problem, or climbs in a competition.

**performance day:** A climbing day devoted to sending a route or performing well in a competition.

**pinch:** Any hold used with thumb and fingers in opposition.

**plyometrics:** A fast, loaded eccentric, or negative, contraction just prior to a concentric, or positive, contraction.

**pocket:** A hole in the rock where fewer than four fingers will fit.

**power:** Force combined with speed of movement (power equals force times speed).

**power endurance:** The common name climbers use for anaerobic endurance.

**pyramid:** A list of the routes or boulder problems sent in the last twelve months in descending order from hardest to easiest. It is also a list of routes targeted for completion within a scheduled improvement plan.

**recruitment:** The percentage of muscle fibers that can be brought to bear in a single contraction.

**redpoint:** Sending a route or boulder problem after rehearsing it one or more times.

**send:** To climb from the start to the finish of a route without weighting the rope and using only the rock for support.

**sequence:** The precise series of hand and foot placements, body positions, and movements required to ascend a climb or a portion of a climb.

**sidepull:** Any handhold requiring that force be applied horizontally toward the body.

**sloper:** A handhold that slopes from back to front.

**smear:** A foothold that slopes from back to front.

**stable balance:** Any position or movement in which the center of gravity is positioned well within its base of support.

**stamina:** The ability to repeatedly perform and recover from high-intensity work over the course of a day.

**strength:** The force a muscle generates, regardless of how long it takes to reach that force.

**system wall:** A systematic grid of identical handholds, such as half-inch crimps, spaced at twelve- to fifteen-inch increments in a ladderlike pattern up an overhanging wall.

**threshold bouldering:** Bouldering workout that requires training at or very near your maximum intensity.

**toeing in:** A foothold position where your foot is 90 degrees to the rock and you are standing on the front tip of the shoe.

**training day:** A climbing day devoted exclusively to improving some aspect of one's climbing.

**undercling:** A hold that requires the palm to face up or out.

**variable-intensity repetition (VIR):** Similar to CIR, except that variable-intensity repetitions include predetermined changes in the intensity during the workout.

**"z" clip:** Reaching below the last piece of protection, pulling up slack, and clipping the next anchor.

# References

Baker et al. 1994. Periodization: The effect on strength of manipulating volume and intensity. *Journal of Strength and Conditioning Research*. 8:235–42.

Baum, Kenneth and Richard Trubo. 1999. *The mental edge: Maximize your sports potential with the mind/body connection*. New York: Perigee Trade.

Bobbert et al. 1996. Why is countermovement jump height greater than squat jump height? *Medicine and Science in Sports and Exercise*. 28:1402–12.

Bosco et al. 1982. Combined effect of elastic energy and myloelectric potential during strength-shortening cycle exercise. *Acta Physiologica Scandinavia*. 114:557–65.

Bourdin, Christophe. 1999. Postural constraints modify the organization of grasping movements. *Human Movement Science* 18:87–102.

Broer, Marion. 1966. *Efficiency of human movement*. Philadelphia: W. B. Saunders.

Bunn, John W. 1972. *Scientific principles of coaching*. Englewood Cliffs, NJ: Prentice-Hall.

Collins, Jim and Jerry I. Porras. 1996. Building your company's vision. *Harvard Business Review*. September–October.

Collins, Jim and Jerry I. Porras. 2002. *Built to last: Successful habits of visionary companies*. New York: HarperBusiness.

Cooper, John and Ruth Glassow. 1963. *Kinesiology*. St. Louis: C. V. Mosby Company.

Costill, D. L. et al. 1979. Adaptations in skeletal muscle following strength training. *Journal of Applied Physiology*. 46 (January): 96–99.

Davis, J. A. et al. 1979. Anaerobic threshold alterations caused by endurance training in middle-aged men. *Journal of Applied Physiology*. 46 (June): 1039–1046.

Feldenkrais, Moshe. 1977. *Awareness through movement*. New York: Harper & Row.

Fitt, Sally Sevey. 1996. *Dance kinesiology* 2d ed. New York: Schirmer Books.

Foster, Susan. 1992. Dancing bodies. In *Incorporations*, edited by Jonathan Crary and Sanford Kwinter. New York: Zone Books.

Franklin, Eric. 2003. *Pelvis power: Mind body exercises for strength, flexibility, posture, and balance*. Highstown, NJ: Princeton Book Company.

———. 1996. *Dynamic alignment through movement*. Champaign, IL: Human Kinetics Publishers.

Gilpin, Heidi. 1994. Aberrations of Gravity. *Architecture New York* 5 (March–April).

Goddard, Dale and Uno Neumann. 1993. *Performance rock climbing*. Mechanicsburg, PA: Stackpole Books.

Groves, Richard and David Camaione. 1975. *Concepts in kinesiology*. Philadelphia: W. B. Saunders.

Hakkinen et al. 1989. Neuromuscular adaptations and hormone balance in strength athletes. In *Proceedings of XII International Congress of Biomechanics* No. 8, edited by P.J. Gregor et al. Champaign, IL: Human Kinetics Publishers.

Hay, James G. 1978. *Biomechanics of sports techniques*. Englewood Cliffs, NJ: Prentice-Hall.

Hoffman, Jay. 2002. *Physiological aspects of sport training and performance*. Champaign, IL: Human Kinetics Publishers.

Holloszy, J. O. and F. W. Booth. 1976. Biomechanical adaptations to endurance exercise in muscle. *Annual Review of Physiology*. 38: (March) 273–291.

Huang, Al Chungliang and Jerry Lynch. 1992. *Thinking body, dancing mind*. New York: Bantam Books.

Jensen, Clayne R. and Gordon W. Schultz. 1970. *Applied kinesiology: The scientific study of human performance*. New York: McGraw-Hill.

Jozsa, Laszlo G. and Pekka Kannus. 1997. *Human tendons: Anatomy, physiology, and pathology*. Champaign, IL: Human Kinetics Publishers.

Knudson, Duane V. and Craig S. Morrison. 2002. *Qualitative analysis of human movement*. Champaign, IL: Human Kinetics Publishers.

Knuttgen, H. G. and W. J. Kraemer. 1987. Terminology and measurement in exercise performance. *Journal of Applied Sports Science Research* 1:1–10.

Lydiard, Arthur and Garth Gilmour. 1978. *Running the Lydiard way*. Mountain View, CA: World Publications.

Martin, David E. and Peter N. Coe. 1997. *Better training for distance runners*. 2d ed. Champaign, IL: Human Kinetics Publishers.

Mauss, Marcel. 1992. Techniques of the body. In *Incorporations*, edited by Jonathan Crary and Sanford Kwinter. New York: Zone Books.

McGinnis, Peter. 1999. *Biomechanics of sport and exercise*. Champaign, IL: Human Kinetics Publishers.

Meglin, Joellen. 1986. Ideokinesis as it applies to injury prevention. In *The Dancer as athlete: The 1984 Olympic scientific congress proceedings*. Champaign, IL: Human Kinetics Publishers.

Messenger, Neil, Will Patterson, and Dave Brook. 2000. *The science of climbing and mountaineering*. Champaign, IL: Human Kinetics Software.

Morehouse, Laurence E. and Augustus T. Miller. 1967. *Physiology of exercise*. St. Louis: C. V. Mosby Company.

Myers, Martha. 1986. Perceptual awareness in integrative movement behavior: The role of integrative movement systems (body therapies) in motor performance and expressivity. In *The dancer as athlete: The 1984 Olympic scientific congress proceedings*. Champaign, IL: Human Kinetics Publishers.

Quaine, Franck et al. 1999. A biomechanical study of equilibrium in rock climbing. In *The science of climbing and mountaineering*. Champaign, IL: Human Kinetics Publishers.

Sagar, Heather Reynolds. 2001. *Climbing your best*. Mechanicsburg, PA: Stackpole Books.

Sale et al. 1990. Comparison of two regimes of concurrent strength and endurance training. *Medicine and Science in Sports and Exercise* 22:348–560.

Schmidt, Richard and Craig Wrisberg. 2000. *Motor learning and performance* 2d ed. Champaign, IL: Human Kinetics Publishers.

Schmidt, Richard and Timothy Lee. 1999. *Motor control and learning: A behavioral emphasis* 3d ed. Champaign, IL: Human Kinetics Publishers.

Scott, M. Gladys. 2000. *Analysis of human motion*. New York: Broadway Books.

Sharp, R. L. et al. 1986. Effects of eight weeks of bicycle ergometer spring training on human muscle buffer capacity. *International Journal of Sports Medicine*. 7:13–17.

Siler, Brooke. 2000. *The Pilates body*. New York: Broadway Books.

Sweigard, Lulu. 1974. *Human movement potential: Its ideokinetic facilitation*. New York: Harper & Row.

Thompson, Floyd. 2001. *Manual of structural kinesiology*. New York: McGraw-Hill.

Von Kliest, Heinrich. 1990. On the marionette theater. In *Fragments for a history of the human body,* part one, edited by Michel Feher, Romona Naddaff, and Nadia Tazi. New York: Zone Books.

Watts, Phillip. 1999. Physiological aspects of difficult sport rock climbing. In *The science of climbing and mountaineering*. Champaign, IL: Human Kinetics Publishers.

Werner, Inpe et al. 1999. Blood lactate responses to competitive climbing. In *The science of climbing and mountaineering*. Champaign, IL: Human Kinetics Publishers.

————. 1999. Three dimensional analysis of rock climbing technique. In *The science of climbing and mountaineering*. Champaign, IL: Human Kinetics Publishers.

# About the Authors

Dan Hague founded Sportrock Climbing Centers in the Washington, D.C., area and led the company through its first eleven years. In that time, Sportrock grew to become the East Coast's largest climbing company with three indoor facilities, extensive indoor and outdoor instructional offerings, and a reputation for excellence within the climbing industry. Dan has been climbing for over thirty years and teaching climbing for eleven years. His coaching clients have included many climbers in the junior divisions who have gone on to impressive finishes in local, regional, and national competitions. In addition, he developed the successful Fast Forward Progression, a series of classes that has helped thousands of Sportrock climbers acquire climbing movement skills quickly and effectively. He has spent years evaluating how climbing is learned and has refined his instructional programs accordingly. Dan's own climbing keeps getting better as he ages, having redpointed a number of New River Gorge 5.13s after turning forty.

Douglas Hunter has been climbing for twenty-five years and coaching climbers for fifteen. In the 1990s, he worked as a full-time climber in Salt Lake City, where he coached and instructed thousands of climbers, a number of whom placed in or won national championships, the climbing world cups, and the summer and winter X-games. He has established first ascents of routes and boulder problems in the Gunks, American Fork, and other areas. He made early ascents of renowned test pieces such as Dead Souls and Cop Killer (both 5.14a) in American Fork and has climbed more 5.13s than he can remember. He has developed climbing programs for children and adults alike, has studied movement pedagogy and kinesiology for many years, and has made significant contributions to how climbing is taught in the U.S. Douglas is a graduate of the USC film school and now works in film and television in Los Angeles.

# Index